THE EXTRA VIRGIN KITCHEN

Recipes free from Wheat, Dairy and Refined Sugar

by Susan Jane White

Gill & Macmillan

Gill and Macmillan
Hume Avenue
Park West
Dublin 12
www.gillmacmillanbooks.ie

978 07171 6931 3

First published in hardcover 2014
This paperback edition first published 2015

Design by www.grahamthew.com
Photography © Joanne Murphy
Styling by Orla Neligan
Assistants to photographer and stylist: Liosa MacNamara and Kerrie Mitchell
Food preparation by Susan Jane White
Edited by Kristin Jensen
Indexed by Adam Pozner
Printed by Printer Trento Srl, Italy

This book is typeset in 9 on 12pt Botanika Mono.

PROPS

Avoca: HQ Kilmacanogue, Bray, Co. Wicklow.
T: (01) 2746939; E: info@avoca.ie; www.avoca.ie

Meadows & Byrne: Dublin, Cork, Galway, Clare, Tipperary.
T: (01) 2804554/(021) 4344100; E: info@meadowsandbyrne.ie; www.meadowsandbyrne.com

Eden Home & Garden: 1-4 Temple Grove, Temple Road, Blackrock, Co. Dublin.
T: (01) 7642004; E: edenhomeandgarden@hotmail.com; www.edenhomeandgarden.ie

Article: Powerscourt Townhouse, South William Street, Dublin 2.
T: (01) 6799268; E: items@articledublin.com; www.articledublin.com

House of Fraser: Dundrum Town Centre, Dublin 16.
T: (01) 2991400; E: dundrum@hof.co.uk; www.houseoffraser.co.uk

Harold's Bazaar: 208 Harold's Cross Road, Dublin 6W.
T: 087 7228789.

Historic Interiors: Oberstown, Lusk, Co. Dublin.
T: (01) 8437174; E: killian@historicinteriors.net

Helen Turkington: 47 Dunville Avenue, Ranelagh, Dublin 6.
T: (01) 4125138; E: info@helenturkington.com; www.helenturkington.com

The Third Policeman: 121 Lower Rathmines Road, Dublin 6.
T: 085 8487763; www.facebook.com/t3rdpoliceman

54321

CONTENTS
+ + + + + + + +

SNACKS AND OTHER NUTRITIONAL HITS

SOUPS

SALADS

SUPPERS

EXTRA VIRGIN TREATS

THANK YOU

A big high five to my suave publisher Nicki Howard, whose wisdom and dynamism whipped this book into shape. You're one hell of a lady.

To Catherine, Teresa, Paul and everyone at Gill & Macmillan. Thank you for making this book everything I had hoped, and so much more. I am eternally grateful for your hard work and support.

Design guru Graham Thew – I blush at your brilliance.

A thunderous thank you to photographer Jo Murphy, stylist Orla Neligan and assistants Kerrie and Liosa. I never expected to have so much fun or to make new friends in the process. Working with you all was beyond inspiring.

Mary O'Sullivan, Brendan O'Connor and Anne Harris at *The Sunday Independent* – all brilliant people at the top of their game. Thank you for taking a chance on me.

To lovely Kristin Jensen and Maggie Armstrong for your patience and meticulous proofreading.

Tom Dunne and producer Joe Donnelly – radio was never so much fun. A heartfelt thank you.

My agent Rebecca Morgan for her tenacity, loyalty and tireless enthusiasm. Thank you for putting up with me these past 14 years.

I'm grateful to Oliver and his team at Wall & Keogh in Portobello, where I spend hours sipping gorgeous teas, tapping toes and writing.

To my beloved, the most nourishing superfood my body has ever known. You electrify me. Mostly.

Our adorable boys Benjamin and Marty, whose laughter rings through our home.

To mum. What a marvel.

Many impressive commentators and activists continue to inspire and inform me. My sincere gratitude to you all: Joanna Blythman, Felicity Lawrence, Bee Wilson, Mark Bittman, Michael Pollan, Marion Nestle, Robyn O'Brien, Dr David A. Kessler, Michael Moss, Gary Taubes, Dr Marilyn Glenville, Eric Schlosser, Robert Lustig, Hugh Fearnley-Whittingstall, Dr John Briffa, Dr John McKenna, Colin Tudge, Claudia Hammond and George Monbiot.

And lastly, YOU. I have the best readers in the world. You give flight to my imagination and make it all possible for me. I wrote this book for you.

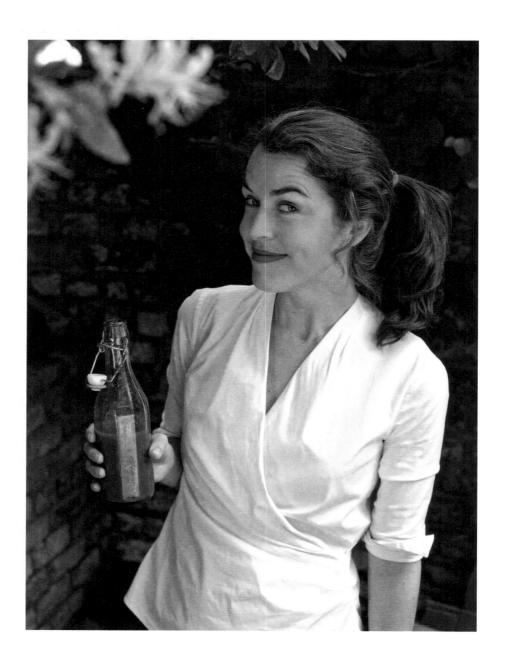

Introduction:

FALLING DOWN THE RABBIT HOLE

My name is Susan Jane. Picture MacGyver in an apron with a grumpy husband who thinks he's a restaurant critic and two ravenous little punks to feed six times a day. Food is my thing, it keeps me happy. People say my energy levels would rival Graham Norton on acid. But I wasn't always so bionic.

Thirteen years ago I was a model student. Literally. Modelling became a valuable source of income at college in Dublin, and later, at Oxford. It's supposed to be a glamorous job, but when you see what models live on — cigarettes and diet cola — you have to wonder.

Back then, I never saw myself as someone who needed to change. I was hyper, stubborn and deluded — what could possibly go wrong? After all, there was nothing out of the ordinary about my diet: jam-filled scones, toast, pasta, breakfast cereals, toast, take-out sambos and more toast. Standard Irish fare. No wonder I tried to regulate my moods with criminal amounts of caffeine.

Let's be honest: consumers are highly submissive. I hardly thought to ask any questions about the ingredients in my energy drink or the Monster Munch I devoured with the giddy determination of a clamper kneecapping a Bentley in the bus lane. I blindly trusted the 'food authorities', whoever they were, and I never imagined that beef burgers, for example, might contain horsemeat, that chicken products could test positive for pork or that our modern diet would lead millions into diabesity. Like Alice in Wonderland, I was jumping feet first into a deep, dark rabbit hole. Except this was no tea party.

First we form habits - and then they form us. It wasn't alcohol or cigarettes that ruined my health, though I experimented as much as any student. It was food. To be more specific: junk food. I convinced myself that only boring people had time to cook. Turns out smarter people *make* time to cook.

One day in the summer of 2005 my body said no, enough. First came the shakes. Horrid urinary infections. Constipation. Mouth ulcers. Exhaustion. But nobody suggested that maybe *I* was contributing to my ill health. My digestive system wheezed like an asthmatic snail, yet diet apparently had nothing to do with it. Ten years ago the medical community dismissed the idea of food sensitivities like industry tycoons scoffing at global warming. Contemplating such an idea was daft. After all, test results had shown I was not coeliac or diabetic. Case closed.

The chronic conditions started to make themselves at home. Thrush. Earaches. Dizziness. Psoriasis. Headaches. Cold sores. But I didn't have time to respect the symptoms and turned to self-medication. I had papers to submit and was hell bent on a place on Oxford Uni's modern pentathlon team. There was literally no time to be sick.

I ended up in hospital, with tubes coming out of … well, everywhere. They sent in doctor after doctor. As the consultants handed me their cards, I noticed they had more and more letters after their names. Yet no one could figure out why my body was as limp as a wet lettuce. I was numb, physically and emotionally.

After twelve courses of antibiotics, several hospitalisations, a course of steroids, anti-fungal colon treatments and many futile vaccinations, I felt unlucky but in no way responsible. Then my white blood cells packed up.

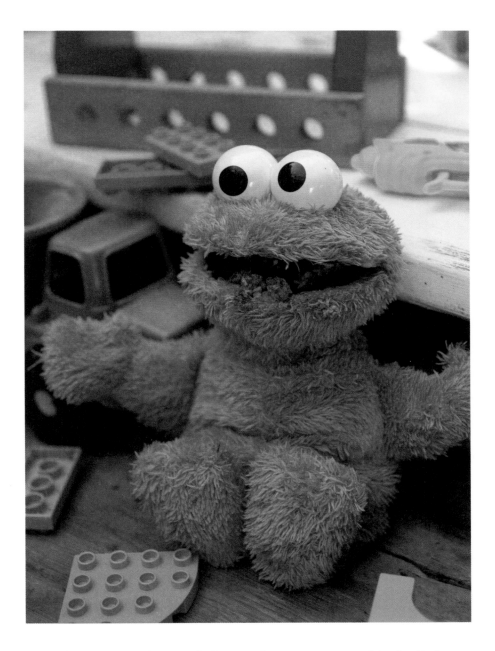

One afternoon in hospital I got chatting to an elderly lady
called Lucy in the cubicle next to me. I wasn't certain why
Lucy had been admitted. She was frail but so sweet in her
papery mint gown, smiling back over the sheets. We talked
for hours. I cried inside when she asked to hold my hand
to give her strength. Lucy cooed about her love of bread
making, yet she was coeliac (so her body could not handle

gluten). I remember thinking how strange that was: ignoring the signals her system was sending.

Across the room, another patient was tucking into jelly and ice cream from the hospital canteen. She was being treated for 'complications' arising from diabetes and obesity. It was like death on a plate, and horribly ironic that the hospital staff were her accomplices. The sight sent a chill up my arms. Both women knew their poison but chose to ignore it. They were digging the way to their graves with their teeth.

A little later, I heard a loud flat bell. Doctors and nurses ran in and sectioned me off from Lucy. I never saw her adorable face again. No one did.

The following morning I looked in the mirror, and what I saw made me cry. I turned away from the mirror, and in that instant - a wrenching minute of pure self-knowledge, accompanied by a sort of grief for the person I was now saying goodbye to - I made the most important decision of my life: to take control of my health. Raising my head, I looked into that mirror once again. And I nodded.

Deal.

My nutritional pilgrimage started with a journey to Dr Joe Fitzgibbon, a doctor who specialises in food sensitivities and fatigue. I travelled six hours by train for every visit. Together we tackled the elimination diet, stripping my meals to very basic foods like meat, fish, pulses, beans and vegetables. Every couple of weeks I reintroduced specific foods to my diet to monitor symptoms, like a food detective. **It felt like someone was sucking the illness out of my body.**

That austere diet made me see the intimate connection between energy levels and the food we eat. Good food keeps you on your tippy toes. Poor food will have you on your knees. Wheat and sugar were lethal in my system, so I waved goodbye to bread, pasta, sugar and all manner of processed food. That was nine years ago.

The first three weeks off wheat, sugar and dairy were horrific. I don't want you thinking I was running barefoot through fields of cornflowers, throwing my arms around trees in a state of orgasmic self-enlightenment. Nor did I ever choose to give up junk food. I had to. My body was falling apart. There was no other choice.

So I tramped around health food stores with a mixture
of confusion and nervous elation, like an ornithologist
sighting a new species of bird. All the time I was busy
mourning for Diet Cola Girl. 'Jaysus, I could buy a bottle
of wine for the price of those berries.' 'I can't afford
that strange flour, it's three times the price of normal
white stuff!'

Eventually I realised there is nothing restrictive about
this way of eating. It's the opposite. Food intolerances
are an opportunity to escape the shackles of processed
food and the excesses of the Wheat-Sugar-Dairy merry-go-
round. There are legions of grains, flours and funky beans
to experiment with in place of boring pasta and bread, and
healthy fats like walnut, coconut, sesame and hemp seed
oils. Discovering this wealth of options was my second
light bulb moment. **My 'restrictive' diet was nothing of the
sort. It was incredibly liberating.**

By continuing to feed our bodies with one-dimensional foods
made from white sugar, white flour and industrially produced
chemicals, we condition our brains to accept crap. Breaking
the habit is challenging, but once you experience the
benefits of eating whole, unprocessed foods, you will never
look back. Make no mistake, it's a love affair like no other.
But don't just take my word for it. See for yourself.

**Here are my favourite recipes. Don't worry - I won't
threaten you with cabbage soup or Lycra tights.** These
recipes are less about denial and more about pleasure:
banana malt ice cream, raw chocolate tortes, chestnut
crêpes, and chia seed fishcakes with curried coconut. If you
approach this book with a sense of adventure, I bet your
palate will be tickled and your mojo will return. In time
your weight will stabilise, you will sleep more soundly and
hum louder. But there's more! We now know that a healthy
diet significantly reduces your risk of developing heart
disease, many cancers and type 2 diabetes. If there was
a pill promising the same, wouldn't you want to take it?
Whole food cooking isn't a pill. It's a ticket.

Of course, you don't have to give up wheat, sugar and
dairy to eat well, and slip-ups are a natural (and
necessary) part of the journey. **Everyone has different needs
and different poisons. That's what makes humans so damn
charming.** But whatever your reasons for exploring new and
nourishing foods away from the circus of convenience, you
are very welcome to the Extra Virgin Kitchen.

Let's do this together.

NIFTY Q&As
==========

Do I need any special equipment before I start?

Definitely - get yourself some tenacity and a sense of adventure. Fleetwood Mac's Greatest Hits is also useful. Or Billie Holiday. Whatever tickles your serotonin.

Where do I buy all these weird things?

In good health food stores and specialist grocers. Most large supermarkets stock 80% of the ingredients listed, such as millet, quinoa, seaweed, tamari and even coconut water. Check out my sources at the back of the book for online ordering.

How come you use cups instead of grams?

Cups are friendlier and make it easier to visualise quantities. I think the metric system alienates people in the kitchen. It has a disempowering effect. Do you know what 65g of dates looks like? Or 325g of flour?

You can pick up measuring cups in the baking aisle of most supermarkets or on Amazon for less than a fiver. Dean & DeLuca probably do frilly ones. Just make sure 1 cup = 250ml as British and American cups differ.

Why don't you use gluten-free flour?

I struggle to see the point of swapping white flour for a 'gluten-free' version. It reminds me of when I used to drink decaf coffee, thinking I was being healthy. Gluten-free white flour is just as processed as its first cousin, the all-purpose white flour.

Admittedly, wholegrain flours are a little trickier to tame into happy biscuits and breads, but their nutritional profile makes them much more desirable. If you've met my husband, you'll understand why I'm attracted to stubborn and contrary ingredients. I find them indecently exciting once you finally conquer them.

Are all your recipes gluten free as well as wheat free?

Not all, but most. Gluten is found in wheat, rye, barley and some oats.

Why don't you use spelt?

Spelt is wheat.

If this cookbook is wheat free, why does it feature lots of buckwheat recipes?

Despite its name, buckwheat is no relation to the cereal wheat. There's no gluten in buckwheat either. How awesome is that?

Any pasta recipes?

No. But plenty of quinoa, which is far tastier. It's like a new friend with super-human powers. Pasta would blush in quinoa's presence.

I live in the US. Ground almonds are the same as almond flour, right?

Almost. Both are healthy and come from almonds, but ground almonds give a heavier finish in baked goodies. Almond flour is much finer and easier to find in the US, but not so much in Europe.

Feel free to try almond flour in place of ground almonds whenever you see a recipe bound for the oven. However, almond flour will not work in any raw recipe, such as the Chia Bonbons, Hazelnut and Raisin Freezer Cookies or Fancy Pants Lúcuma Fudge.

Is margarine okay instead of butter?

Not in my opinion. Be sceptical of pseudo foods tailored to 'reduce cholesterol'. Investigative journalist Felicity Lawrence warns that many manufac-turers use the cheapest possible oils to make margarine and hide under the pretence of being 'healthy'. Most of these oils must be processed or hydro-genated to extend their shelf life, but not your life. 'Cholesterol free' is a similarly deceptive marketing device among companies that use hydrogenated fats. So an ostensibly healthy product can do more harm to your cholesterol than good. Professor Walter Willet of Harvard Medical School slammed this as 'the biggest food-processing disaster in US history'.

How about regular sunflower oil?

For taste reasons, you're welcome to use whatever oil you fancy. However, as a cautious mummy of two growing boys I only use extra virgin, cold-pressed oils that have not been brutalised by processors or adulterated by manufacturers. When in doubt, leave it out.

Isn't coconut oil fattening?

It is a fat, yes. But it's a good fat. Our relationship with fat is perverse. We need it in order to manufacture brain cells and hormones (without which everyone would be suffering from depression). However, choose judiciously.

There are good fats and bad fats. Extra virgin, cold-pressed coconut oil is a good fat.

The saturated fat in coconut is made up of medium chain triglyc-erides (MCTs), the mere mention of which makes triathletes indecently excitable. These MCTs are metabolised quickly by the body and can be used as an alternative source of energy to carbohydrates. MCTs are also easier to break down than the longer chain triglycerides in olive, sunflower or canola oil. More impor-tantly, coconut's MCTs are composed of lauric and capric acids. These heroic anti-viral, anti-fungal and anti-bacterial agents are also present in mother's milk to give her baba the best start in life.

Can I fry with olive oil?

Frying at a high temper-ature will denature almost any oil. It doesn't matter if you use the best cold-pressed extra virgin oil money can buy. Heating, as opposed to warming, chemically disfigures oil and spoils many health benefits. Basically, you are creating unhealthy free radicals that are liable to fraternise with your arteries.

If you suffer from cholesterol or weight problems, it might be worth writing this on the inside of your kitchen cupboard to remind you!

We use coconut oil because of its high smoke point. This means it's a more sturdy oil to cook with than, say, linseed or sunflower oil. When I'm gently sweating veg, I'm happy to use olive oil, as the heat never reaches a perilous point.

Ghee is clarified butter, which many lactose-intolerant cooks find they can eat without side effects. Just like butter, ghee is solid at room temperature and holds a higher smoke point than most oils. We always have some in our fridge.

I love agave and use it all the time. Is it good for me?

Let's be clear - no sugar is healthy. Agave is touted as a low glycemic fructose syrup that does not require insulin to break it down. A health boon, right? But science is rarely that simple. Eating this page wouldn't require insulin either. Hardly a reason to include it in our diet. It's fair to say that agave is not a health food, but a useful food. This is an important differentiation. Evidence suggests that a diet rich in *liquid* fructose has a deleterious effect on the body. The addition of high fructose corn syrup (HFCS), for example, has caused much controversy between health scientists and food manufacturers. While agave does not fall within the same category as HFCS, it is still classified as fructose.

Agave wouldn't be my first choice of sweetener unless I was diabetic (and even still, moderation is critical). Try raw, unadulterated organic agave if possible. Other issues to consider include processing methods and added ingredients. Agave piracy dates back to 2008, when several supermarket brands of agave were found to be highly processed and contaminated with other forms of syrups. It's hardly surprising that manufacturers want a slice of success when a new food enjoys such attention. This applies to all newfangled foods. Keep your antennae finely tuned and your gut on speaking terms with you! As with all sweeteners, no matter what you choose, moderation is key.

What's so terrific about maple syrup anyway? Isn't it just as bad for you as sugar?

No. Unless you plan to neck a pint of it. Maple syrup is a wonderfully wholesome natural sugar. But if you're diabetic, it's off limits.

Maple syrup is harvested naturally from maple trees and contains surprising amounts of iron and calcium. It's one of the only sweeteners that helps alkalise the body - other sugars can be highly acidic to the system. Acidic systems have been shown to leach calcium from our bones, while alkaline systems actually enhance calcium absorption. This is useful information for those who suffer from arthritic or osteo conditions.

A pal in Québec, Canada, is struggling to find local maple syrup. Rumour has it the middle-class Chinese are buying up all of Canada's stocks. This has consequences for us too, one of which is a rise in the price of this deliciously sticky nectar. Another is the surge of imposters on the market. To avoid being duped by 'maple-flavoured' syrup, always interrogate the labelling. It should have one ingredient: 100% pure Canadian maple syrup. Grade B is preferable.

What's the story with brown rice syrup? Healthy or not?

Okay, so, no sugar is healthy. The key is to find one that works for you and use it moderately or sparingly.

Despite brown rice syrup being a fairly processed product, it has low levels of glucose (about 5%) and high levels of the more complex carbohydrate maltose (around 55%). This gives brown rice syrup an attractive glycemic load. Alicia Silverstone, author of *The Kind Diet*, totally digs it. As a result, Hollywood does too.

It's made by fermenting the cooked grain with cultured enzymes to break down the carbohydrates. The liquid by-product is boiled to make a sweet, sticky syrup. Like all trendy products, there are good versions and seriously processed versions. It's worth doing your own research. Sticking to organic seems sensible given the volume of

agrichemicals used in rice production. There were issues with arsenic in the soil a few years back too.

What on earth is coconut sugar?

Coconut blossom sugar is a relatively new unrefined sugar on the Western market. Stunning stuff. Not as sweet as regular cane sugar, it offers a burnt toffee kick. It's not heavily processed either. The sap of the coconut flower is dehydrated to form honeyed crystals. While coconut sugar can be classified as a palm sugar, it is not to be confused with regular palm sugar, which is produced differently and is no friend to the diabetic. Coconut sugar is thought to have a low glycemic value. Good news for hyperactive children, diabetics and bored sedentary workers.

But watch out! My cynical side predicts that adulterated forms will begin to appear on our shelves. Look for trusted brands and ask your local health food stockist for advice if you're suspicious. Coconut sugar is pricey and will attract piracy. Them is the facts of life. Rapadura

sugar is much more difficult to adulterate and is a very good sub for coconut sugar if glycemic load does not concern you.

If rapadura is a sugar, what's it doing in this book?

You'll notice that rapadura sugar features in just three recipes. I wanted to introduce readers to a range of healthier sugars in place of the nutritionally void white variety.

Rapadura is a unique extra-fine sugar made from dehydrating sugarcane juice. It is caramel in colour with a deep mineral taste to it. Find it online and in all good food stores. Pricey, but worth experiencing.

However, if your diet obliges you to stay off sugar, this would mean quarantining all forms of good and bad sugars, including rapadura, honey, maple syrup, brown rice syrup and even fruit. My cookbook only manages to evict nasty white sugar from our kitchens.

I'm diabetic. Is this book for me?

Absolutely. However, it's important to stick to your low GL principles. Wherever you see maple syrup, use raw agave or experiment with xylitol. Coconut sugar is apparently low GL, but at the time of going to print, there was insufficient independent research to corroborate this for me. I urge you to do your own research. Remember that dried fruit, date syrup, maple syrup, apple syrup and honey are all high on the glycemic index and therefore unsuitable. Stevia is an interesting and popular source of sweetness for many diabetics, but I don't like the taste. Perhaps you will have better luck than me.

Can I use barley malt extract in place of maple syrup? It's so much cheaper.

Sure. Although I haven't tried barley malt in all my recipes, I can assure you it gives tremendous results in baking. Even raw chocolates work with barley malt. Just remember that it's only half as sweet as honey and maple syrup. This syrup is made from fermenting and boiling barley, in a similar way to brown rice syrup. Some of the original nutrients found in barley are transferred to the nectar. While barley malt is not as sweet as maple syrup, it's unusually malty and licky-sticky.

Barley malt is a complex sugar, meaning that it takes quite some time for it to be broken down by the body. Simple sugars, like white sugar or corn syrup, are absorbed immediately, resulting in blood sugar spikes and yo-yo moods. For evidence of this, spend 30 minutes at a children's birthday party. It's pretty mental.

Cutting out convenience food is difficult. How can I cope with cooking all the time?

With great music, the sort that makes your blood pelt around your body and electrifies your fingertips. Nothing is a chore when your favourite tunes massage your neurotransmitters. It's key to cooking.

I also throw lots of suppers and treats into my freezer, ready to plunder on lazy days. Be selfish with your time - conquer many meals in one session, rather than cooking three times a day. With practice, you'll motor through these recipes.

How do I know if I have a food intolerance?

If you've already bought this book, chances are something's not agreeing with you. Find a registered dietician or doctor to do an elimination diet with you. I'm not a huge fan of allergy testing, simply because it didn't bring any relief to me. For best results, become your own food detective (with the encouragement of and direction from a professional).

Why are soya and tofu controversial? I'm confused. Are they the same thing?

Tofu is made from the soya bean. You're probably familiar with other soya bean products, such as soya milk, miso soup, soya sauce and tempeh. Milk is extracted from the soya bean and used to make soya curd, referred to as tofu. It's not unlike cheese making. Made this way, tofu is supposedly replete with isoflavones, a big pal of calcium. Isoflavones have been found to assist in bone density as well as hormonal imbalances. So far, so good.

Once soya's health benefits became clear outside of Japan, consumer demand rocketed. I think its explosive rise here in the West encouraged food companies to find cheaper ways of producing it. Consequently, soya's reputation has been muddied with chemical isolation techniques, synthetic adulteration and genetic modification, all of which raise serious questions about the beneficial effects of the end product. That's why soya is so controversial. The chemically altered soya is a whole different creature to the whole-bean soya associated with the Asian diet. Frustrating, isn't it?

The only way you can tell the difference is to read the manufacturer's label on food before you buy. I've been advised to avoid soya protein isolates. Up to 60% of packaged supermarket foods use this synthetically debased soya as a cheap bulking agent. So don't be fooled into thinking soya is synonymous with health.

To tap into soya beans' bone fide health benefits, my advice is to stick with organic, non-GM tofu and eat it no more than once a week. Even the Japanese don't eat as much soya as we do. There are also ethical issues to consider. Animal feed is largely composed of soya, which drives demand for soya plantations. We are witnessing the destruction of hundreds of thousands of wildlife acres to satiate demand for soya production. In short, the world has gone bonkers for the stuff. If you can live without it, all the better.

Do you eat Quorn?

Nope, never. Cutting down on meat seems to be a much more sensible approach. Swapping one bad habit for another makes little sense.

Are these recipes suitable for children?

Definitely. Just leave out the salt, black pepper, garlic or tamari - and add these to your own plate. Good nutrition is the best health insurance you can offer your family.

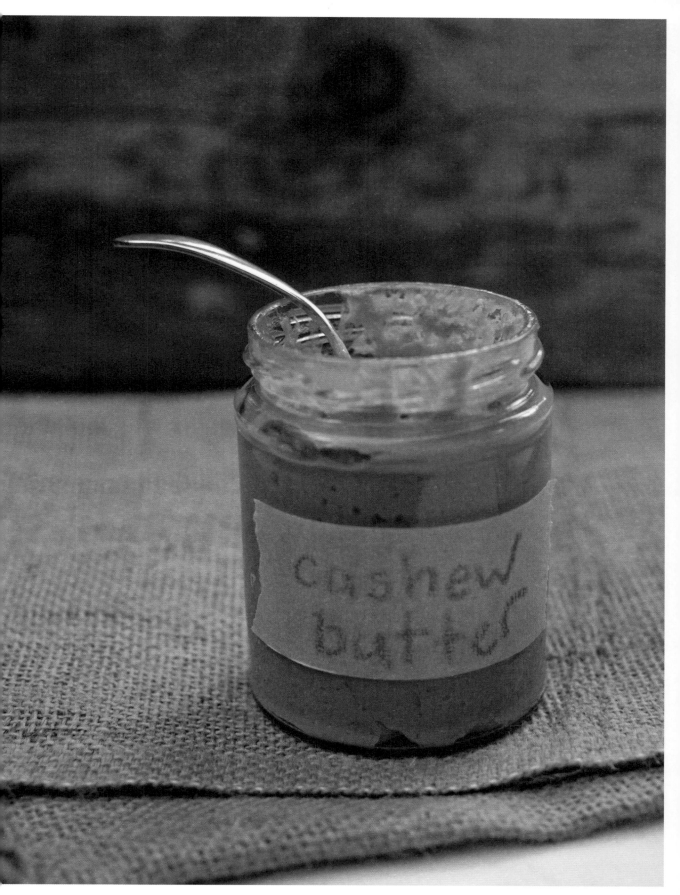

YOUR KITCHEN'S ARTILLERY
* *

HERE ARE YOUR NEW ALLIES IN THE KITCHEN, IN ORDER OF IMPORTANCE.

Measuring cups

You'll notice I measure in cups, handfuls and drizzles, which makes it easier to visualise quantities as you read the recipe and write your shopping list. I've always found grams and ounces alienating. It may as well be trigo-nometry to me. Like most tactile people, I function on a sort of visual mathematics. We use British/Australian cups where 1 cup = 250ml.

Tenacity

Available deep down, often in the same aisle as drive and desper-ation.

Pestle and mortar

If you don't have a pestle and mortar, find an Asian food store. You'll pick up an excellent deal, save yourself a small fortune and instantly acquire bragging rights in the pub. A pestle and mortar propels you into an underground club of serious cooks. Think Jamie Oliver meets Thomas Keller. No good meal can be made without a bit of muscle action in the kitchen. I guess the bottom of a heavy saucepan would also work, but it might scare the bejaysus out of the neighbours.

Food processor

Mine's a Magimix from my mother-in-law. The lady's got style. I use it every day.

Hand-held or personal blender

Also referred to as a soup gun or whizzy thing, hand-held blenders give a much smoother finish than a food processor (unless you have a swanky Vitamix). Particularly important for hummus (page 114). Pick one up for a tenner.

Heavy-based saucepan or large sauté pan

Heavy-based saucepans spread heat evenly, which helps prevent burning or ingredients 'catching' on the bottom of the pan and driving your patience batty. Le Creuset are the Bentleys of the kitchen. Look out for them during sale season or in discount stores like TK Maxx. The bigger, the better.

Oven thermometer

This is like a lie detector for ovens. Available online on Amazon and in kitchen stores.

Spiraliser

Mine is a Lurch, and it's definitely love. Not essential to your kitchen, it's more of a nerdy toy. Expect one to set you back about €40 or €50.

Tefal 8-in-1 Rice Cooker

To make perfectly fluffy quinoa, measure 2 cups of quinoa to level 2 in the basin. Season with a few turns of the sea salt and peppercorn mill. Press the 'grains' programme. The rice cooker will steam the grain and produce the most perfect quinoa you're ever likely to taste.

For details on how to cook almost every brown rice on the market using this rice cooker, visit my blog at www.susanjanewhite.com.

Empty jam jars

To transport food into work with you.

Ideas for Breakfast

'Keep your face to the sunshine,
and you will never see the shadows.'
Helen Keller

1 British cup = 250ml

The breakfast roll is dead. Who wants to hoover up
chemically enhanced meat, bleached rolls and puddles
of cholesterol?

We've designed this chapter for anyone who dreads the
shrill of their alarm clock. Some recipes involve a little
forward planning, but will ultimately gift you with more
snoozage and go-go juice (the High-octane Banana Nutmeg
Flapjacks on page 34 last all week in the fridge,
for example).

Only 6 seconds to fuel up? No problem. Stick your hand
in the freezer to loot your store of ready-made goodies
from this book: Lemon and Pistachio Pie (page 224), Office
Bombs (page 62), Your New Wheat-free Bread (page 51), Goji
Berry Smudge (page 207), Strawberry Shortbread (page 231),
Hazelnut and Raisin Freezer Cookies (page 228), Blackberry
Tart (page 235), Black Bread with Sun-dried Tomatoes (page
54), Barley Grass Balls (page 66) or Chia Bonbons (page 64).

I swear you won't miss your breakfast cereal and milk.
In fact, I bet you'll look back on your favourite cereal
packet like a bad ex and wonder what on earth you ever saw
in it. It was a love affair controlled by a sugar rush, and
little else. Good riddance.

**Visit page 12 to learn more about my alternatives to refined
cane sugar.**

THE ONLY GRANOLA RECIPE YOU'LL EVER NEED

****

A bowl of DIY granola and nut milk is a great way to start the day. It takes just 20 minutes to make and the benefits last all week. The beauty of making your own granola is the satisfaction of knowing exactly what went into it - none of the cheap fats, preservatives, sugar or gunk regularly found in commercial ones.

For your inner Mary Poppins, tie a ribbon around a jar of granola and give it as Christmas pressies. Parachute some blue cornflower petals in there too, available online and from Fallon & Byrne in Dublin.

2 cups nuts (260g) nuts
  (pecans, walnuts, Brazil
  nuts, hazelnuts)
2 1/2 cups (225g) jumbo oats
1 cup (100g) quinoa flakes
1 cup (130g) combination of
  sunflower and pumpkin seeds
5 tablespoons ground
  linseeds or ground almonds
1 teaspoon sea salt flakes
3/4 cup (190ml) raw honey or
  maple syrup
3/4 cup (190ml) extra virgin
  coconut oil
grated zest of 1 orange
2 cups (280g) dried fruit
  (cranberries, dates,
  raisins, unsulphured
  apricots)
1 rough cup (100g) dried
  banana, chopped

Makes 20 servings

Preheat the oven to 170°C/150°C fan/340°F. Line 2 baking trays with parchment paper.

Roughly chop any big nuts (pecans are fine left whole). Toss the nuts in a large bowl with the oats, quinoa flakes, seeds, ground linseeds and salt. Feeling adventurous? A tablespoon of cinnamon or dried ginger will add another flavour layer.

Gently warm the honey, oil and orange zest together. Pour over the bowl of oats and coat well. You won't be adding the dried fruit until after baking.

Spread thinly on the baking trays and transfer to the middle shelf of the oven. Bake for 17-20 minutes. Shake the trays after 8 minutes to prevent burning. You're aiming for a light golden colour. Oats and nuts taste bitter if you let them turn brown.

Remove from the oven and allow to cool and solidify completely before tossing through the dried fruit. Store in an airtight container for 2-3 weeks. Great with the Brazil nut milk on page 75 or cultured coconut yoghurt. Makes enough to last all week for a large family.

MANGO, BLACKBERRY AND BUCKWHEAT PORRIDGE

****

This is no ordinary porridge. But then again, this is no ordinary cookbook. Every recipe is designed to feed your battery and have you high-jumping those afternoon slumps.

Despite its name, buckwheat is not related to wheat and it does not contain gluten. That's a high five and a back flip for coeliacs.

1/2 cup (100g) buckwheat
  grain, soaked overnight
squeeze of lemon juice
1 small apple, grated
a bite-sized chunk of
  coconut cream*
1/2 mango, sliced (or
  soak some dried mango
  overnight)
handful of blackberries
  (optional)
maple or apple syrup, to
  serve

Serves 1

* You can use coconut milk in place of water, but it works out to be a lot more expensive. Coconut cream comes in a block and you can chip off bits as you need it. Just store it in the fridge.

Soak the buckwheat overnight in water and a squeeze of lemon juice. In the morning, pour off the excess water (and debris), then rinse in a sieve to separate the grains once more. This process breaks down the phytic acid in the cereal and makes it more digestible as well as quicker to cook.

Bring 1 cup of water to the boil. Add the soaked buckwheat, grated apple and the shavings or chunks of coconut cream. Cook for 15–20 minutes at a put-putter rather than a ferocious boil. It will thicken and become creamy with time.

Best adorned with juicy mango slivers, messy blackberries and DIY apple syrup (see page 25). While mangos can be pricey, you can sniff out massive boxes of them in Asian stores every June, July and August for buttons. Soaked dried mango works for the rest of the year.

METRO MUESLI WITH CHIA JAM

****

Rushed for breakfast? Time for muesli-making, darling. Not that fancy expensive stuff you pass wistfully in trendy delis. I mean your very own creations, transported in a snazzy jar with a spoon, appetite and sleepy smile. It makes the M50 actually enjoyable.

Oats don't always have to be eaten as molten-hot porridge. Soaking oat flakes overnight in a liquid (water, milk, apple juice) makes them delectably sweet and more digestible. Prepping this breakfast is an easy habit to acquire, sparing those brain cells first thing in the morning. But don't take my word for it. Try it and see.

Gastroenterologists - the specialists who look after your pipes - recommend getting between 25-35g of dietary fibre every day. A bowl of Metro Muesli with Chia Jam will give you an almighty 22g of fibre before the day even dawns. Add grated apple for an extra 5g or banana for 3g. Want to know the average daily intake in Ireland? A measly 10g. Highly processed diets are devoid of fibre. Given that colon cancer and heart disease are this country's top killers, it's probably time to make friends with a new breakfast regime.

This is just a variation on Bircher muesli. Stir all the ingredients together except the cinnamon. Use whatever ingredients to hand that you feel really work for you - a tablespoon of buckwheat? Blueberries? Grated apple? Cacao nibs? Banana? Hazelnuts? The following morning, scoop into a jar and crown with cinnamon before you dash out the door. Don't forget a spoon.

If you have the time, try making some chia jam. It's a quirky variation to the sugar-laden stuff. Soak the listed ingredients for 30 minutes or overnight. Store in a jam jar for up to 3 days. Ta-da!

For the muesli:
2/3 cup (60g) jumbo oats
1/3 cup (50g) raisins
1 cup (250ml) water, apple
  juice, soya or nut milk
2 tablespoons linseeds
squeeze of lemon juice
sprinkle of pumpkin seeds
sprinkle of sunflower seeds
sprinkle of ground cinnamon

Serves 1

For the chia jam:
1/2 cup (125ml) apple juice
dash of lime juice
2 tablespoons chia
1 tablespoon raw honey
1 tablespoon acai or
  beetroot powder

Makes 6-8 servings

DECENT MILLET PORRIDGE AND APPLE SYRUP

****

Millet is not a fabulously tasty grain. My nostrils balked and my palate winced the first time I made porridge with it. But by teaming millet with strong flavours, you'll bring out this grain's best quality - its texture.

Millet's nutritional kudos and affordability are good enough reasons to introduce it to your breakfast table. Sprinkle with coconut blossom sugar for the food nerd in you, but living in Ireland means I'm able to get my hands on Highbank Orchard Syrup. This is our answer to maple syrup, made from 100% local organic apples and love.

Cook the millet and water on a medium heat for 3-5 minutes before adding the creamed corn and salt. That's it!

To make your own apple syrup, press the apples and boil the juice for 25 minutes until it resembles a viscous syrup. Store in an airtight jar and summon when required. Ideally, you'll need to use fresh apple syrup within 4-5 days.

This delicious sticky nectar is rich in potassium, the mineral that helps evacuate hangovers.

For the porridge:
1/3 cup (40g) millet flakes
2/3 cup (165ml) water
1/3 cup (75g) puréed
  sweetcorn
pinch of salt flakes

Serves 1

For the apple syrup:
12 apples

Makes 6-8 servings

DOUBLE DECKER AMARANTH AND BANANA PUD

****

Amaranth is another one of those supergrains that have the Hollywood glitterati genuflecting. It has serious nutritional gravitas, rivalling quinoa as the number one seed. Amaranth's got more muscle than wheat, clocking in four times the amount of calcium and twice as much iron. And with generous stores of lysine, you can kiss cold sores toodle-loo. Not bad for half a cent per gram.

A caveat for the cook: bananas used in this recipe need to be over-ripe. Any green areas on the banana skin means they have not ripened fully and will make the pudding bitter. Look for older bananas with blackened sweet spots.

Please don't try this recipe with coconut milk or almond milk. Something offensive happens.

1 cup (200g) amaranth grain
1 1/2 cup (375ml) water
1/4 teaspoon sea salt
3 tablespoons maple syrup
3 tablespoons tahini or
  almond butter
2 large eggs, beaten
500ml soya, hemp or oat milk
2 very ripe bananas, chopped
1/2 cup (75g) raisins
1 teaspoon vanilla extract
1 tablespoon rapadura or
  coconut sugar
1 tablespoon ground cinnamon

Serves 6-8

Preheat the oven to 160°C/140°C fan/325°F.

In a small saucepan with a tight-fitting lid, bring the amaranth, water and salt to a soft boil. This means a gentle putter rather than a violent bubble that will blow the lid off and scare the bejaysus out of your budgie. Cook for 15 minutes, until the water is fully absorbed. Amaranth is not a dry, fluffy grain when cooked. Expect something that looks like a gluey couscous.

While the amaranth is doing its thing, prep the rest of the gear. Blend the maple syrup and nut butter together until smooth, then add the eggs. Pour this mixture into the milk and add the chopped bananas, raisins and vanilla.

Remove the amaranth from the heat, stir briskly and add in the milky mixture. Give it all a gentle stir.

Pour and scrape the pudding mix into a medium-sized pie dish (about the size of a magazine page). You're aiming for a pudding at least 1 inch deep, but no more than 2 inches. Pyrex rectangular glass dishes give the best result for custardy puds like this one. Cook for 40 minutes in a conventional oven. It should wobble slightly in the centre when removed. Halfway through cooking, mix the rapadura sugar and cinnamon together and sprinkle it on top.

CHIA AND CHAI BREAKFAST PUDDING

****

I make this for my little monsters and their mighty appetites. While chai tea is not essential, I recommend using it through the wintry months. Sweet chai contains cardamom, cinnamon, ginger, anise, fennel and cloves - all of which are warming spices for your belly.

Using a fork, whisk together the chia seeds, milk and coconut oil. Tear open the sweet chai teabag and stir it through. Allow the chia pudding to set overnight, either in the fridge or on the countertop. Serve in the morning with layers of banana and blueberries. A sneaky drizzle of brown rice syrup is awfully good too.

3/4 cup (125g) chia seeds
2 cups (500ml) almond (or other) milk
1 tablespoon melted coconut oil
1 teabag sweet chai (or cinnamon)
1 banana, sliced
handful of blueberries
drizzle of brown rice syrup (optional)

Serves 3

BADASS BREAKFAST BARS

****

These fibre-rich breakfast bars are sure to have your arteries applauding. No butter, cream, sugar or stodgy white flour — just pure, unadulterated whole foods the way Mother N intended.

The attraction of low-glycemic food like oats is that it breaks down slowly, releasing a steady stream of energy into the body. Picture drip-feeding your diesel tank so that it never runs empty. This makes oats an excellent diabetic food, but also gold for athletes, weight watchers, hyper children and anxious cabinet ministers.

More geek speak? Oats' cargo of soluble and insoluble fibre has the nifty ability of servicing our pipes in more ways than one. There ain't nothing sexy about constipation, especially given that our skin often takes over as an excretory organ. Yes, oats will make you regular, but they'll also sat nav your pipes for cholesterol and escort it out of your body like a bad-tempered bodyguard.

It's important to note that oats need to be cooked or soaked in order to tap into their nutritional benefits. Muesli straight out of a bag with milk does not count.

4 1/2 cup (670g) combination of dried apricots, prunes and pitted dates
juice of 1 lime
4 tablespoons pumpkin seeds (optional)
5 cups (450g) oat flakes*
1 cup (100g) ground almonds
1 cup (140g) rye* flour
1/2 cup (50g) ground chia or ground flaxseeds
1 teaspoon unrefined organic salt
1 cup (250ml) freshly squeezed orange juice
1 cup (250ml) extra virgin coconut oil
5 tablespoons barley malt extract, maple syrup or brown rice syrup*

Makes 20-25 bars

Preheat the oven to 180°C/160°C fan/350°F. Line a 20cm square baking tin (or something similar) with greaseproof baking parchment.

Place your apricots, prunes and dates in a saucepan and pour in enough water to come just below the level of the fruit. Bring to the boil, then lower the heat and simmer for 15-20 minutes with the lid on. If steam escapes, add a touch more water. Once cooked, stir through the lime juice and mix until the fruits are almost smooth. Set aside.

While the fruits are doing their thing, briefly pulse the pumpkin seeds in a blender or a coffee grinder. You can chop them up with a sharp knife if you prefer less washing up, or buy them pre-milled.

* For the gluten-sensitive brigade, I find using brown rice flour, maple syrup and gluten-free oats works well.

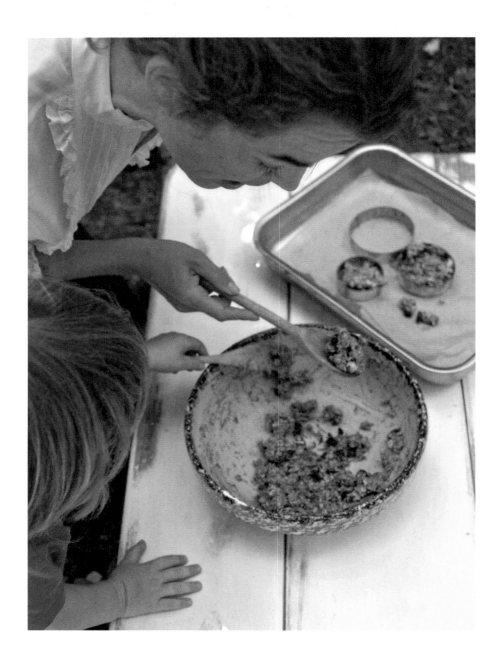

In a mixing bowl (and wearing a deliciously
frilly apron), mix together the pumpkin seeds,
oats, ground almonds, rye flour, chia/flaxseeds and
salt. If your oats are big, pulse them in a food
processor first with the pumpkin seeds. Finer oat
flakes give better results, but be careful not to
pulse into an oatmeal or flour.

In a separate bowl, mix the orange juice, oil
and sweetener and pour into the dry ingredients,
stirring until everything is glistening.

Using dampened fingers, press two-thirds of the
oat mix into the lined tin. It's really gooey and
sticky, so ramp up the radio to take the edge off
impatient fingers. Spread the jammy apricot mix
over this base. Gently press the remaining oat
mix on top of the apricot mix. You'll need to
do this with your fingers again. Take a curtsy -
only if you're wearing a frilly apron, otherwise
you'll look a bit silly - and admire your
brilliance.

Place on the centre shelf of the oven and bake
for 40 minutes, until lightly golden but not
browned. Allow to cool before slicing into
squares. Store on top of kitchen paper inside
an airtight tin or in the fridge. The smell of
these Badass Breakfast Bars will draw children
away from their Nintendo like the Pied Piper
- straight into an apron. Who knows, maybe
you'll have the next MasterChef hatching in your
kitchen?

These keep well in the fridge for up to 10 days.
In other words, a lot of happy breakfasts.

HIGH-OCTANE BANANA NUTMEG FLAPJACKS

****

Commercial breakfast bars are full of sugar, cheap hydrogenated fat and salt - none of which your brain cells will appreciate. With increasing financial pressure on producers to lower their production costs, it's hard to trust anything with a wrapper and a marketing department nowadays. These homemade breakfast bars are more like supersonic flapjacks and store really well in the fridge for 2 weeks.

Don't be put off by coconut oil's saturated fat content. These fats are in the form of medium chain triglycerides. MCTs readily convert to energy, in contrast to longer chain triglycerides such as sunflower oil. This is done through our cells' mitochondria - the gateway to our body's fuel. No wonder sporting stars choose this oil over any other. What a shame no one told Lance Armstrong.

1 cup (150g) Medjool dates
  or pre-soaked regular
  dates
2 cups (180g) oats
1 cup (100g) ground almonds
3/4 cup (55g) broken banana
  chips (not dried banana)
1/2 cup (65g) chopped pecans
1/2 cup (75g) raisins
handful of sunflower seeds
1-2 teaspoons grated nutmeg
1 teaspoon Maldon sea salt
  flakes
3/4 cup (190ml) extra virgin
  coconut oil
1/2 cup (125ml) honey, brown
  rice syrup or barley malt
  extract

Makes 20 flapjacks

Preheat the oven to 170°C/150°C fan/340°F. Line a tin no bigger than a magazine page with parchment paper.

Chop the dates and combine with the remaining dry ingredients in a large bowl. Merrily mix.

In a saucepan, gently melt the coconut oil with your choice of natural sweetener for around 5 minutes, until nicely melded. Strangely, maple syrup does not work in this recipe.

Create a hole in the centre of your dry ingredients and add the deliciously syrupy coconut oil. Energetically mix, preferably with sashaying hips and a bit of Bell X1. This helps every last bit of your gooey mix to glisten. Pour into the prepared tin and press down firmly with your fingers. Licking of utensils and bowl most definitely encouraged. Lightens the washing up.

Bake for 35 minutes, until lightly golden - any darker in colour and the oats will turn bitter. Remove from the oven and allow to rest for 10 minutes before refrigerating them. Resist cutting until they have chilled. Otherwise you will be left with a frustratingly messy affair, which no amount of Bell X1 can remedy.

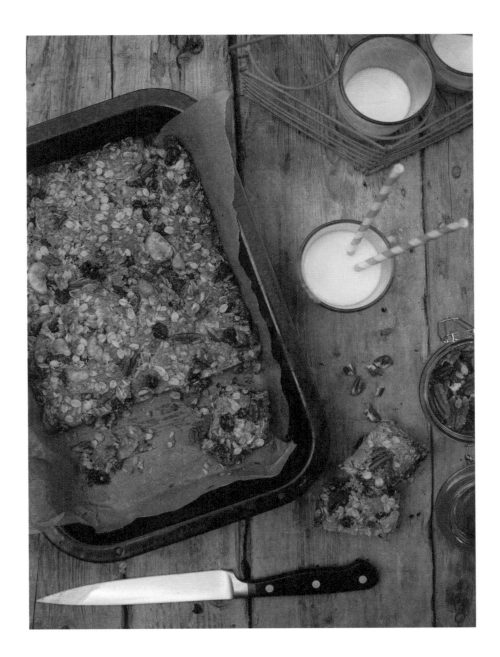

MAPLE AND CARDAMOM PEACHES

****

Peaches are bursting with vitamins that keep our bodies jolly. Niacin in particular helps improve circulation to the brain - something most of us would appreciate on a Sunday morning.

And you know the disappointing, fluffy peaches you sink your teeth into? Those infuriating peach imposters? No need to hurl them in the bin. Collect yourself, and scald the living daylights out of them instead. A peach's sweetness will sing once heated. Such delicious reprisal.

If you're using fresh ginger in place of dried ginger, try peeling a thumb-sized piece and freezing until firm. This makes it super easy to grate and ensures the ginger's stringy fibres don't corrupt your brekkie. Grated frozen ginger gives any dish a heart-thumping ping - my number one tip for boring lentils and despondent salads.

4 massive peaches
2 tablespoons maple syrup
1/2 teaspoon ground cardamom
1 teaspoon fresh or dried
  ginger
cultured soya or coconut
  yoghurt, to serve
squeeze of lemon juice, to
  serve

Serves 4-8

Preheat your grill or barbecue. It's wise to clean any residue from yesterday's messy chicken wings - not a good companion to today's breakfast.

Cut the peaches in half and remove the stone. This is noticeably easier with ripe peaches, as under-ripe peaches refuse to let loose their centre stone. Then, using a lunchbox and lid, mix the maple syrup and spices together. Pop the peach halves inside and shake the box to coat the fruit.

Place the gooey, coated peaches under a grill or over the barbecue flames and cook for a few minutes on each side, depending on how hot it is. You'll be the judge of that. Remove each one gently, as they are decidedly delicate now. Tuck in with yoghurt and lemon juice. Chill for up to 3 days in the fridge.

6AM TODDLER COOKIES

****

Ever up at 6am with your teeny tots? These cookies will keep them quietly active while nourishing their little motors. There's hardly any mess - notice there's no flour or eggs.

Preheat the oven to 180°C/160°C fan/350°F. Line a baking tray with greaseproof paper.

Grate the apple into a large mixing bowl. If you're crafty enough to do this without getting your knuckles involved, high five your toddler. Toss through the remaining ingredients, coating everything really well with the mashed banana. Make approximately 16 cookies by taking a table-spoon of the dough and flattening it between your hands, just like Play-Doh. A bit of *Blue Peter* may be required.

Place on the lined baking tray and bake for 12 minutes, or a little longer if the cookies are a bit bigger. No need to cool on a wire wrack - let them find your breakfast table immediately. Minor caveat - scoff them all on the same day, as they tend to misbehave after 24 hours.

1 medium apple
1 cup (90g) porridge oats
  (not jumbo)
1/2 cup (75g) sultanas or
  raisins
1/2 cup (125g) mashed banana
2 teaspoons baking powder
1 teaspoon ground cinnamon

Makes 16 cookies

STICKY CINNAMON AND PRUNE CAKES

****

Unless you were born before 1945, a prune cupcake sounds as appealing as a jug of turnip juice. But balk not. My friend the prune has more antioxidants than a blueberry. Prunes are a lot cheaper too. Add to this the nutritional superpowers of flaxseeds, apples, bananas, pecans, olive oil, carrots, cinnamon and rye, and you've got yourself a love bomb. Just what your body needs to survive a morning in the office.

8 squishy prunes, destoned
  and chopped
1 medium banana, mashed
1/4 cup (30g) pecans
6 tablespoons freshly
  pressed apple juice
4 tablespoons raw agave,
  barley malt extract, maple
  or yacón syrup
2 tablespoons milled
  flaxseeds (linseeds)
2 tablespoons extra virgin
  olive oil
1 cup (60g) loosely packed
  grated carrots
1 1/4 cup (175g) rye flour
2 teaspoons baking powder
1 teaspoon ground cinnamon

Makes 9-12 muffins

Preheat the oven to 180°C/160°C fan/350°F. Line a muffin tray with 9-12 paper cases.

In a large bowl, mix the prunes, banana, pecans, apple juice, sweetener, flaxseeds and oil together. Stir through the grated carrots and set aside.

In a separate bowl, introduce the rye flour to the baking powder and cinnamon. Make sure the baking powder doesn't stick in one place. Make a well in the centre of the flour and scoop the wet prune mixture into it. Mix thoroughly. I always find singing loudly helps. Spoon into your prepared muffin tray, but don't fill the cases too high or they won't cook in the centre.

Bake for 30-35 minutes (or half that time if using a smaller fairy cake tray). Remove from the oven and watch hungry nostrils dance. These muffins benefit from cooling down for 20 minutes to solidify and rest. Very difficult to resist looting, so remove self from kitchen and find distraction elsewhere.

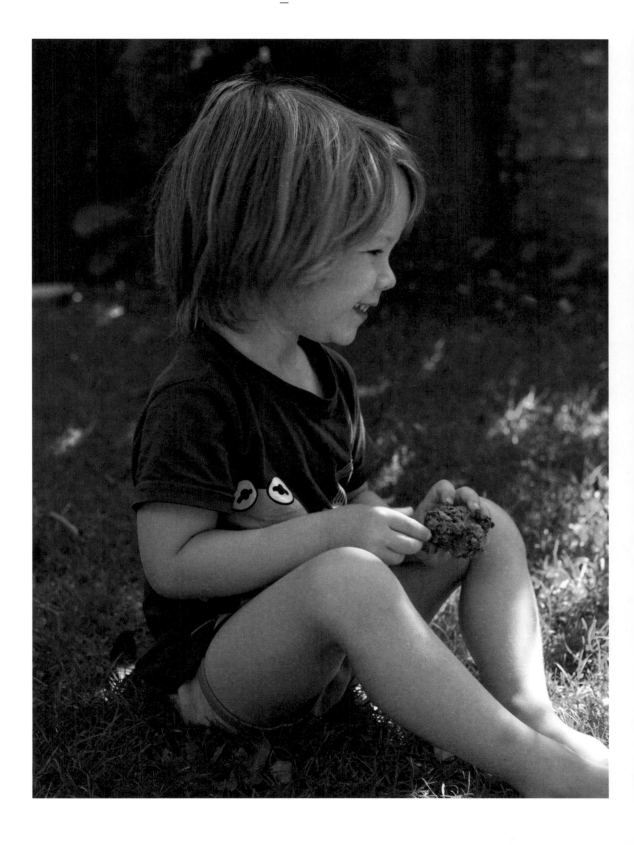

SCRAMBLED TOFU WITH CARAMELISED ONION AND SHIITAKE MUSHROOMS

****

This is vegan speak for a full fry. Good for lazy evenings and sedate brain cells. Just make sure your tofu is biodynamic and organic to avoid the dodgy mechanical isolation techniques many processors use. (For more on this, see pages 13-14).

Shiitake mushrooms are good for the immune system, according to Dale Pinnock, aka The Medicinal Chef. Their polysaccharides play funny games with our frontline defences, resulting in some serious moves against invading pathogens. The herb turmeric has been implicated in the reduction of tumours, amyloid plaque in Alzheimer's and many other inflammatory conditions, such as arthritis, so we've stuck a good tablespoon in for you. There's raw garlic too, vaunted for its healing powers. Think Pac-Man in your bloodstream. In other words, this is a good dish to have up your sleeve alongside your emergency Kleenex.

1 onion
about 8 shiitake (or other)
 mushrooms
2 tablespoons extra virgin
 olive or coconut oil
about 8 cherry tomatoes
splash of tamari, plus extra
 to serve
1 x 300g block firm
 biodynamic tofu (we use
 Demeter)
1 garlic clove, crushed
1 tablespoon ground turmeric
2 teaspoons ground cumin
1 teaspoon nutritional yeast
 flakes or a pinch of salt
cayenne pepper, to serve

Serves 3

Slice or dice the onion and shiitakes, depending how you like to eat them. In a warm frying pan, add the oil, onion, mushrooms and cherry tomatoes and cook for 10 minutes, until the onions turn glassy and translucent. If your frying pan looks overcrowded, watch out. Steam won't escape and will waterlog your breakfast instead of caramelising it. I like to roast or grill my tomatoes with a lick of balsamic vinegar and olive oil and add them to the mushrooms before plating up. While I find this method best, it does add to the washing up.

Once the onions and mushrooms are cooked, add a splash of tamari and stir briskly as the pan sizzles. This will dress the mushrooms in some finger-licking umami. Add the block of firm tofu and crumble it under a wooden spatula. Let the garlic, turmeric, cumin and yeast flakes join the party, digging any white pieces of tofu into the bright yellow turmeric glaze. As soon as it's warmed through, serve with cayenne pepper, tamari soya sauce and some cracking company.

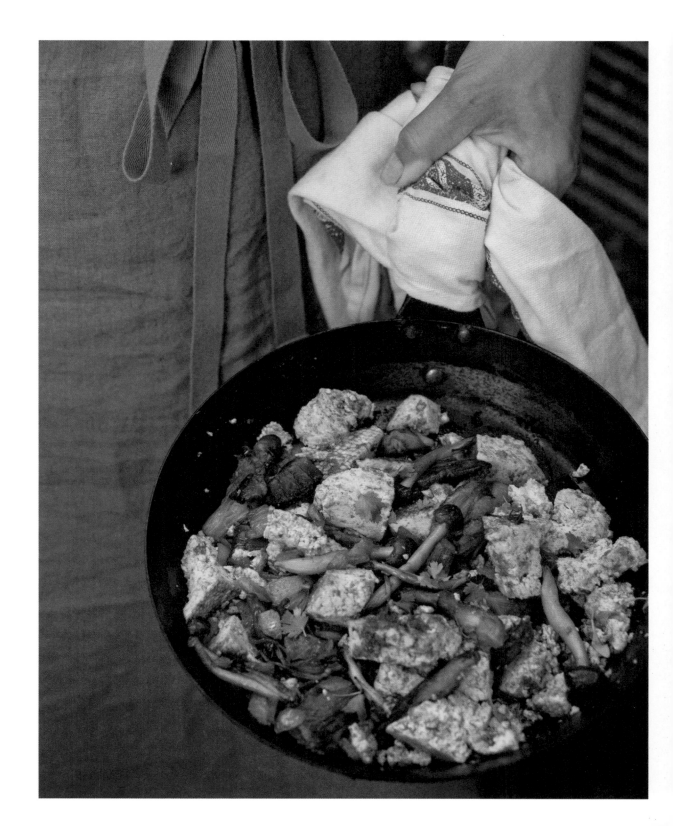

BAKED SWEET POTATOES

****

Ambrosial, warm and comforting - everything a breakfast should be on a chilly morning. Sweet potatoes are superheroes of the soil. Expect to ramp up your frontline defences after breakfasting on these. You'll find lots of beta carotene, zinc, vitamin E and vitamin C within its amber flesh. These are the nutrients responsible for fancy immune ripostes. Think Catherine Zeta-Jones and Zorro. The sniffles won't stand a chance.

2 medium sweet potatoes
a little time

Serves 1-2

Throw the potatoes into the oven, whole and in their skins. Bake at 200°C/180°C fan/400°F for 60-90 minutes, depending on their size. There's no need to pierce or slit the potato skins. Sweet potatoes will steam beautifully in their own jackets if you leave them alone. Remove when very soft to touch. Sweet potatoes benefit from overcooking rather than undercooking.

GREEN EGGS

****

Matcha is the Rolls Royce of green teas. The whole tea leaf is ground into a powder, as opposed to diluted in a teabag. This might help explain why matcha has significantly more antioxidants and pomposity than regular green tea. This neon green powder also houses a gob-smacking amount of protective catechins. Health scientists get indecently excited about these compounds. Be careful not to fall for all the hype of 137 antioxidants per sip, bottomless libido and eternal life. But it does make scrambled eggs more interesting.

Green eggs take 3 minutes from start to finish. Double up to serve a friend.

Gently warm the coconut oil in a heavy-based pan on a medium heat, making sure the oil doesn't reach smoke point. Butter and cream are supposedly the best allies to making the perfect scrambled eggs, but something very special happens when they cavort with coconut oil instead. You're about to find out.

Break the eggs into a bowl and whisk briefly with a fork. Add them to the heated pan and let them cook halfway through before stirring them. I like my eggs luscious and floppy, so I take them off now and plate up. El Hubador prefers his fluffy and seriously scrambled, so I leave his on for a further 10 seconds and stir with a vigour usually reserved for rowing a sinking boat. Stir through the chives or chervil and season once cooked. Whatever way you like yours, just remember not to add the matcha powder until the scrambled eggs are served up. Use a sieve to sprinkle the green powder over them like angel dust.

2 teaspoons extra virgin
   coconut oil
3 eggs
2 teaspoons chopped chives
   or chervil
generous pinch of salt and
   crushed black peppercorns
1/4 teaspoon matcha green
   tea powder

Serves 1

MISO EGGS AND SOYA SAUCE

****

4 teaspoons extra virgin
  coconut oil
5 eggs
2 teaspoons live,
  unpasteurised miso
splash of tamari

Serves 2

Gently warm the coconut oil in a heavy-based pan on a medium heat, making sure the oil doesn't reach smoke point. Butter and cream are supposedly the best allies to making the perfect scrambled eggs, but something very special happens when eggs fraternise with coconut oil.

Break the eggs into a bowl and whisk briefly with the miso. Add to the heated pan and let the eggs cook halfway through before stirring them. I prefer mine soft and floppy, so I fold the eggs over like an omelette and plate up. If you prefer them cooked for longer, stir briskly until the eggs look fluffy. This usually makes the miso silky smooth as opposed to lumpy.

Whatever way you like yours, just remember not to add the tamari until the scrambled eggs are served up. Otherwise you'll end up with murky-looking eggs, which don't go well with hangovers.

IDEAS FOR BREAKFAST

MILLET AND CHESTNUT CRÊPES WITH PASSIONFRUIT SYRUP

****

This recipe is borrowed from Béatrice Peltre's award-winning blog, La Tartine Gourmande. Turns out Bea married my mother-in-law's cousin's son. That makes me practically French. Three times removed, of course, but what's a number, right?

Combine the flour, sugar and salt in a large bowl. The sugar is an important addition, so please do leave it in the recipe. Break the eggs into the centre of the flour and slowly whisk while pouring in the milk. Continue to whisk until the batter is silky. Stir in the coconut oil and vanilla. Cover with a plate and place in the fridge to rest for 1 hour, or overnight.

When ready to use, stir again. In a crêpe pan or frying pan, melt a little more coconut oil. Swirl to coat. Add enough batter to barely coat the bottom. You may have to shake the pan a little. Cook for 1-2 minutes on a medium to high heat. Once it starts bubbling and the batter looks cooked through, flip the crêpe and cook for 1 extra minute on the other side. Repeat until you run out of batter, adding a little coconut oil between each crêpe. Keep the crêpes warm on a plate as you work, covering them with a towel.

To make the syrup, just combine the pulp of the passionfruit with your choice of sweetener and drizzle over your creations. Homemade apple syrup is like a flavour grenade, so try to give the recipe on page 25 a go.

1/2 cup (65g) millet flour
1/4 cup (25g) chestnut flour
2 tablespoons cornflour
2 tablespoons rapadura or
  coconut sugar
pinch of sea salt
2 eggs
1 cup (250ml) hemp, oat or
  almond milk
1 tablespoon extra virgin
  coconut oil, melted, plus
  extra to cook
1 teaspoon pure vanilla
  extract
2 passionfruit
2 tablespoons raw honey,
  apple or date syrup

Makes 10 crêpes

SMOKED SALMON BLINI WITH HEALTHIER HOLLANDAISE

****

If you could do one thing to improve your health this year, swap your nasty margarine and commercial salad dressing for this incredibly sumptuous mayonnaise. When made with warm coconut oil, it rivals the most heavenly hollandaise to ever kiss a blini.

For the 'hollandaise':
2 egg yolks
1/4 cup (60ml) flaxseed oil
   or Udo's Oil
1/4 cup (60ml) extra virgin
   coconut oil, melted
2 big garlic cloves, crushed
1-2 tablespoons
   unpasteurised cider
   vinegar
1/2 cup (125ml) extra virgin
   olive oil
6-8 anchovies, roughly
   chopped

For the buckwheat blini:
1 cup (140g) buckwheat flour
1 teaspoon baking powder
salt and freshly ground
   black pepper
1 egg
2/3 cup (165ml) almond, hemp
   or oat milk
extra virgin coconut oil,
   to fry
8-10 slices of smoked salmon

Makes 8-10 big blinis

To make the 'hollandaise', run the motor of your food processor with the egg yolks. Keeping the motor on low, gradually add a steady stream of flaxseed oil and watch it thicken ever so gradually. Add it drop by drop – don't rush or you will end up curdling it, as I have done through impatience and overexcitement many a time. This can take up to 4 minutes. Repeat with the coconut oil. When it gets very thick, it's time to add the crushed garlic and cider vinegar to thin it out and give it an edge. Keep the motor running.

Next, slowly add the olive oil, watching the mayo thicken again. Always add the olive oil after the coconut oil and not the other way around. Olive oil can turn bitter if overly whisked.

Finally, add the anchovies and pulse briefly – you don't want to pulverise the anchovies. Taste and adjust the sharpness of the cider vinegar to your preference. If it's too sharp, turn on the motor again and add a little more olive oil.

Scoop into a screw-top jar and refrigerate for up to 3 weeks. A jar is approximately 12 portions.

To make the blini, sieve the flour, baking powder and a generous amount of seasoning into a bowl. In a separate cup, beat the egg with the milk and gradually pour into the dry ingredients, whisking all the while to prevent lumps. The batter lasts for 2 days in the fridge, so advance preparation is easy.

Heat some extra virgin coconut oil in a large non-stick frying pan on a medium to high heat. Drop enough of the blini batter to form a drop scone and fry for 20-30 seconds, until set.

Several can be done at once. Flip to cook the other side. The mixture is usually runny on one side, so flip with haste. Try not to leave them cooking too long or they will dry out. Taste the first one when cooled and decide for yourself. Hot blini will always taste moist, but they quickly lose their juiciness upon cooling. Bear this in mind too.

Repeat until there is no batter left. Dollop with the hollandaise and a blanket of smoked salmon. Pretty special stuff.

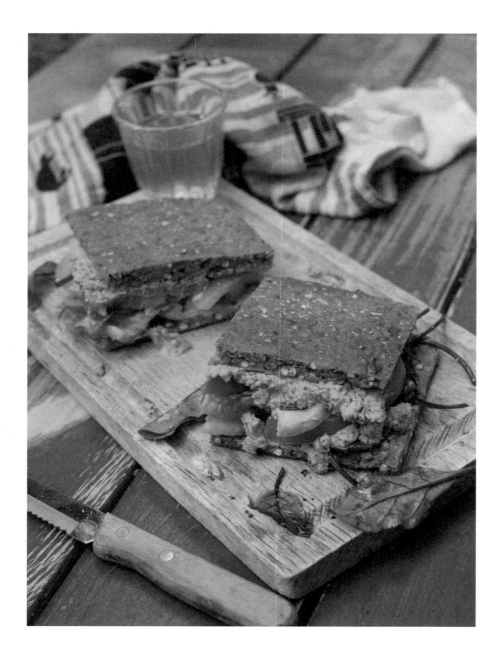

YOUR NEW WHEAT-FREE BREAD

****

Few pleasures in life can compete with tearing open a hot focaccia. I'm not suggesting you quarantine or banish such pleasures. On the contrary, let's celebrate these delights for what they are and enjoy them from time to time.

For a wholegrain and nourishing alternative, I recommend inaugurating this recipe to your life. And your freezer. It tastes like Irish brown bread, but without the bloating often associated with wheat.

Preheat the oven to 200°C/180°C fan/400°F. Line a shallow tin just smaller than a magazine page with greaseproof paper. We're going to bake this in a tray rather than a loaf tin, so when it's cooked, we'll cut it into squares. Each square can be used for a sambo, sliced horizontally like a bap.

Sieve the flours, baking powder, seasoning and spices into a large bowl to introduce air and make it fluffy. Try not to omit the spices, as they are central to this bread. Add the milk, millet flakes, sunflower seeds, whole buckwheat grains and honey (if using). It should be a pouring consistency and be quite runny. Pour the batter into the lined tin.

Bake for 35-40 minutes, depending on the depth of the tray you are using. Remove from the oven, allow to cool on a wire rack and divide into quarters. Looks really slick. Once you taste this buckwheat bread, you'll never want to buy bread again. Freeze in quarters, ready to split horizontally and toast every morning.

1/2 cup (70g) buckwheat flour
1/2 cup (50g) organic soya flour
2 teaspoons baking powder
1 teaspoon Herbamare seasoning, celery salt or sea salt
1 teaspoon ground ginger
1 teaspoon ground cinnamon
2 cups (500ml) almond milk, oat milk or hemp milk
3/4 cup (90g) millet or barley flakes
3/4 cup (90g) sunflower seeds
1/2 cup (100g) whole buckwheat grains
1-2 tablespoons honey, barley malt or maple syrup (optional)

Makes 1 loaf

RYE BANANA BREAD WITH HOMEMADE NUTELLA

****

Rye is rich in B vitamins, the chaps that act as spark plugs for energy ignition. This grain is also thought to have a higher concentration of cancer-protective lignans than any other cereal crop. Even more inter-esting, rye is the grain of choice for body-builders because of its specific amino acid profile, which seems to fancy muscle mass. But don't worry - you won't end up looking like a Transformer by nibbling away on this banana bread. You've got to lift insatiable amounts of weights to do that.

If you're looking for a totally gluten-free or grain-free recipe, just swap the rye flour with more coconut flour. It will be a little drier, but still crazy delicious. Barley malt syrup also works well, but honey doesn't for some strange reason.

However tempted you may be, please don't add walnuts or pecans. Nuts dry out the mixture.

For the bread:
1/4 cup (35g) coconut flour
1/4 cup (35-50g) rye flour
handful of dried dates
2 teaspoons ground cinnamon
1 teaspoon baking powder
1/2 teaspoon Maldon sea salt
  flakes
3 eggs, beaten
1 cup (240g) roughly mashed
  bananas (about 3 bananas)
5 tablespoons (75ml) melted
  coconut oil
2-3 tablespoons coconut
  sugar
2 teaspoons apple cider
  vinegar or lemon
1 teaspoon vanilla extract

For the homemade Nutella:
1/3 cup (90g) hazelnut butter
  (about half a small jar)
3 tablespoons cacao or cocoa
  powder
2 tablespoons maple or brown
  rice syrup

Makes 1 loaf

Preheat the oven to 180°C/160°C fan/350°F. You'll need a small to medium bread tin, lined and ready.

To make the Nutella, whip the ingredients together in a cup using a fork.

For the banana bread, get two large bowls. In the first one, stir the flours, dates, cinnamon, baking powder and salt together. In the second bowl, add the remaining ingredients and blend well.

Using a balloon whisk, beat the wet mix into the dry mix and transfer to your loaf tin. If you have banana left over, a few thin slices on top give it the Martha Stewart treatment. They also turn sweet and squishy in the oven.

Bake for 40 minutes. Cool on a wire rack and smother with Nutella or reverence.

BLACK BREAD WITH SUN-DRIED TOMATOES

****

Omega-3 oils are to hormones what Edward is to Jedward: indispensable. Our bodies cannot make omega-3, so we need to regularly include it in our diet. As always, food sources are preferable to supplements. You'll find a decent supply of omega-3 fatty acids in this bread. Flaxseeds are also said to be one of nature's highest sources of cancer-protective plant lignans. These groovy compounds are linked to happy hormones, lower blood cholesterol and boisterous antioxidant behaviour. Quite the hat trick for a tiny seed.

If you know someone who is gluten intolerant or coeliac, please jot this recipe down and gift it to them. It contains no flour or grains, making it perfect for paleo disciples too. But you don't have to be a paleo geek to appreciate this bread - it's incredibly good for you and seriously tasty.

I prefer to use blackstrap molasses instead of honey for three reasons. First, it gives the best baking results. Second, it's super rich in iron and B vitamins for energy. And third, it's much cheaper.

2 cups (220g) milled
 flaxseeds (linseeds)
3 teaspoons dried oregano
2 teaspoons baking powder
4 eggs
1/2 cup (125ml) hemp or
 almond milk
4 tablespoons extra virgin
 olive or macadamia oil
2 tablespoons blackstrap
 molasses or honey, warmed
 until runny
10-12 small sun-dried or
 sun-blushed tomatoes
handful of black olives,
 stones removed

Makes 1 loaf

Preheat the oven to 180°C/160°C fan/350°F. Lightly oil or line a small baking tray that's a few inches smaller in height than an A4 page. Brownie tins are perfect.

Combine the ground flax, oregano and baking powder together in a large bowl. Set aside.

In a separate bowl, mix the eggs, milk, oil and molasses until thoroughly united.

Chop up the sun-dried tomatoes and olives and add them to the wet ingredients. Now add wet to dry and immediately pour into your greased baking tray. Spread evenly and sprinkle a little more dried oregano on top.

Bake for about 25 minutes, then remove from the oven and its tin. Allow to cool for 25 minutes on a wire rack. Tickle with black olive tapenade, some super-garlicky hummus or serve alongside your favourite bowl of soup. This bread freezes exceptionally well, ready to grill when there's nothing in the cupboard.

See photo of Black Bread on page 96.

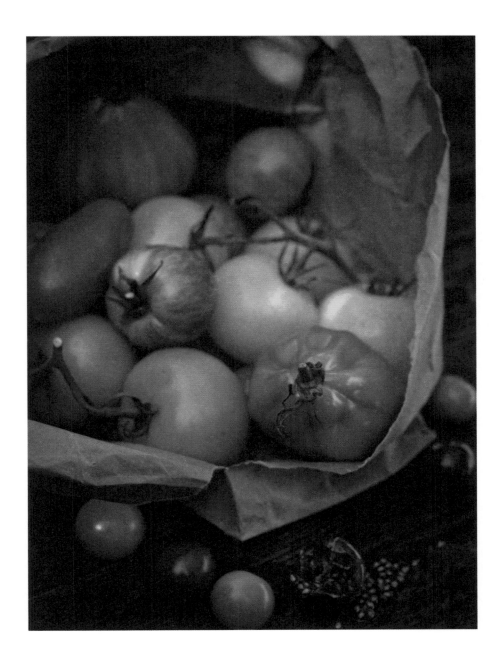

IDEAS FOR BREAKFAST

MULTISEED BREAD WITH CARAWAY SPICE

****

Trying to cut down on butter and baguettes? Difficult, isn't it? Now's a good time to create fresh associations with the food you eat in order to break the unhealthy ones.

David A. Kessler has written a gripping book about how junk food hijacks our brain chemistry and controls our behaviour. Reading even one chapter of Kessler's The End of Overeating feels so liberating and empowering. Kessler cautions us that certain cues activate brain circuits that guide behaviour. Instead of attacking the behaviour (overeating, smoking, reaching for more butter, insert vice here), recognise the cue.

For example, can you watch TV without reaching for a snack? Or have a coffee without smoking a cigarette? In other words, it's the cue that needs reformulating if we are to successfully ditch the junk in our diets. It's not enough to put a fatwa on the food. We need to acknowledge the prompts. So what are your cues?

Kessler's advice is to create fresh associations in an attempt to retrain our behaviour and palate. I recommend putting caraway and aniseed into your bread. Such a simple change will help keep your mitts off that errant butter dish. Caraway and aniseed are so much tastier when paired with olive oil. Your taste buds will breakdance.

Start by lightly toasting the pumpkin and
sunflower seeds on a baking tray in the oven for
12 minutes at 180°C/350°F with no oil. Leave to
cool. I recommend toasting more than you need, as
hot, crunchy seeds are often looted in my house.

Once cooled, transfer the toasted seeds and
linseeds into a large mixing bowl with the sugar,
warm water and yeast. Let these guys laze for 10
minutes before adding the remaining ingredients.
Mix into a firm dough and leave for another 10
minutes.

Now briefly and lightly knead the dough. Leave in
the bowl, covered with a clean cloth, for 1 hour
in a warm spot. Transfer to a suitable loaf tin
lined with non-stick parchment. You'll need to
squish in the sides a little. Leave to rise for
another hour. This will depend on the type of
yeast you have used, so as soon as it looks about
20% bigger, you're in business.

Bake for 45 minutes at 200°C/180°C fan/400°F.
Remove from the oven and from its tin and cool on
a wire rack. Best sliced thinly.

You'll love this multiseed bread. It tastes
incredible warm from the oven, but you can gently
toast some slices the next day to achieve similar
results. For a funky change, add a teaspoon of
ground fenugreek, aniseed and fennel seeds.

3/4 cup (100g) pumpkin seeds
3/4 cup (90g) sunflower seeds
3/4 cup (115g) linseeds
1/4 cup (40g) rapadura or
  coconut sugar
300ml warm water
2 teaspoons fast-action
  organic yeast
roughly 3 cups (400g) rye
  flour
2 tablespoons extra virgin
  olive or macadamia oil
1 tablespoon caraway seeds
1 teaspoon sea salt flakes

Makes 1 loaf

Snacks and Other Nutritional Hits

'Health is beauty. If someone takes care of themselves,
you can see the health shining from within them.'
Anna Friel, actress

1 British cup = 250ml

The definition of madness is doing the same thing over and
over again but expecting different results. If your body
isn't functioning as well as you'd like it to, take a look
at what you're putting into it. Eating foods that promote
good health will have you on your tippy toes. Eating foods
that promote poor health will have you on your knees. It's
as simple as that.

Many of these snacks can be stored in the freezer, lined up
like soldiers for when the munchies attack. This is an important feature of a clean diet. If you don't have back-up,
you're sure to fall under enemy fire.

Of course, there will be occasions when we fraternise with
the enemy (insert vice here). No matter. Move on and bap-
tise a few of these recipes to get you back on track. Today
is the first day of the rest of your life.

HOT AND SMOKY SEEDS

++++++++++++++++++++++++++

Touche Éclat and espressos must be keeping our economy afloat. Over half of us reportedly suffer from some sort of sleep disorder. So when it comes to nodding off, what are the smarter options? If self-hypnosis and camomile tea never worked for you, take a close look at your diet and see if you are getting enough B vitamins (especially B6), zinc and the amino acid L-tryptophan.

Foods rich in tryptophan can be an effective sleep aid without having to subscribe to dodgy narcotics. Tryptophan is the building block for an important snoozy hormone called melatonin. Without it, our eyes will struggle to shut.

Here's the good news. You'll find tryptophan, B vitamins and zinc in pumpkin seeds. As a result, scientists have begun to put pumpkin seed extract in multivitamin pills and sleeping aids. Bear in mind that it's easier and cheaper to keep a stash of pumpkin seeds in your fridge. But don't expect to fall straight to sleep if you eat them. Think of pumpkin seeds as couriers, delivering the cargo your body needs later tonight.

roughly 1 1/2 cups (200g)
  combination of pumpkin and
  sunflower seeds
2 tablespoons tamari
1 tablespoon mirin
  (optional)
1 teaspoon dried chilli
  flakes
1 tablespoon dried nori
  flakes (optional calcium
  boost)

Makes 1 1/2 cups

Preheat the oven to 180°C/160°C fan/350°F.

Toss the sunflower and pumpkin seeds on a baking tray and roast for 8-10 minutes. Now it's time to add the tamari, mirin and chilli flakes. Coat well, using a wooden spatula to stir the seeds about so as not to scrape your tray. Return to the oven for an extra 1-2 minutes of toasting.

Remove from the oven to cool and stir through the nori flakes (if using). Shards of Crispy Kale (page 63) also work. Once cooled, the seeds become crunchy again. Refrigerate in a screw-top jar and sprinkle over salads and soups or keep a stash in your pocket. They can last for up to 6 weeks.

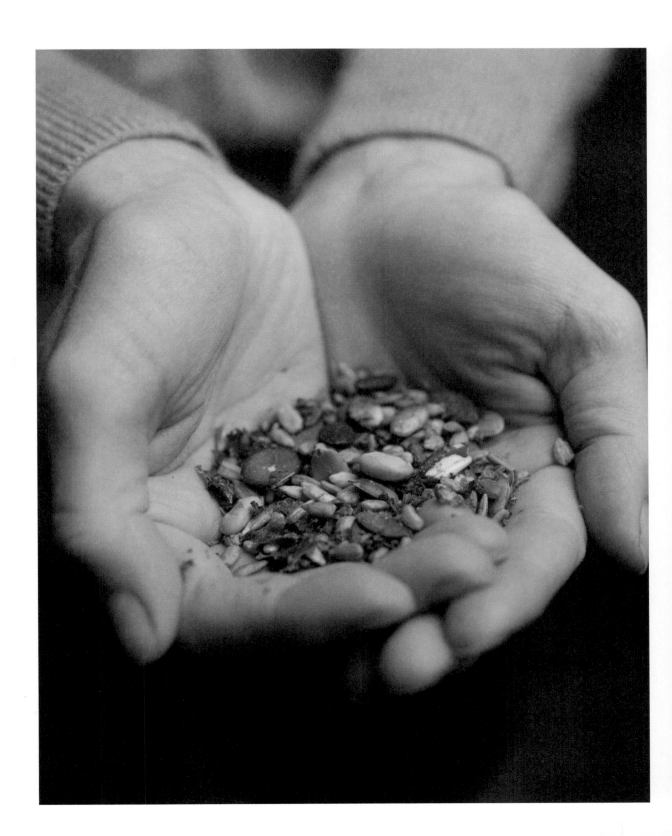

OFFICE BOMBS

+++++++++++++++

Office Bombs love lunchboxes, gym bunnies and little mitts. They take just minutes to prepare, but the benefits last all day. These snacks were designed to drip feed your battery consistently instead of one big sugar surge. Perfect fodder to help high jump that 3 o'clock afternoon trap.

If you can't find the large packets of milled sunflower and pumpkin seeds, just whizz enough of both seeds until they resemble fine breadcrumbs.

2 raspberry leaf teabags, opened
2 cups (240g) combination of milled pumpkin and sunflower seeds
1 cup (150g) raisins, chopped
1/2 cup (45g) ground almonds (or more ground seeds)
1/2 cup (125ml) tahini
1/2 cup (125ml) maple syrup, honey or brown rice syrup
4 tablespoons raw cacao nibs
5 tablespoons carob powder
pinch of good-quality salt, like pink Himalayan
desiccated coconut, to coat

Makes 30

Blitz everything except the desiccated coconut in your food processor just long enough for the mixture to start clumping together. You may need to scrape down the sides as you go along. Alternatively, with the assistance of some tunes or tenacity, beat the ingredients together with a simple metal fork.

Roll the dough between your palms into golf ball-sized treats. Drop them into a bowl of desiccated coconut to turn them into Office Bombs. They'll keep for 3 weeks in the fridge, 3 months in the freezer or 3 seconds in your hands.

CRISPY KALE

+++++++++++++

I experimented with 19 batches of kale crisps and over 40 guinea piglets. My taste buds had to be validated. After all, kale is a green leafy vegetable, the kind that tends to repel even the intrepid herbivores among us. Suddenly it was casting a spell upon rambling little fingers.

Not one of my guinea piglets gagged when I divulged its core ingredient. A couple of gasps could be heard, and a few silent screams. The under-10s thought these 'crisps' were a really naughty snack. One plate later, they had wolfed down more greens than the entire week.

There are a couple of variations you could try. Below is the most basic. Nutritional yeast flakes have an umami buzz. It's cheese to vegans, and replete with that elusive vitamin B12. If your local health food store is out of yeast flakes, use garlic granules and smoked paprika instead.

Preheat the oven to 180°C/160°C fan/350°F.

Flatten the kale leaves and use the point of a knife to remove the tough centre ribs. Tear the leaves into bite-sized pieces.

Using your hands, massage oil into each leaf. Spread across a baking tray. Don't worry about flattening the leaves out; they're better bunched up. Bake for 8-12 minutes. Check after 6 minutes and toss to prevent charring.

Grind the yeast flakes into a powder using a pestle and mortar. Remove from the oven and sprinkle the powdered yeast over the now-crispy kale. Scoff while warm. I'm not sure if crispy kale keeps in a sealed container. It never gets that far. Also awesome with sweet brown rice, avocado and tamari as a swift supper.

2 good handfuls of bone-dry curly kale
2-4 tablespoons extra virgin olive or coconut oil
1 tablespoon nutritional yeast flakes

Serves 4

CHIA BONBONS

++++++++++++++++

Chia seeds are an easy way to get those much-coveted omega-3 fats without having to neck back flax oil or pharma bullets.

What's so snazzy about omega-3s? A deficit in omega-3 fats has been linked to angry skin conditions, poor concentration levels and delinquent hormones. Without omega-3s, it seems we manufacture substandard cells. Not an attractive proposition. Think gazelle or tortoise: which would you rather be?

So will taking omega-3 fats cure mental atrophy, PMT and sagging boobs? No, but strong evidence suggests it can help. That's enough.

It's worth noting that the type of omega-3 fatty acids found in chia is slightly different to those found in oily fish. Chia contains ALA, the precursor to EPA and DHA fatty acids. You've probably come across these confusing terms at the pharmacy when choosing omega-3 supplements. In short, it has been argued that EPA and DHA are easier for the body to absorb. As a result, the omega-3s present in oily fish like mackerel are thought to be superior to those found in plants such as chia and flax. But chia offers a suite of other goodies, including more calcium than milk, banks of potassium, bone-building boron and cholesterol-reducing fibre.

4 tablespoons tahini
nearly 1/4 cup (60ml) maple
  syrup
1/2 cup (45g) milled chia
  seeds
1/4 cup (25g) ground almonds
2 tablespoons cocoa or raw
  cacao powder
5 tablespoons desiccated
  coconut

Makes about 30 bonbons

Beat the tahini and syrup together with a fork. Please note that honey won't work in this recipe. Once the tahini mixture is all glossy and luscious, measure in the chia seeds, ground almonds and cocoa powder and encourage them to party. A wooden spoon is useful.

Put the coconut in a bowl or shallow plate. Roll a small cherry-size ball of mixture between the palms of your hands to form a bonbon. Drop each one into the coconut and roll it around to coat, then let it set on a cold plate. You could try different coatings, like beetroot powder, lúcuma powder or ground hazelnuts. Store in the fridge and plunder at will.

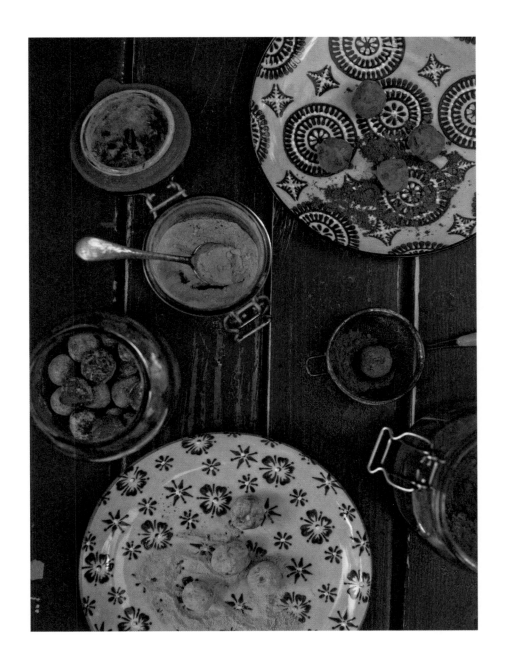

BARLEY GRASS BALLS

++++++++++++++++++++++

Instead of those dodgy energy drinks, make a big batch of these and store them in the office fridge.

Barley grass is like a mini farm of nutrients. Is it exceptionally rich in any one nutrient? No, but its broad nutritional spectrum makes it a first-rate tonic for dull days. I suspect that eating profuse quantities of green leafy vegetables would offer similar results. Let's agree that barley grass is a lot quicker and easier to prepare.

4 tablespoons ground almonds
4 tablespoons milled pumpkin
  and sunflower seed combo
2 tablespoons tahini
1-2 tablespoons runny honey
1-2 tablespoons barley grass
  powder
sprinkle of goji berries
  (optional)

Makes about 16 big bonbons

Mush everything together with a fork until it looks like thick cookie dough. Roll a teaspoon of the mixture into little bonbons between your palms. Store in an airtight jar in the fridge and liberate when required.

DR SMOOTHIE

++++++++++++++

Here's an easy way to start the day with a halo on your head. It doesn't involve broccoli, lycra or resetting your alarm clock. Just fruit, live yoghurt, oats and an appetite. Okay, and maybe a sense of humour if you forget to put the lid on the blender.

1 very ripe banana or
  avocado
1 cup frozen berries
1 cup (250ml) freshly
  pressed apple juice
1/2 cup (125ml) organic live
  soya or coconut yoghurt
4 tablespoons oat flakes
1 tablespoon ground chia or
  flaxseeds

Serves 2-3

The joy of this recipe is that you don't need a special juicer, just your magical whizzy machine. Blend everything together and leave for 1 hour or overnight before scoffing. Bring Dr Smoothie into work in a jam jar, or savour it on the road when your nerves begin to fray in the tailback traffic. Harness its happiness and you'll be surprised how mellow you'll feel by 8am.

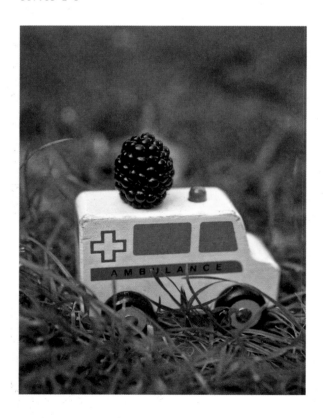

PROTEIN GRENADES

+++++++++++++++++++++

These grenades will save you money, fuel your muscles and feed insatiable appetites. More importantly, they're unequivocally better than the commercial sports muck at supermarkets and specialist sports stores.

Hemp protein powder is outrageously tasty, and legal. It comes directly from the hemp plant and contains all eight essential amino acids as well as a nice dose of omega-3 and iron. Iron is responsible for making haemoglobin, which transports oxygen around the blood. No iron, no energy. Omega-3s are important post-training, as they help quench inflammatory markers and heal bruised tissue.

And finally, a word on linseeds. They help your pipes. A lot. And offer another round of omega-3 artillery.

Not bad for a bonbon.

Using a fork, mush everything together in a bowl. Sunwarrior's vegan protein powder is awesome too, but it may dent your bank account.

Roll into mini bonbons and maybe coat each protein grenade with more desiccated coconut. Store in the refrigerator, preferably behind the vegetables, where your housemates will never find them.

2 tablespoons crunchy peanut butter
1 tablespoon hemp seed (protein) powder
1 tablespoon pea protein powder (we use Pulsin)
1 tablespoon ground linseeds
1 tablespoon desiccated coconut
1 tablespoon raw agave, honey or maple syrup
1 tablespoon goji berries (optional)

Makes 8

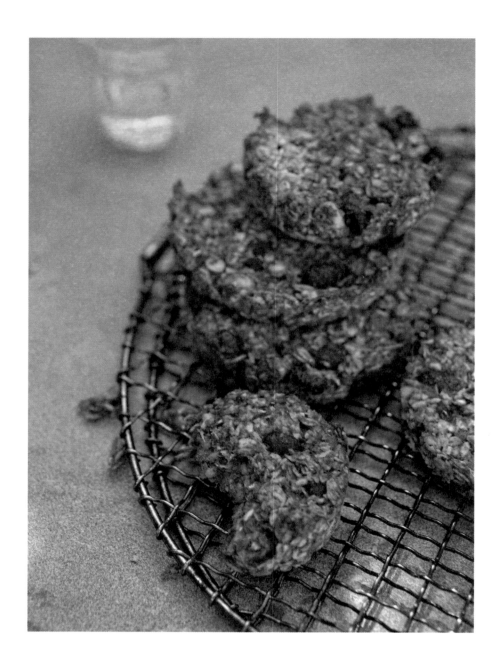

APPLESAUCE AND CINNAMON COOKIES

++

Satisfying and chewy, these are designed as everyday cookies, the sort you throw in your bag as you dash out the door. Or sneak into tedious board-rooms.

Raisins are pumped with resveratrol, which acts as a free radical assassin. Free radicals cause damage to our skin and to our arteries by helping LDL cholesterol set up home. Nasty things.

Preheat the oven to 180°C/160°C fan/350°F. Line a large baking tray with parchment paper.

Chop the apples into bite-sized chunks and place in a small saucepan with 1/4 cup of water and your dates or prunes. Cover with a tight-fitting lid and boil for 15 minutes, being careful the apples don't stick to the bottom of the pan. Once the fruit is soft enough to mush, remove from the heat and blitz with a hand-held blender. Measure out 2/3 cup and set aside. Any leftover purée can be frozen for the next batch of cookies or served on top of yoghurt.

Next, finely chop the roasted hazelnuts. There's little point buying pre-chopped hazelnuts, as their good oils turn rancid much quicker. In a large bowl, stir together the chopped hazelnuts, oats, raisins, coconut, linseeds and cinnamon. In a smaller bowl, beat the fruit purée and nut butter together thoroughly, followed by the milk and vanilla. Fold this glossy batter into the dry ingredients and mix thoroughly.

Place a large cookie cutter on the paper-lined tray and spoon the dough into the cookie cutter, filling until it's at least 2cm deep. Press and smooth with the back of the spoon. Gently lift the cookie cutter up and repeat with the rest of the dough.

Bake for 30 minutes, before they turn brown. Remove from the oven and cool on a wire rack. They can be eaten right away if, like me, you don't have the willpower to wait.

2-3 apples
8 dates or prunes, destoned
4 tablespoons roasted hazelnuts
1 3/4 cup (160g) jumbo oat flakes
3/4 cup (115g) raisins and/or dried cranberries
3/4 cup (60g) desiccated coconut
2 tablespoons milled linseeds or milled chia seeds
1-2 tablespoons ground cinnamon
1/4 cup (65g) nut butter, like hazelnut, almond or macadamia
1 cup (250ml) organic soya yoghurt, almond milk or hemp milk
2 teaspoons vanilla extract

Makes about 12 big cookies

SPIRULINA SHOTS

+++++++++++++++++++

Ever heard of an algae called spirulina? It smells a bit like fermented horse urine. This is usually overlooked once its magic starts to kick in. A favourite among ambitious models, spirulina offers a shortcut to cleansing the body. This curious green powder is home to immodest amounts of protein, calcium, zinc, iron, essential fats and energy-releasing B vitamins. Spirulina is hailed for helping with everything from lazy limbs to waning libidos.

Manufacturers recommend adding spirulina to yoghurts or smoothies. Here's a better way to shoot it back without assaulting your senses, or the kitchen floor.

2 apples (or 1 cup freshly
  pressed apple juice)
2 teaspoons spirulina powder

Serves 1

Juice your apples if you have one of those groovy machines. Cucumber is also good. Spirulina powder clings to the bottom of cups, so I recommend pouring half the juice into a cup, followed by the spirulina, then the remaining juice. Whisk with a fork. No need to hold your nose - it's surprisingly nice. Or perhaps I'm still asleep when I knock it back.

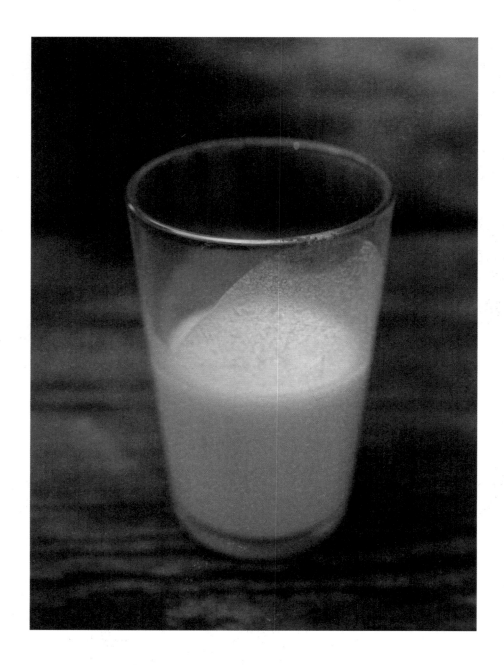

NUT MILK

++++++++++

Brazil nut milk is gorgeous. A Vitamix is the ultimate accessory when making it - and a clean muslin from Mothercare. Since I don't have a Vitamix, my kitchen walls are regularly redecorated. It hasn't stopped me making nut milk every other week. I drink the milk straight away or soak muesli in it overnight.

Start by soaking the Brazil nuts overnight or for 24 hours. Rinse and drain. Add 4 fresh cups (750-1000 ml) of water to your Vitamix or food processor along with the vanilla and blitz until silky smooth. In theory you could add a drop of maple syrup, but I don't think it needs it.

Pour this messy lot into a large jug, using the muslin cloth as a strainer to catch the shards of nuts. A very fine sieve also works. That's it.

1 cup (140g) Brazil nuts
1/2 teaspoon vanilla extract
 or powder (optional)

Makes 1 litre

STRAWBERRY AND BANANA SHOELACES

++

These popular children's snacks are called fruit leathers in the US and are usually pumped with sugar and preservatives. DIY versions are easy to make and noticeably tastier. The downside is that they take 6 hours to slow cook. The upside? A strawberry-scented house!

2 cups (330g) strawberries,
  stems removed
1 banana
1 tablespoon milled flaxseeds
  or milled chia seeds

Makes 15 shoelaces

Blitz all the ingredients in a powerful blender until smooth and glossy. If your strawberries are not fully ripe, you may need to add 1 tablespoon of honey to compensate for any bitterness. I also tried an apple and strawberry combo, which didn't work so well. Looks like banana might be key.

Line a Swiss roll tin (a roasting tray with a lip) with parchment paper. Spread the banana and strawberry mix evenly over the parchment with a spatula, making sure it's as smooth as smooth can be. This is the most important step.

If you are lucky enough to own a dehydrator, use your Teflex tray and dehydrate at 42°C for 5-6 hours. I use my oven at 60°C/40°C fan/140°F. Depending on the thickness (5mm is perfect), I cook it for 6-8 hours. You will know when it is done - touch and see whether it is still tacky. Remove from the oven once it feels dry to touch. Allow to cool on the parchment before cutting into shoelaces with a scissors, paper and all. The parchment can be removed straight away or later, when the chislers attack them.

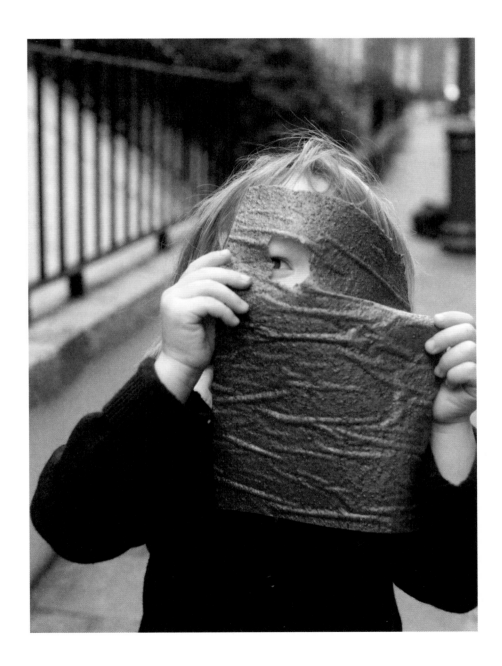

SNACKS AND OTHER NUTRITIONAL HITS

BUCKWHEAT PANCAKES

++++++++++++++++++++++++

Buckwheat pancakes taste sweeter and more wholesome than regular pancakes, and are unquestionably more interesting. White flour is nutritionally bland in comparison.

If you're a fan of Japanese take-out, chances are you've already tasted buckwheat in the form of soba noodles. Buckwheat, despite its name, is not wheat at all. It appears to be a relative of rhubarb and is entirely gluten free.

Russians make blini from buckwheat flour (see page 48) and smother them in caviar for their elevenses. Certainly beats a KitKat.

1 cup (140g) buckwheat flour
generous pinch of seasoning,
  like Herbamare
2 cups (500ml) water
extra virgin coconut oil,
  to fry

Makes 9 x 20cm pancakes

Stir the flour and seasoning together in a deep jug. Add a little of the water until it forms a smooth paste. Add the remaining water and whisk, ensuring no lumps appear. Leave to settle for at least 20 minutes. This makes flipping the pancake much easier when you go to cook the batter.

Heat your non-stick frying pan (non-stick is essential) with 1/2 tablespoon of coconut oil for each pancake. Using a soup ladle, pour just enough batter onto your hot pan to coat the whole surface. Too much batter will make the pancake too thick to flip. You may need to tilt the pan to cover the whole surface with the batter.

Flip when the underside is cooked. A few practice shots are generally necessary - this is pretty common, so don't beat yourself up over it. The added bonus is munching the unsuccessful ones! By the third or fourth pancake, your results will be flawless.

While the other side of the pancake is cooking, go make yourself some scrambled eggs as a filling. Serve on top of a buckwheat pancake and roll up like a wrap. Any leftover pancakes can be used as cold wraps for lunch at school or the office tomorrow. Try boiling baby potatoes and stirring through crunchy peanut butter, crushing a few spuds along the way to help create a softer filling. A couple of torn salad leaves or fresh coriander will make it look like you hired Gordon Ramsay to make your lunch.

SUPERFOOD SPREADS - BRAZIL NUT RED PESTO

++

Traditionally, a pesto is made by crushing ingredients to a smooth paste. We're speeding things up here with a cheat's version. The addition of anchovies provides omega-3 oils to our diet as well as boosting brain power with its DMAE phospholipid content. DMAE is believed to convert into the brain nutrient choline, which is useful for remembering important things like the boss's dog's name or where you parked the cursed car. Pregnant mothers feeding on choline-rich foods can also raise their baby's chances of becoming the next president of Mensa.

Throw all the ingredients into a food processor and pulse until it's nicely chopped up and chunky. If the tomatoes were jarred, you won't need additional olive oil. Refrigerate in a screw-top jar until ready to ravage.

12 sun-dried tomatoes
1 x 50g tin of anchovies
handful of Brazil nuts
drizzle of extra virgin
  olive oil

Makes 5 portions

SUPERFOOD SPREADS - DIBIS W'RASHI

+++

This is an Iraqi dish that children love to eat with smashed banana or bread. You can make your own date paste by boiling the fruit in a little water for 15 minutes, then whizz until sumptuously smooth.

Whip the tahini and date syrup together with a fork. Add a spot of sea salt if it's not going to find your toddler's mouth. This is good enough to eat straight from a spoon. If stored in a jar in the fridge, this dip will keep for 2 weeks.

4 tablespoons tahini
2 tablespoons date syrup or
  homemade date paste (see
  above)
pinch of sea salt

Makes 6 portions

Sweet and Salty Chilli Sauce

Fig and Sesame Butter

Dibis W'rashi

Masala Walnut Butter

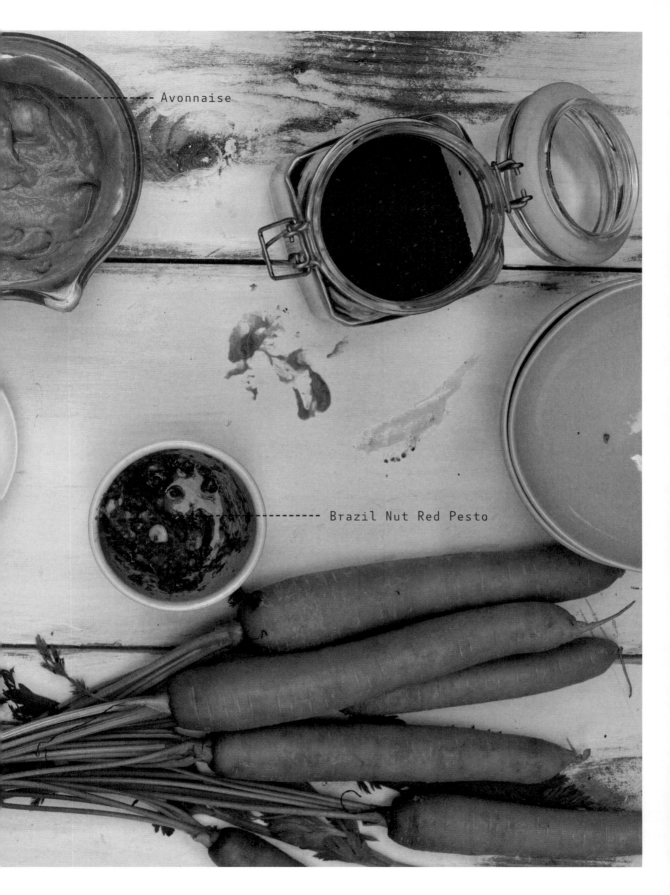

Avonnaise

Brazil Nut Red Pesto

SUPERFOOD SPREADS – MASALA WALNUT BUTTER

++

When pounded to a pulp in a pestle and mortar, walnuts' natural omega oils are released and meld together to make a decadent butter, heaps healthier than the dairy equivalent. While it's true that walnuts are made up of approximately 60% fat, their natural omega-3 oils power your brain, not your waistline.

Look out for stale or oxidised walnuts. They're about as bitter as Simon Cowell. Try to keep walnuts in the fridge and source from reputable stores with a high turnover.

1 good mugful (150g) of
  walnuts
1 garlic clove
1 teaspoon garam masala
sprinkle of Maldon sea salt
  flakes
1 teaspoon lemon juice
raw carrots, cucumbers or
  peppers, as dippers

Makes 5 portions

Break up the walnuts and add to your trusty pestle and mortar alongside the garlic, spice and salt. Pound for about 5 minutes, until you've got an oily butter. If it's still crumbly, keep on going.

Add 1 tablespoon of water and the lemon juice. Water tends to change the colour of the mixture from biscuity brown to light beige. Don't worry – you're on the right track. It's really up to you how creamy or thick you want it. As a guide, 2 tablespoons of water should be ample. Taste and decide if you'd like more spice or crushed garlic.

Tuck in using strips of carrot, cucumber or pepper. As a dinky starter for a supper party, you can make great pass-aroundies by filling a teeny Brussels sprout leaf with this whip and crown with a juicy redcurrant.

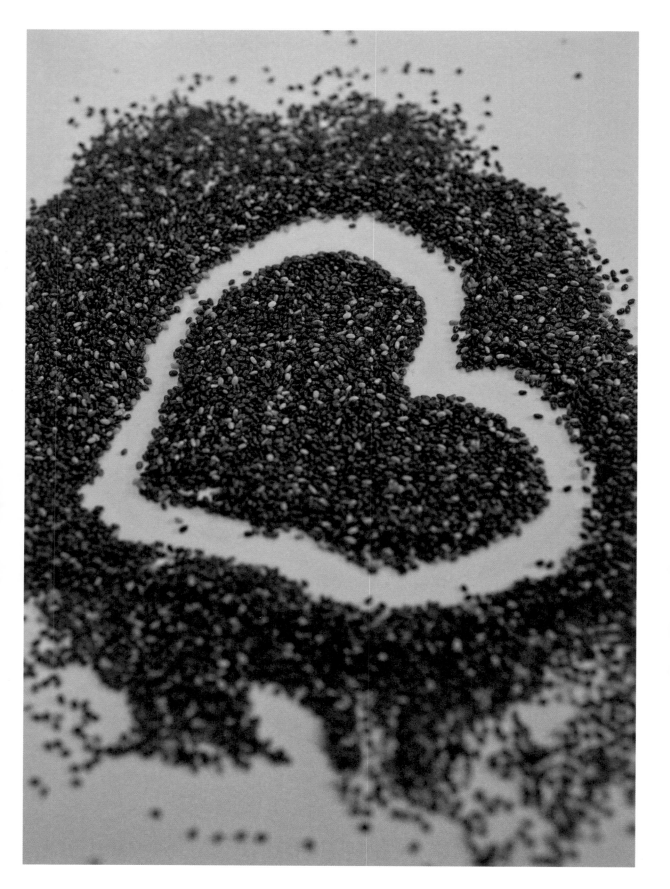

SUPERFOOD SPREADS - OMEGA PARSLEY BUTTER

++

Think about it - your skin is made from the inside, not the outside.
This recipe specifically combines pumpkin seeds' rich source of zinc,
lemon's vitamin C, hemp's protein, the essential omega fats from seeds and
parsley's stock of chlorophyll. In other words, it's a real beauty bullet.

Mince the garlic, or grate it with the teeny-tiny part of your grater. Follow with the lemon rind, then squeeze its juice. Give everything a jolly good whizz in the blender until smooth. Store in a scrupulously clean jam jar, with an extra drizzle of olive oil on top. In theory, it should keep for 2 weeks in the fridge. In practice, well, that's another thing. Super tasty on avocados, oatcakes, sliced cucumber, tomato, bread sticks or Sunday's roast chicken.

1 small garlic clove
1/2 unwaxed lemon
bunch of parsley, finely chopped
3 tablespoons hemp seeds
3 tablespoons pumpkin seeds
2 tablespoons extra virgin olive oil
1 tablespoon hemp or linseed oil
1 tablespoon sunflower seeds
1/2 teaspoon good-quality sea salt

Makes 6 portions

SUPERFOOD SPREADS - FIG AND SESAME BUTTER

++++++++++++++++++++

Great source of calcium, iron and finger-licking. Oh, and beautiful bowels.
My little ones take it to nursery in place of peanut butter.

Remove any stalks from the dried figs, then whizz all the ingredients together in a food processor. Add 1-2 tablespoons of water if you fancy a softer finish. Water won't thin the spread down, but rather, reduce its richness.

Throw all the ingredients into a food processor and pulse until it's nicely chopped up and chunky. If the tomatoes were jarred, you won't need additional olive oil. Refrigerate in a screw-top jar until ready to ravage.

6 dried figs, soaked overnight
4 tablespoons raw tahini
1-2 tablespoons honey or maple syrup (optional)

Makes 6-8 portions

SUPERFOOD SPREADS - SWEET AND SALTY CHILLI SAUCE

++

This is a smashing dip for chicken wings and dunky thangs.

2-3 tablespoons barley malt
  extract, raw agave or
  yacón syrup
2 tablespoons fresh miso
  paste
2 tablespoons cold-pressed
  toasted sesame oil
1/2 teaspoon cayenne pepper

Makes 5-6 portions

Whip the ingredients together in a cup with a fork. Serve in a soup bowl to facilitate easy dunking. Leftovers can be stored for 1 week in the fridge.

SUPERFOOD SPREADS - AVONNAISE

+++++++++++++++++++++++++++++++++++++

Fairly deadly with tinned tuna, raw carrots and flax crackers. I love using Herbamare veggie salt in this, from the Swiss naturopath Alfred Vogel. Find it in most good health food shops.

1 large ripe avocado
2-3 tablespoons water
1 teaspoon lemon juice or
  cider vinegar
black pepper, to taste
celery salt, to taste

Makes 2 portions

Purée all the ingredients together. You'll need to use a hand-held blender to achieve a super-smooth consistency, like mayonnaise. Taste and adjust the seasoning to your preference. Eat straight away, as avocados tend to discolour quickly.

SUPERFOOD SPREADS - HOMEMADE NUTELLA

+++

Makes a great gift to someone feeling poorly.

Whip the ingredients together in a cup using a
fork. If you're not planning to eat this DIY
Nutella straight away, you can refrigerate it in
a clean jam jar for up to 3 weeks. Once chilled,
it can be difficult to spread, so add a teaspoon
of hot water and beat the Nutella until it's
glossy again.

1/3 cup (90g) hazelnut butter
  (about half a small jar)
3 tablespoons cacao, cocoa
  or carob powder
2 tablespoons maple syrup

Makes 6 portions

SUPERFOOD SPREADS - PEANUT BUTTER, BANANA AND MAPLE SPREAD

+++

*I usually sneak leftover beans into the mix when I have them. My son is
none the wiser, but his bowels certainly are.*

Mash all the ingredients together and serve
on oatcakes. This spread is best scoffed right
away, as the mashed banana starts to darken with
oxidation.

1 ripe banana
2 tablespoons pure peanut
  butter
a drop of maple syrup
oatcakes, to serve

Serves 2-4

Soups

'It's better to pay the grocer than the doctor.'
Michael Pollan

1 British cup = 250ml

Soups are magical potions. They can resuscitate flat batteries and pump life through our bodies faster than a voodoo drum. There's something special about slurping a hot bowl of sunshine and feeling your veins ignite. When food is in liquid form, we not only digest it rapidly, we also absorb nutrients much quicker. Here are some of my favourite recipes to get your toes tingling. No need for cream, butter or flour - just a little love and a wooden spoon.

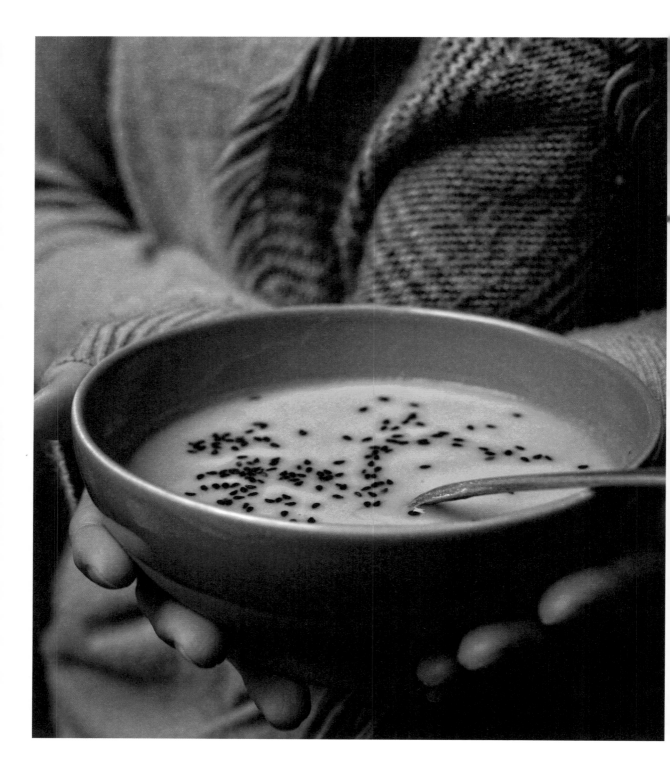

LEMONGRASS, COCONUT AND SWEET POTATO SOUP

==

Lemongrass is the easiest of exotic Asian herbs to deal with in a Western kitchen. I tend to have problems pronouncing the others, let alone soliciting them into a pan. Lemongrass is widely available in supermarkets now, which either means we are becoming more courageous behind the apron or more mournful of our carefree days backpacking around Thailand.

Organic coconut milk is best, otherwise the milk can be hijacked with all sorts of preservatives and stabilisers. If you think this is just claptrap, I urge you to buy both and compare. You'll notice a trippy purple hue in many non-organic milks.

Gently warm a dollop of extra virgin coconut oil in a sauté pan. Add the sweet potatoes, onions and garlic and leave to sweat quietly while you prepare the remaining ingredients. This process sweetens the veg naturally as long as you don't brown them.

Bash the fat, fibrous end of the lemongrass stalks with the base of a saucepan or heavy object. Of course, a pestle and mortar would be perfect, but not as cathartic as a flying saucepan after a long day in the office. Add the smashed stalks to the sweet potatoes and onions along with the stock and coconut milk. Bring to a simmer and cook for 10 minutes, until soft.

Remove the lemongrass and discard. Purée the soup with a hand-held blender until delectably smooth. Tickle with cayenne to give delicious heat and a splash of lime for a sharp kick. Finally, dazzle with the torn coriander, a splash of tamari and your holiday photo album. Guaranteed to transport you straight back to the coconut-lined beaches of Koh Samui.

good blob of extra virgin coconut oil
2 sweet potatoes, peeled and diced
1 onion, diced
3 garlic cloves, chopped
1-2 lemongrass stalks
2 cups (500ml) vegetable stock or water
1 x 400g can organic coconut milk
pinch of cayenne (optional)
squeeze of lime juice
handful of fresh coriander leaves, torn
tamari, to serve

Serves 4

HITCHCOCK AND NUTMEG SOUP

==================================

Thank goodness you can now buy raw pumpkin from supermarkets in wedges, just like melon. Hacking into a whole one is a little too Hitchcock for me. Besides, you'd need to be Mr Universe to dice up a pumpkin.

Roasted, this saffron-coloured vegetable is deliciously sweet and mapley to taste. As soon as you socialise it with your palate, you'll wonder why we only eat it at Halloween. Be careful not to buy the monstrous decorative pumpkins, which are only good for ghoulish faces.

Nuts like me - short for nutritionists - love pumpkin because of its super-sonic carotenoids, its liver-loving antioxidants and astral amounts of vitamins C and A. Winter bugs won't stand a chance. Of particular impor-tance to the hypertension-istas or balding men among us, pumpkin sports more potassium than the humble banana: five times as much.

2 onions, chopped
5 garlic cloves, left in
  their paper houses
1 x 1-1.5kg pumpkin
good splash of extra virgin
  olive or coconut oil
3-4 cups (up to 1 litre)
  chicken or vegetable stock
whole nutmeg, to garnish
buckwheat blinis (page 48)
  to serve

Serves 8

Preheat the oven to 200°C/180°C fan/400°F.

Toss the chopped onions onto a large baking tray with the whole cloves of garlic in their papery pods. Slice the pumpkin into wedges, discard its stringy nest and seeds and dice the flesh into bite-sized pieces. Leave the skin on if it's an organic pumpkin. Tumble with the onions and garlic, giving it all a good lick of oil. (You may need to use 2 trays to avoid overcrowding.) Roast for 45 minutes, or until the pumpkin is soft and caramelised around the edges. Shake the tray once or twice during roasting, just so your nostrils can party.

Once the pumpkin is seriously tender and sweet, scoop into your food processor alongside your onions. You'll need to squeeze the garlic from their papery shells - swipe a little taste for yourself. It's pretty cosmic roasted this way. Blend on high. Add enough stock to give the desired consistency of your soup. Whizz carefully now, trying not to scald yourself or redecorate the kitchen walls. Pour into big bowls and grate fresh nutmeg on top.

ROASTED GARLIC AND WILD NETTLE SOUP

==

Children are fascinated with nettle soup because it curiously fails to sting their tongue. Use this alleged sorcery to your advantage. If the nippers stay up later than bedtime, threaten to turn them into purple ferrets. In the meantime, learn this recipe by heart so that when you return from the fields, this ingenious alchemy can begin.

1 whole head of garlic,
  cloves peeled
glug of extra virgin olive
  oil
Maldon sea salt flakes
a crack of black pepper
4 onions, diced
1 leek, chopped any old way
roughly 1/2 carrier bag of
  nettle leaves*
2 litres homemade chicken or
  vegetable stock
1 cup (140g) frozen petits
  pois (optional)

Serves 12

** Please use rubber gloves
when you pick the nettles!*

To roast the garlic, preheat your oven to 180°C/160°C fan/350°F.

Toss the garlic cloves in a bowl with the olive oil and seasoning. Stack 6 squares of tinfoil on a work surface and place a sheet of parchment paper on top. This prevents the garlic from colouring or burning and turning bitter. Put the cloves in the middle of the paper and fold the parchment and foil over it like a tent, scrunching the edges. Make sure it's sealed well. Place the package in the centre of the oven and roast for 45 minutes.

Remove from the oven and allow to cool for at least 30 minutes. If you open the package too early, you will lose all that fabulous juice or burn yourself with plumes of steam.

If this all seems a little much, feel free to use crushed raw garlic in place of creamy roasted garlic. They taste very different, but are both fabulous in their own ways.

To make the nettle soup, sweat the onions and leek in olive oil over a gentle heat for 10 minutes, until the onions look translucent. If the veg catches on the bottom of the pan and starts burning, splash some water in and turn the heat down. Using a heavy-based saucepan is best.

Rinse the nettles under running water and remember to wear your rubber gloves. Spring nettles are sweetest. Toss the nettles into your pot of veg and add the stock, salt flakes and cracked pepper. Bring to the boil, immediately reduce the heat to a gurgling simmer and cook for 5-6 minutes. Any longer, and you risk murdering the taste. Remove from the heat and sprinkle in

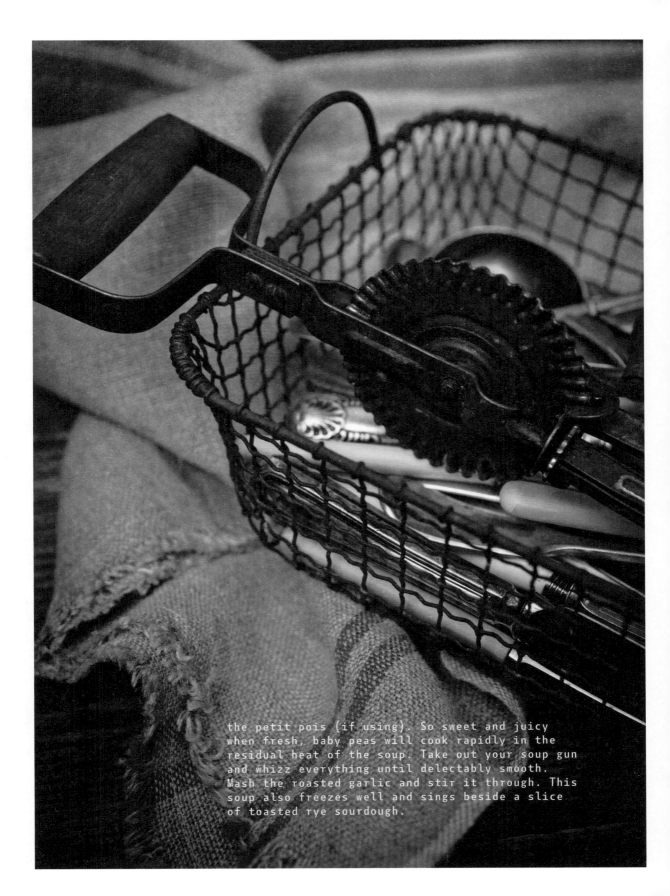

the petit pois (if using). So sweet and juicy
when fresh, baby peas will cook rapidly in the
residual heat of the soup. Take out your soup gun
and whizz everything until delectably smooth.
Mash the roasted garlic and stir it through. This
soup also freezes well and sings beside a slice
of toasted rye sourdough.

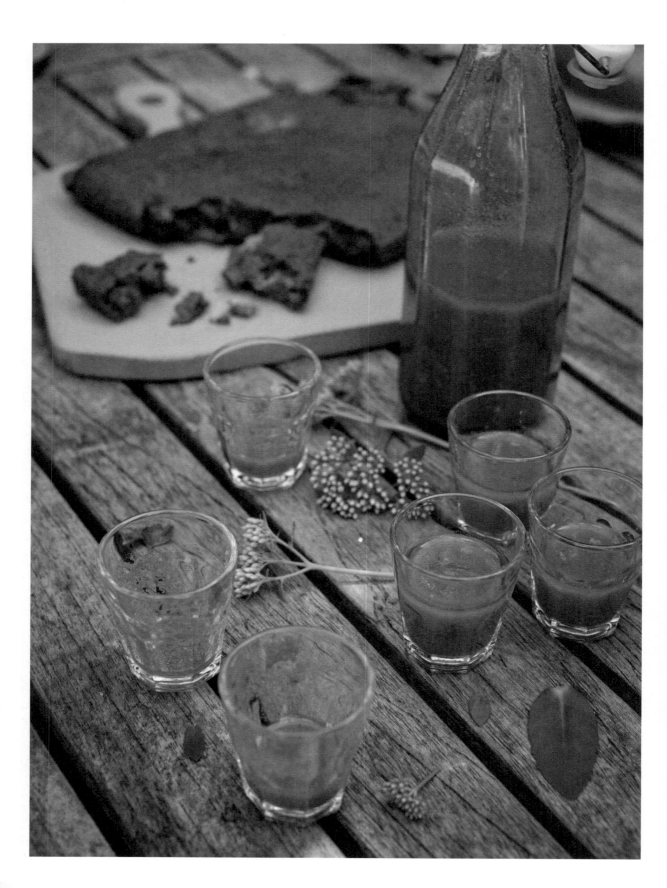

PICNIC GAZPACHO

==================

Tomatoes practically blush with virtue, like a rosy cherub with puppy fat. You've probably noticed the praise they enjoy in medical circles. In fact, the European Commission is backing a five-year research project called Lycocard to explore the role that tomatoes play in reducing the risk of developing cardiovascular disease and prostate cancer.

Lycopene, a carotenoid found in tomatoes, is thought to have raging antioxidant properties. We like antioxidants because they help to counteract mischief-making oxidants in our bloodstream. These meddlesome oxidants are often the result of poor dietary choices like processed fats, sugar, artificial additives and synthetically created preservatives. Cheap pre-packaged meals are full of the above, making your blood feel like sludge.

Now that we know lycopene can help zap villainous oxidants, we should be plotting to take more. Gazpacho is a chilled tomato soup. It's absurdly refreshing on a summer's day, especially if heat tends to muffle your appetite. When temperatures soar, the Spanish swill pitchers of gazpacho. Their tickers are all the merrier for it.

Too simple, really - whizz and serve. You'll need to start with the cherry tomatoes and garlic. Just give them a jolly good whizz in a high-speed blender until they're really smooth. Add in the spring onions, red pepper, cucumber, passata, lemon juice and a crack of black pepper and pulse very briefly. Gazpacho is best when it's thick and chunky, like a soupy salsa. If you accidently purée until kingdom come, don't panic. Blame heat stroke. Garnish with a smile and crumbled egg, announcing it is in fact salmorejo.

Chill in the refrigerator for at least 1 hour and spoon into 4 shallow soup bowls. Serve with a drizzle of top-quality olive oil, ice cubes, a few basil leaves and The Gypsy Kings' greatest hits.

1 small punnet (250g) cherry
  tomatoes, quartered
2 garlic cloves,
  crushed
3 spring onions, sliced
1 red pepper, deseeded and
  diced
1 cup diced cucumber
500ml tomato passata
juice of 1 small lemon
fresh crack of black pepper
top-quality extra virgin
  olive oil, to serve
ice cubes, to serve
basil leaves, to garnish
  (optional)

Serves 4

SMOKY BLACK BEAN SOUP

=============================

I love this soup. Your taste buds will back flip and your cardiologist is sure to wildly applaud. We already know the virtues of beans. Add to this tomatoes' heart-protective carotenoids, olive oil's cholesterol-busting tendencies and yeast flakes' cargo of B vitamins and you've got yourself a defibrillator in a kitchen pot. Just don't leave out the cumin or smoked paprika. They give this soup an extraterrestrial kick.

2-3 cups (200-300g) chopped
  leeks
1 garlic clove, sliced (not
  crushed)
4 tablespoons extra virgin
  olive oil
1 teaspoon ground cumin
1 teaspoon smoked paprika
2 x 400g tins black beans,
  drained and rinsed
1 x 400g tin cherry tomatoes
6 cups (1.5 litres)
  vegetable stock or
  seasoned water
1 tablespoon tomato purée
1 tablespoon nutritional
  yeast flakes (optional)
1-2 teaspoons honey or
  coconut sugar
splash of tamari

For the pseudo crème
  fraîche:
1 cup (250ml) natural or
  coconut milk yoghurt
1 garlic clove, crushed
handful of parsley, chopped
a few turns of the black
  pepper mill

Serves 6-8

Using a large heavy-based saucepan on a low heat, sweat the leeks, garlic and olive oil for 8-10 minutes, until soft and sweet. Toss in your cumin and smoked paprika and stir briskly, allowing their aroma to hit your hungry nostrils, then add the remaining ingredients. Turn the heat up until the soup starts to gurgle, cover and lower the heat again. Allow to putter away for 5 minutes.

Ladle into large bowls and top with a pseudo 'crème fraîche' made from natural yoghurt, crushed garlic, parsley and smashed black pepper.

CHILLED AVOCADO AND WATERCRESS SOUP

===

Instead of artery-clogging cream, you'll find that avocado can deliciously thicken soup while cranking up your meal's nutritional value. Avocados are especially high in vitamin E, nature's antidote to damaged skin. Combined with this soup's stellar vitamin C content, you're looking at an anti-ageing elixir. Although I'm not suggesting you apply it as a face mask.

Many of us need to increase our calcium intake from alternative sources to dairy. Watercress should help.

Start by gently warming the olive oil in a large pan. Add your onion and garlic to the oil and cook on low for around 10 minutes, until the onion looks fairly translucent. This process is called sweating and helps to sweeten root vegetables for soups.

Add the petits pois, watercress and stock. Cook for 5 minutes, until the water starts to violently boil. Remove from the heat and pulse with a hand-held blender. It will turn a brilliant green. Pour into a wide-brimmed, pre-chilled bowl and allow to cool in the fridge for 1 hour. An ice bath is helpful.

Preheat the oven to 180°C/160°C fan/350°F. Toast the almond flakes on a flat oven tray for 4-6 minutes, until lightly coloured but not brown. Set aside.

Once the soup is chilled, scoop out the flesh of your chilled avocado and add before serving. Give everything another blitz and serve immediately with an untidy smattering of toasted almond flakes.

2 tablespoons extra virgin olive oil
1 onion, diced
2 garlic cloves, minced
450g frozen petits pois
125g watercress
4 cups (1 litre) homemade vegetable or chicken stock
flaked almonds, to serve (optional)
1 medium avocado, chilled

Serves 4

90-SECOND BARLEY MISO SOUP

===================================

Miso is one of Japan's culinary trophies. Made from fermenting soya beans or grains with a live culture, miso is high in enzymes, good bacteria, female-friendly isoflavones, cancer-fighting selenium and that elusive vitamin B12. Look for unpasteurised miso in the refrigerator section of all good food stores. You'll notice there are lots of varieties and grains to choose from, a bit like wine. Some are sweet, others are earthy and full bodied. I've even noticed happy versions with fermented hemp for the die-hard hippies among us.

Miso paste is my secret weapon in the kitchen. When a sauce, soup or dressing misbehaves, in goes a tablespoon of barley miso and out comes Beethoven's seventh symphony.

A small nutritional caveat – never boil fresh miso. Its flavour and bacterial culture will get the guillotine. Instead, add a little of the liquid to a cup with the miso and dissolve into a smooth paste. Pour this brew back into the soup or sauce and then serve without any further cooking.

1-2 teaspoons unpasteurised
  barley (or other) miso
1 spring onion, sliced
sprinkle of petits pois
1 quail's egg (optional)
pinch of arame seaweed
  (soaked for 10 minutes) or
  nori flakes

Serves 1

Mix the miso paste in a soup bowl with 2 table-spoons of hot water until dissolved. Pour over boiled water from the kettle and add the spring onions and peas. Crack a raw quail's egg into the centre (if using). The heat from the soup will quickly cook the teeny tiny egg. It's pretty awesome to watch.

If that doesn't appeal, play with additions such as warm almond milk, soaked arame or nori flakes. Reach into the freezer and grab a slice of Your New Wheat-free Bread (page 51). No need to cook tonight.

JEWISH PENICILLIN

=========================

There's nothing quite like a bubbling cauldron of chicken stock wafting through the kitchen on a Baltic winter evening. Sends my nostrils into a frenzy of hunger. Stock is quite happy to sit on the hob and gurgle away for several hours, enveloping your senses while you get going on that bumper box set of The Wire.

Let's be honest: most of us still grab ready-made stock cubes instead of making our own. But that's like comparing Peter Andre to Damien Rice. The first ingredient in an average chicken stock cube is salt. What a rip-off. Then comes artery-clogging hydrogenated fat, followed by sugar - exclamation mark - unspecified starch (aka more sugar), monosodium glutamate (MSG) and dubious 'flavourings' are star ingredients. Even the canned varieties are based on these cheap, phony stocks.

This recipe is liquid gold. Simmering the bones helps draw out the chicken's natural minerals and collagen to fuel our bodies. Its potency is further enhanced with garlic, ginger and turmeric's anti-viral, anti-bacterial and anti-inflammatory compounds. Our grannies and our granny's grannies used it to soothe indolent limbs and hazy eyes in place of popping flu pills.

Ask your local butcher to save his free-range or organic chicken carcasses for you instead of dumping them. Just make sure to return his generosity with a great big flask of steaming hot goodness and a seraphic smile.

Break up your chicken carcass as much as you can and cover with cold filtered water in a large saucepan. Add all the ingredients to the pot and bring to a bubbling simmer, uncovered. Lower the heat so that the liquid is only shuddering. Skim off and discard the foam that appears on the surface over the next 60 minutes - there's no need to become a slave to it, however.

Once the broth has a rich, chickeny flavour, usually in 4-8 hours, turn off the heat. Strain. Allow the broth to settle and throw out the bones and veg. Store in the freezer to make soup at a later date or tuck straight in.

Give this stock your own signature stamp by adding grilled mushrooms, slices of avocado and chilli, broken buckwheat noodles or freshly chopped parsley before serving. Although it's so darn delicious on its own, it rarely needs any doctoring.

1 organic chicken carcass
3 onions, peeled and roughly chopped
3 celery sticks, roughly chopped
5 garlic cloves, peeled
2 bay leaves
thumb-sized piece of fresh ginger, peeled and chopped
3cm piece of fresh turmeric root, peeled
1 teaspoon unrefined salt flakes
freshly cracked black pepper, to serve

Makes 1-2 litres

Salads

Healthy eating should never tax your taste buds.

1 British cup = 250ml

Relax. You're in the right place. Cleaning up your diet
doesn't need to involve neon leotards or cauliflower
smoothies. No one should be threatened with that.
This chapter is more about pleasure than denial. We could
all improve our diets, but we don't have to sacrifice
flavour.

The food we eat is inescapably linked to our concentration
levels, our mood, our libido and yes, our love handles.
We eat about five times a day. That's over 1,800 opportu-
nities each year to positively affect our energy and weight.
Salads are a great place to start. Let me prove it.

SPIRALISER RECIPES - MAKING SPAGHETTI FROM COURGETTES

○○○

I love spiralisers. These dinky machines make you feel like Handy Manny in the kitchen. Instead of prepping pasta, you can grab a courgette, fix it to a spiraliser, and kaboom! Courgette spaghetti! And if you don't fancy forking out for another kitchen gadget, you could use a potato peeler to scrape ribbons from the vegetables instead.

A naturally shy vegetable, courgettes carry flavour rather than provide it. The trick is to avoid the large, bitter ones. You can dress courgette spaghetti up with your usual tomato passata, a bit of garlic, olives, spinach and look! That's your five a day busted in less time than it takes to reheat a dodgy take-out. Investing in a spiraliser might be the best €40 you'll spend this year.

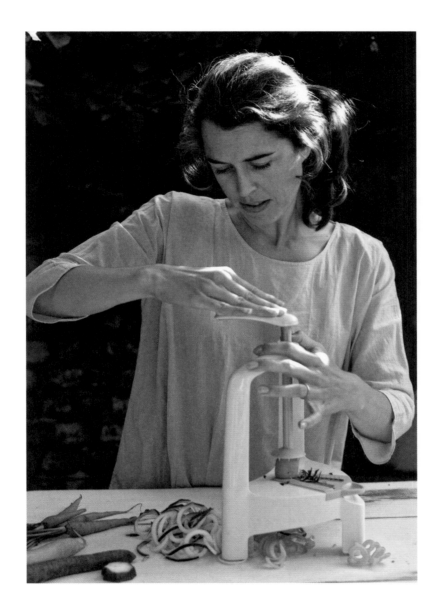

SPIRALISER RECIPES - THE HAPPY COURGETTE

○○○

Crunchy, chewy, smooth yet zippy, this is one happy courgette.

1 fat carrot
1 small to medium courgette
1/4 cup (4 tablespoons)
  walnuts
1/4 cup (4 tablespoons)
  dried cranberries
handful of flat-leaf parsley,
  dill or chervil

For the dressing:
3 tablespoons organic
  natural soya yoghurt
2 tablespoons red wine
  vinegar or apple cider
  vinegar
1 tablespoon Dijon mustard
1/2 garlic clove, minced

Serves 2 as a salad or 3 as
  a side

Spiralise the carrot and courgette into a large bowl. Loosely toss together with the walnuts, cranberries (raisins and grapes love this recipe too) and herbs.

To make the dressing, whisk together the yoghurt, vinegar, mustard and garlic. Tumble into the prepared carrot and courgette. Dig in.

SPIRALISER RECIPES - WASABI PEA CARBONARA

OOOOOOOOOOOOOOOOOOOOOOOOOOOOOOOOOOOOOOOOOOOOOOOOOO

This is a good creamy dish with a delicious sting of wasabi. When you're rehydrating dried mango, just add enough water for them to soak it up. Leave for a few hours, or overnight if possible.

Pour boiling hot water on top of the frozen peas and leave to sit while you spiralise the courgette and carrot into a bowl. Drain and add the peas to your courgette and carrot spaghetti.

In a separate bowl, purée the avocado, the rehydrated mango pieces and their soaking liquid, the wasabi, green tea (if using) and the lemon or lime juice. Taste, and add a dash more juice if you think it's required. Pour this sumptuous green ganache over the courgette spaghetti and coat it thoroughly. If you think there is too much sauce, spiralise another carrot into the mix.

Divide between bowls and have your friends guess the ingredients!

1/2 cup (70g) frozen petits pois
1 small to medium courgette
1 fat carrot
flesh of 1 avocado
handful of dried mango, rehydrated in water (see note above)
2 teaspoons organic wasabi paste
1 teaspoon matcha green tea powder (optional)
squeeze of lemon or lime juice

Serves 4-5 as a starter or side

SPIRALISER RECIPES - FLAKED SALMON WITH SPICY POMEGRANATE NOODLES

○○○

One of my all-time favourite salads. The key lies in good-quality pomegranate molasses, so beware of imposters!

2 fillets organic salmon or
  wild trout
extra virgin raw coconut
  oil (or whatever oil you
  prefer)
1 fat carrot
1 small to medium courgette
2 tablespoons pomegranate
  molasses
2 tablespoons almond butter
2 tablespoons cold-pressed
  toasted sesame oil
2 tablespoons Bragg Liquid
  Aminos or 1 tablespoon
  tamari
1 small garlic clove, minced
  or crushed
good pinch of cayenne pepper
pomegranate seeds, to
  garnish

Serves 2

Preheat the oven to 200°C/180°C fan/400°F.

Prepare the salmon by wrapping the fillets in a parcel of tinfoil and drizzle with the oil. I use extra virgin raw coconut oil, but use whatever you're happiest with. Make sure there's lots of space above the fillets - it's more like a tent than a parcel. They steam in their own juices this way.

Transfer the tent of salmon onto a baking tray and roast for 10-15 minutes, depending on how big the fillets are. Check by pulling the flesh apart. If they're not done, just reseal your tent and pop them in the oven again. When you've become familiar with this method of cooking, crank it up another level by adding smashed lemongrass, maple syrup, chilli, cumin, kaffir lime leaves or whatever tickles your appetite on any given evening.

While the salmon is cooking, spiralise the carrot and courgette. In a separate bowl, beat together the remaining ingredients to make your spicy dressing. Toss through your spiralised noodles and divide between 2 bowls. When the salmon is done to your liking, flake the flesh over each bowl of noodles, then sprinkle over the pomegranate seeds. Awesome meal on a warm summer evening.

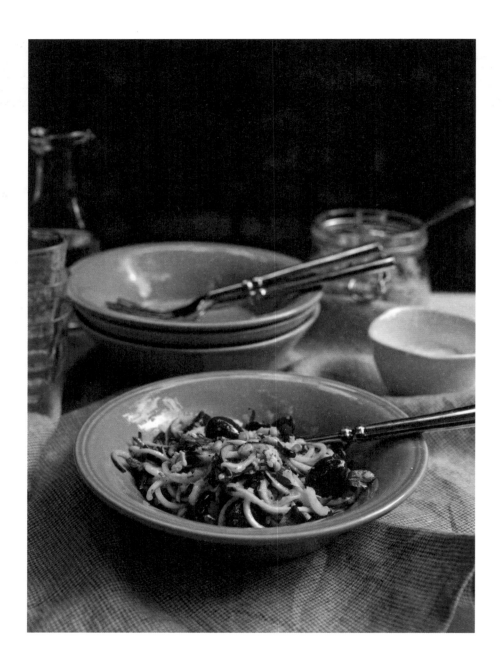

SPIRALISER RECIPES – GARLICKY TAGLIATELLE WITH BLACK OLIVES AND PINE NUT RICOTTA

ooooooooooooooooooooooooooooooooooooooooooooooooooooooooooooooo

Sick of stodgy pasta and cheese? Preparing courgette and carrot tagliatelle takes less time than boiling pasta, and also delivers your entire vegetable RDA. Admittedly the pine nut ricotta demands a bit of Mary Poppins in the kitchen, but if you plug in some Ricky Martin he'll visit your fingertips. My hubby sneaks some diced anchovies and tomatoes in here too.

Put the courgette and carrot through the middle blade of your spiraliser or use a potato peeler to create long, thin ribbons.

In a separate glass, whisk together the parsley, garlic, olive oil and lemon juice. You won't need it all, so freeze the remainder for another evening.

Tumble enough of the dressing into your tagliatelle and toss thoroughly to coat each strand. Sprinkle in the chopped olives. Crown with a generous drop of pine nut ricotta and a few turns of the black pepper mill. A simple smattering of pumpkin seeds is a filling alternative to the ricotta.

1 courgette
1 carrot
roughly 1/2 cup flat-leaf parsley or chervil
3 garlic cloves, crushed or finely grated
1/2 cup (125ml) extra virgin olive oil
juice and zest of 2 small lemons
handful of black olives, roughly chopped
pine nut ricotta (page 143) or pumpkin seeds

Serves 2

SPIRALISER RECIPES - RED PEPPER AND WALNUT (MUHAMMARA) NOODLES

○○○

Last time I made these noodles, I necked the entire batch. My husband's roar was heard several postcodes away.

2 fat carrots
2 small to medium courgettes
3 red peppers (or 1 jar of roasted peppers)
1 cup (120g) walnuts
1/3 cup (25g) wheat-free breadcrumbs
3 garlic cloves, minced and mashed to a paste with 1/2 teaspoon salt flakes
4 tablespoons tomato purée
1 tablespoon pomegranate molasses
1 teaspoon ground cumin
pinch of dried chilli flakes
1/2 cup extra virgin olive oil
fresh lemon juice, to taste (optional)

Serves 6 as a starter or side

Spiralise the carrots and courgettes. Large courgettes can taste bitter and fluffy, so it's worth hunting down the smaller ones.

Let's get making the muhammara. To prep the peppers, place them directly on the middle shelf in a very hot oven. Let them roast for around 40 minutes, until they're on the brink of collapse. Don't worry if their skin is blistered or black. It's what's inside that counts. Gently remove the roasted peppers from the oven by pulling the stalk of each one and catching them in a large bowl. Cover the bowl with cling film for 10 minutes. This makes it much easier to remove their skins. Without ouching yourself, pinch off the skin and discard along with the stalks and seeds.

To prep the walnuts, smash them in a pestle and mortar until their natural oils begin to be released. Or you could use the base of a saucepan, so long as the neighbours aren't in.

Purée the rest of the ingredients except the olive oil and lemon juice to a smooth, creamy dip. Now stir through the olive oil. Any sooner, and your muhammara will look like something Peppa Pig has expelled. Stir through the walnuts.

Taste, and adjust with a squeeze of lemon or more chilli flakes if you fancy. Tumble into your prepped noodles and divide between your serving bowls. Black olives and hummus make for groovy companions.

SPIRALISER RECIPES - CURLY CARROTS

ooooooooooooooooooooooooooooooooooooooooooo

My boys chase each other with giant shoelaces of raw carrot. They think it's hilarious. I look on with the wonder of an astronomer sighting a new galaxy. Who would have thought raw carrots could be so much fun?

When they have playdates, Benjamin and Marty beg me to make 'curly carrots' for their unsuspecting guests. Everyone ditches the Lego, sits on the floor and chomps on ribbons of carrots as if they were liquorice laces.

Use the smallest plate on your spiraliser to make carrot laces. The carrot needs to be fat, or else you'll be left with brief curls of carrots instead of long, curly laces.

1 fat carrot
some currants or pomegranate
  seeds

Makes 3-4 snack portions

SPIRALISER RECIPES - CARROT RIBBONS AND SPRING PESTO

ooooooooooooooooooooooooooooooooooooooooooooooooo

Leftover pesto can be frozen in jars. Make sure to press the pesto down firmly with the back of a spoon to remove any pockets of air (trapped air can cause contamination and foul tempers). Top the pesto with a little more oil, making a seal.

Start by picking the wild garlic leaves over and discarding any coarse stalks and grass. Whizz in a food processor along with the pumpkin seeds, olive oil, salt and lemon juice. Transfer to a scrupulously clean jar and set aside. This takes 6 minutes, tops.

Head and tail the carrots. Make sure they are straight to facilitate smooth spiralising. Put them through your spiraliser and collect the curly carrots in a bowl. Toss through the wild garlic pesto and tuck in. It's honkingly good stuff. Use the smallest plate on your spiraliser to make carrot laces. The carrot needs to be fat, or else you'll be left with brief curls of carrots instead of long curly laces.

50g freshly picked wild
  garlic leaves
25g pumpkin seeds
1/2 cup (125ml) extra virgin
  olive oil
1/2 teaspoon Maldon salt
  flakes
small squeeze of lemon or
  lime juice
2 fat carrots

Serves 2

MOON-DRIED TOMATOES AND SPROUTED HUMMUS

○○

I'm a devotee of buying local and organic. This doesn't make me a sermonising tree-hugger or a hemp-wearing hippy (although I do have a crush on Woody Harrelson). I'm a fan because organic farming nourishes the soil naturally without the use and abuse of chemicals. Organic methods help protect Mother Nature's playground and preserve nature's biodiversity. (Though science is rarely ever that simple.)

By now you've probably heard about colony collapse disorder and the disappearance of honeybees in many parts of France, Britain and the United States. This phenomenon has been increasingly linked to neonicotinoid insecticides. Not good news. Honeybees are critical for the pollination of many of our favourite foods, such as almonds, apples, beetroot, asparagus and blueberries. Scientists say the disruption of pollination could wipe out entire crops, threaten our agriculture and bring the world into an ecological crisis. According to the USDA, one-third of the American diet relies on bee pollination.

So what can we do? For a start, we can choose to support farmers who grow vegetables without the indiscriminate use of agrichemicals. Check out local organic farmers' markets. By doing so, we not only support our winged friends, we also support nature, our local economy, our health and even our taste buds. Secondly, think about becoming a beekeeper. (The first might be easier to manage.) For more information, visit the beautiful site www. helpsavebees.co.uk.

For the moon-dried tomatoes:
about 16 cherry tomatoes, halved
1 garlic clove, finely chopped
3 tablespoons extra virgin olive oil
1 teaspoon coconut blossom sugar or maple syrup
1/2 teaspoon sea salt flakes
handful of fresh coriander leaves

For the sprouted hummus:
1 cup (225g) dried chickpeas
1-2 garlic cloves, crushed
1/2 cup (125ml) chilled water
4-8 tablespoons lemon juice
4 tablespoons tahini or cashew nut butter
2-3 tablespoons ground cumin
2 tablespoons extra virgin olive oil
1 tablespoon tamari
1/2 cup finely chopped parsley, coriander, basil or black olives

Serves 4

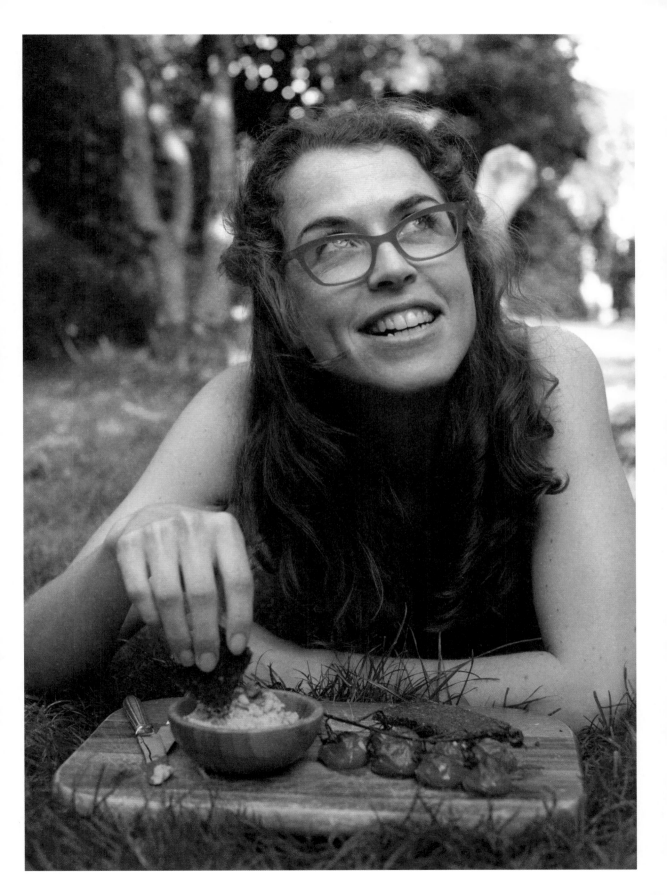

Preheat the oven to 220°C/200°fan/425°F.

Coat the halved tomatoes generously with the garlic, oil, sugar and salt. Sit the tomatoes cut side up in an ovenproof dish and pour the remaining juices over. Pop in the oven and immediately turn off the heat. Leave overnight or for a day without opening the door.

For the sprouted hummus, simply sprout your dried chickpeas by soaking them in water overnight. Drain them the following morning and place the chickpeas on damp kitchen paper along the windowsill for the day. When you return from the office, you can canter straight into your kitchen and whizz up this hummus. Purée everything except the herbs in your food processor for 3 minutes. Add more iced water to help loosen it up if necessary.

Herbs are best chopped finely and stirred through the hummus instead of blending them. Otherwise, it can look as if Kermit the Frog crawled into your blender. The green tops of spring onions are a stealthy money-saver instead of using pricey fresh herbs.

Serve the tomatoes with loads of freshly chopped coriander leaves and the sprouted hummus.

IRISH SUPERFOOD SALAD

oooooooooooooooooooooooo

This is a cosmic combo of truly tasty, local ingredients. It happens to be healthier and cheaper than popping vitamin pills. Plus you get to soak up the applause showered upon you by your dinner guests.

If you're feeling particularly lazy, use vacuum-packed beetroot in place of potatoes. No need for cooking.

Scrub and wash the baby potatoes, cover in cold salted water and bring to the boil for 15-20 minutes. Pierce them with a fork to check whether they are cooked. For the last 5 minutes of cooking the potatoes, add the eggs to cook simultaneously as a nifty time-saver. Once the eggs are boiled and the potatoes are cooked, drain and discard the cooking water. Allow to cool.

While the spuds are cooking, flake the mackerel fillet into a bowl with your chosen salad leaves, olive oil, the juice of half the lemon, lemon zest, nori flakes and capers (if using).

Halve the cooked baby potatoes. Peel and quarter the boiled eggs. Gently toss everything together and serve straight away or divide into paper deli boxes for lunch. Try not to reuse your old Tupperware if you're having lunch with that hottie from the office next door. You'll find smart recyclable containers by the salad counters in food stores and delicatessens. Politely, er, borrow them on your next shopping trip.

handful of baby Irish
  potatoes
2 large eggs
1 fillet smoked mackerel
handful of fresh rocket or
  watercress
decent splash of extra
  virgin olive oil
zest and juice of 1 small
  unwaxed lemon
sprinkle of dried nori flakes
  (optional)
a few capers (optional)

Serves 3

BASIL BUTTERBEANS

ooooooooooooooooooo

We love butterbeans because they look like something out of a Roald Dahl storybook. They're also cheap and keep in the cupboard for over a year. The trick with cooking beans is to soak them overnight. Unsoaked beans can taste dry and crunchy, even if you double the cooking time.

Here are a couple of tips to help you introduce butterbeans to the dinner table: Toddlers will eat them whole. Teens don't notice them mixed through a can of baked beans. And leery grandparents won't suspect anything different in their mashed potato (FYI, butterbeans mash beautifully). For everyone else, this recipe is sure to convert them.

1 cup (170g) dried
  butterbeans
3 tablespoons extra virgin
  olive oil
zest of 1 small lemon
a few basil leaves, chopped

Serves 4 as a side

Cover the butterbeans with water and soak overnight. The next day, drain the beans, cover with fresh unsalted water and boil for 90 minutes, until very tender. Taste a bean - you're aiming for the texture of a baked potato. When you're satisfied, drain the beans and stir through the remaining ingredients. Also excellent with dribbly tomatoes and mint.

DINING AL DESKO BEET SALAD

○○○○○○○○○○○○○○○○○○○○○○○○○○○○○

I love the summer. It's probably my favourite day of the year. I queue up to sit in the park and sear my beautiful blue skin. For the other 364 days of the Irish calendar, I like to keep toasty indoors and dine al desko. Loads of us do it.

But keep those sambos away from me or I'll be snoring by 3pm. Food should give you energy, not take it away. Try this recipe and see for yourself. The ginger will give your circulation a good giddy up.

Chop the veggies into bite-sized chunks. Two or three beets from a vacuum packet should suffice, depending on their size. Quantities are up to you.

Steam the chunks of carrot until tender. It won't need more than 5 minutes in a pot with a tightly covered lid and a minimum amount of water. You could also leave it raw for extra nutrition and crunch, but this renders talking over lunchtime next to impossible.

Toss the veggies, apple and walnuts together with a splash of olive oil and a squeeze of lemon juice. Grate some ginger over everything using the same part of the grater that you would use for lemon zest. Taste, and adjust the seasoning to your liking. Wrestle into a plastic lunchbox or empty container. Just don't forget the fork.

1 vacuum packet of beetroot
1 large carrot
1 celery stick
1/2 apple, diced
handful of walnuts
splash of olive oil
squeeze of lemon juice
3cm piece of fresh ginger,
   peeled
salt and pepper

Serves 2

'F%*K ME' SALAD

ooooooooooooooo

Here's a fragrant supper of fiery prawns, honeyed papaya and mint, all kissed with toasted sesame oil. Anyone who tastes it usually responds with a whispered 'f%*k me!'

Chillis are devious little vegetables. They raise our body temperature and help release natural endorphins to keep our blood gurgling with excitement. I recommend the powdered form to give your lips a delicious sting and swell the senses. Guessing the heat of a fresh chilli is riskier than cycling backwards in a Grand Prix. Double the quantities if you plan on sharing this dish.

rice or mung noodles for 1
1 small papaya
1/4 cucumber
1/4 red onion
handful of cooked prawns
freshly torn mint leaves

For the Thai dressing:
juice of 1 lime
1 tablespoon fish sauce (nam pla)
1 tablespoon toasted sesame oil
2 teaspoons raw honey or maple syrup
pinch of cayenne or freshly sliced chilli

Serves 1

Cook the noodles according to the manufacturer's instructions on the packet (these can vary greatly). Cut the papaya in half, and again into slices. This will make it easier to cut into chunks for the salad. Treat it like a melon. While the seeds are deemed edible, they are deeply unpleasant. Known for its rich enzymes and potent anti-inflammatory compounds, papaya will help keep your liver on speaking terms with you. Especially if you're Irish.

Slice the cucumber thickly, then cut each slice into quarters. Slice the red onion thinly into rings. Toss the papaya, cucumber and red onion joyfully together with the prawns and mint.

Whisk together the remaining ingredients to make a Thai dressing good enough to drink. Pour over your medley of papaya and allow the flavours to infuse. By now, your noodles will be ready. Drain and rinse briefly with cold water to separate the starchy bits. Tumble into the happy medley and serve with a fork and straw. If you're bringing this into work, expect office pillagers to descend. Arm yourself with an extra sharp fork.

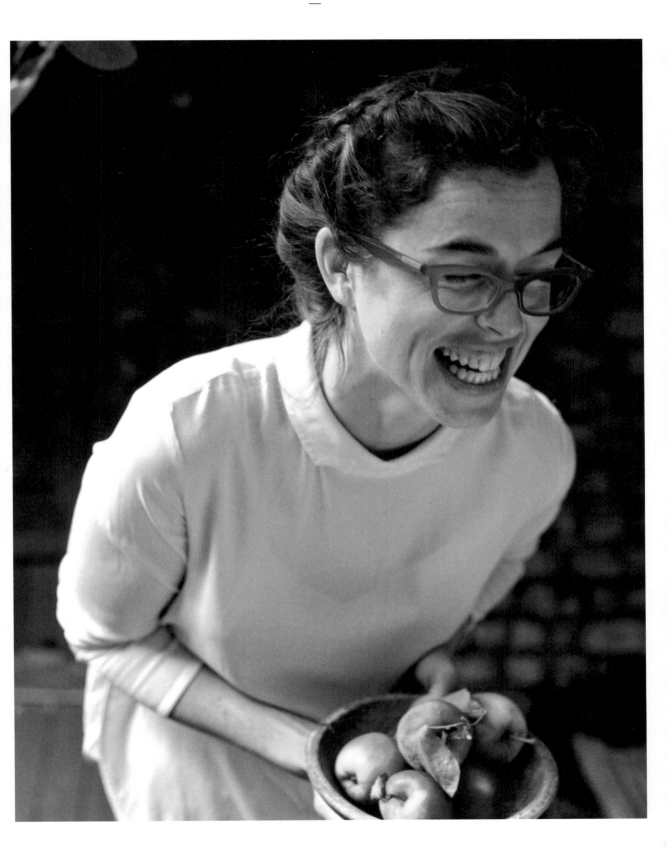

SAY HELLO TO OPRAH'S OCEAN VEG

ooooooooooooooooooooooooooooooooooo

Seaweed is the next big thing. Our dear Oprah is a massive
fan of these 'ocean vegetables'. We Irish seem to think
it's only useful for deflecting annoying children on the
beach. In fact, seaweed is full of anti-ageing nutrients
and disease-fighting lignans.

Listen up, rusty bones! Sea veggies' calcium supply is good
for healthy bones and teeth, without the artery-clogging
effects that dairy-rich diets can yield. Then there's iron
- a mere 10 grams of mixed sea vegetables can give you just
under half the recommended daily allowance of this blood-
building mineral. Ocean veg can be a good source of vitamin
B12. Meat-eaters get lots of B12, but vegetarians struggle
to keep up.

There are many types of sea vegetables to choose from,
guaranteed to make Brittas Bay more exciting this year.
Here are a few to get you started. All are harvested wild
and are free from chemicals, preservatives and, yes,
sometimes taste.

The most common type of sea vegetable on our menus is <u>nori</u>, the shiny green wrapping around sushi. Nori is unusually rich in protein. You'll get loads of nori in Asian food stores for a fraction of the high street price. Best crumbled on top of brown rice.

<u>Agar</u> and <u>carrageen</u> are used in place of artificial stabilisers and gelling agents. I use them to set panna cotta and fruit jellies - a crafty way of getting important minerals into children's party food.

<u>Kombu</u> and <u>sugar kelp</u> are the dark ones that gave me nightmares as a nipper. Thick, slippery strands of goodness. Who would have thought? Pop them into slow-cooking stews at the very beginning. I find they can take a long time to break down. It's rumoured that adding kombu to beans can help reduce the incidences of trouser-trumpets. That's Latin for flatulence.

We always add <u>wakame</u> to stews about 30 minutes before cooking is finished. It brings a good smack of umami for the taste buds as well as a suite of fancy minerals. Like most ocean veg, a packet of wakame will last 3 years in the cupboard.

<u>Dulse</u> is particular to Ireland. This sea veggie has a chewy texture and deep purple hue. Best purchased in powdered form and sprinkled on food. The more courageous cooks can play with it in broths and soups. Cornucopia Café in Dublin has an excellent one on their menu.

<u>Arame</u> is the sweetest and most elegant of the sea vegetables. Jet-black angel strands of goodness. No need to cook - simply soak for 10 minutes and socialise them with broccoli, Brazil nuts and soya sauce for a speedy lunch, or with sautéed garlic mushrooms as a side.

SESAME SEA SALAD

ooooooooooooooooooo

Arame doesn't taste as weird as it sounds. It is the easiest and prettiest seaweed to prepare. Consider it essential for your kitchen's emergency programme, especially designed for occasions when the oven decides to misbehave and you have a hot date to feed. Or a starving in-law. Equally as terrifying. The result is Ready Steady Cook meets Heston Blumenthal.

a handful (20g) of dried
  arame
3 carrots, grated
3 spring onions, chopped
1/2 apple, grated
juice of 1/2 lemon
3 tablespoons sesame seeds
3 tablespoons currants
3 tablespoons extra virgin
  olive or sesame oil

Serves 4 as a side dish

Soak the arame in cool filtered water for 10-15 minutes.

Meanwhile, toss the grated carrots, spring onions, apple, lemon juice, sesame seeds and currants together. Gloss it up with a good splash of olive or sesame oil. When the sea veggie has swelled to twice its size, discard the water and comb through the salad. Serve alongside fish or hummus. Watch out, though - kids tend to spit out the spring onions!

SPROUTING - THE BEAN ZOO

○○○○○○○○○○○○○○○○○○○○○○○○○○○

Here's a new hobby for a healthier, glossier you.

The task? (1) Purchase a Vogel three-tier germinator for about the same price as a yoga class. (2) Stock up on dried mung beans, alfalfa seeds and whole lentils. These are the easiest chaps to start with. (3) In each tier, sprinkle 2 tablespoons of your chosen bean, seed or lentil. (4) Let the germinator pay homage to the natural sunlight adorning your windowsill and tickle with water twice daily. Ta-da! Your very own bean zoo, providing oodles of entertainment, fascination and nutrition.

Depending on the bean, seed or lentil, sprouting can take from as little as 36 hours to 7 days. Your jolly germinator will come with an index of sprouting timelines. The trick is to refrigerate them as soon as they have sprouted, preventing them from growing too large and bitter. The shorter the sprouting time, the crunchier and sweeter they taste.

Bean sprouts provide a talented array of protein, vitamins, minerals and raw enzymes without the hassle of cooking. This is what I call *real* fast food. Word of wisdom - don't bother trying egg, fish or linseed oil with sprouts. Something alarmingly unpleasant happens.

SUPERMAN'S SALAD

ooooooooooooooooo

Choose from eight different varieties of sprouts to vivify your lunchtime and your liver. All sprouts need is a little lick of olive oil, juicy fruit and chopped herbs before throwing them into Tupperware.

Take about 4 segments of grapefruit and peel the white pith away from their juicy flesh. Chop each segment into approximately 4 pieces. This could take a while - my grapefruit usually finds its way into my mouth. Roughly tear your chosen herbs and toss with the grapefruit, sprouts and olive oil.

Further combos to try:
In place of pink grapefruit and chives, try olives, lemon juice and parsley; chopped banana, coconut flakes and coriander; Brazil nuts, steamed broccoli and soya sauce; roasted veg and rocket; yoghurt, curry powder, raisins and grated carrot; tofu, rice noodles, chilli and sesame oil; or avocado, pistachios and dried apricots.

1 pink grapefruit
handful of fresh chives,
   mint or coriander
1 mug of sprouted beans
2 tablespoons extra virgin
   olive oil

Serves 1-2

NECTARINE AND LITTLE GEM SALAD WITH GOJI BERRY CREAM

○○

1-2 Little Gem lettuces
1/2 apple or nectarine,
  depending on the season
handful of pumpkin seeds
handful of sunflower seeds
a few turns of the black
  pepper mill

For the dressing:
6 tablespoons extra virgin
  olive oil
2 tablespoons lemon juice or
  apple cider vinegar
2 tablespoons goji berries
1 tablespoon raw honey,
  brown rice syrup or raw
  agave
pinch of cayenne

Serves 2

Break the leaves from the lettuce heads into the largest bowl you have. Gently tumble with the chopped apple, seeds and black pepper. You can toast the seeds to bring out their nuttiness: heat a non-stick pan on high and toast the seeds for 30 seconds. They are done when you hear the pumpkin seeds pop off the pan. A few chilli flakes will give a delicious nip.

Using a hand-held blender, purée the dressing ingredients to make a glossy sauce almost like a mayo but lighter in consistency. If your blender is as contrary as mine, it's worth soaking the goji berries in a little water first for 25 minutes. This should make the ride a little smoother. Pour over the salad and lightly toss together using your fingertips. An implement like a spoon or fork can bruise the leaves and make a salad quickly look tired.

Pile on the centre of a large plate. A turn or two of the black pepper mill is all it needs now. And maybe a bit of adulation. The pine nut ricotta on page 143 is fairly swell on top.

BOND GIRL SALAD

○○○○○○○○○○○○○○○○

If we are what we eat, then most people are cheap, fast and easy. But good nutrition doesn't have to compromise your wallet or your wristwatch. Raging hot actress Halle Berry swears by her 5-factor rule: meals have to use 5 different ingredients and be ready to eat in 5 minutes.

A few examples: smoked salmon, poached egg, fresh cress, cucumber and jarred capers; grated raw carrot, coconut, sultanas, curry powder and sesame oil; or tinned mackerel, spring onion, rocket leaf, tomato and avocado. Your brain gets a good workout! No refined muck, of course, just 5 wholesome ingredients. That means if you couldn't find a particular ingredient 100 years ago, it doesn't count.

Try this Indonesian-style slaw to get you started. It takes a lot less than 5 minutes to make and is a great side dish with fish.

3 handfuls of finely sliced
  red cabbage
1 cup (150g) chopped
  pineapple
1/2 cup (125ml) natural
  yoghurt
1/4 cup (35g) sultanas
1 tablespoon curry powder
sprinkling of red-skinned
  peanuts

Serves 2-3

Tumble all the ingredients together. If you have a red onion loitering in the larder, throw that in too. Use whatever natural yoghurt you have - coconut, soya, goat, sheep. The hotter the curry powder is, the better. Something cosmic happens to pineapple when fire touches its orbit.

PROBIOTIC CELERIAC SLAW

ooooooooooooooooooooooooooooo

Celeriac may look like a Harry Potter concoction, but it's actually as common as turnip. Watch out for it on your next trip to the grocers. You'll notice that the rest of these ingredients are probably resident in your fridge already, save the offensive-sounding berry. Physalis look like massive amber raisins and have a sherbety smack.

Sprightly little berries buzzing with goodness and charm, physalis supply immune-enhancing beta carotene and vitamin C to help slay bugs. Throw them into salads and conversation to impress. However, it would be prudent to enunciate carefully. Get it wrong, and you will sound as if you enjoy STDs.

If you want to upgrade the quantities of this slaw for a party, the ratio of apple to carrot to celeriac is 3:2:1. In other words, remember to grate three times the amount of apple to the amount of grated celeriac. You're in control.

Let all the ingredients converse in a large bowl. If you're planning on having leftovers the next day, dunk more yoghurt into the slaw before plating up. There's no need for additional probiotic powder - you'll get plenty in the natural yoghurt. I originally devised this recipe for a client finishing several courses of antibiotics, so we whacked up the probiotic element to nourish her intestinal flora.

3/4 cup (65g) grated apple

1/2 cup (40g) grated carrot

1/2 cup (80g) whole walnuts, finely chopped

1/2 cup (125ml) natural soya yoghurt or coconut milk yoghurt

4 tablespoons grated celeriac

3 tablespoons sultanas and/ or dried physalis

1 tablespoon chia seeds (optional)

1 tablespoon smooth or wholegrain mustard

1/2 tablespoon probiotic powder, like Udo's (optional)

Serves 2 for lunch or 3 as a side

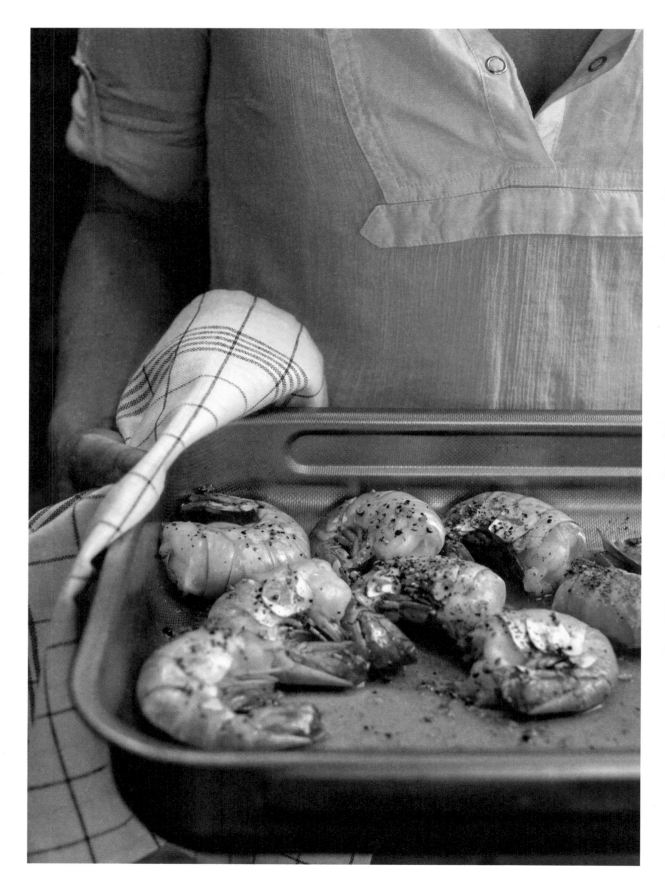

CURRIED CAULI, BANANA AND SPINACH WITH FLAKED FISH

○○

Use any fish you like, but we find salmon, mackerel, hake and cod easiest to flake. Prawns work deliciously well and can be thrown in a hot oven on a separate roasting tray to the cauli. Pan-fried squid is quickest - only 90 seconds to flash-fry in a little extra virgin coconut oil. Ask the fishmonger to prep your squid into rings for you.

Jack up the oven to 210°C/190°C fan/410°F.

Find your biggest roasting tray and briefly melt the oil in it in the oven for a few moments.

Meanwhile, split your cauliflower in half and break into clumsy chunks. Peel and chop the blackened bananas. Remove your roasting tray from the oven, tumble in the cauli, banana, curry powder and turmeric and coat everything really well. Roast for 20-25 minutes, shaking from time to time if you remember to. When the cauliflower starts to char, she's done. Remove the tray and mix through the baby spinach.

Meanwhile, to cook the fish, dot a large piece of tinfoil with coconut oil or your favourite oil. Place the hake or cod on top, fold the edges of the foil towards each other and seal them together, leaving lots of air above the fish. The fish will steam naturally in this 'tent' as long as both sides are sealed. Bake in the same oven as the cauliflower for 15 minutes, until the flesh can be pulled away. It's easy to overcook fish - I find the alarm on my phone to be a good ally in the kitchen. Once you reckon the fish is cooked, remove from its foil tent, season well and sprinkle with extra spices if you fancy. Set aside until the cauli is ready.

To serve, flake your hake or cod on top of the tray of cauliflower and add a little squeeze of lemon or lime if you have it.

3 tablespoons extra virgin coconut oil
1/2 large head of cauliflower
2 blackened, over-ripe bananas
3 tablespoons Indian curry powder
1-2 teaspoons ground turmeric (optional for colour and nutrition)
handful of baby spinach leaves
1 large fillet of hake or cod, bones removed
salt and pepper
squeeze of lemon or lime juice (optional)

Serves 3

BEGINNER'S BUCKWHEAT WITH GRATED APPLE, CHILLI AND PUMPKIN SEEDS

ooooooooooooooooooooooooooooooooooooooooooooooooooooooooooooooooooo

Instead of boring pasta, which often tastes more like soggy Kleenex than good-quality wheat, give buckwheat a shot. It's a teeny triangular grain, confused by shades of red, brown and green. The all-familiar Japanese soba noodles and Russian blini are made from buckwheat. Chances are you already like its nutty flavour.

Despite its name, buckwheat is not wheat. Hollywood's glitterati love its slow-release carbs and avalanche of beautifying bioflavonoids. Buckwheat even has lysine, that elusive amino acid responsible for preventing outbreaks of cold sores.

More good news? Once you have the ingredients sourced, this dish takes a mere 12 minutes to rustle up from package to plate.

A handy habit is to store fresh ginger, skin peeled, in your freezer so you never run out of it. Then, with the part of the grater that you normally use for zesting lemons, grate the ginger straight from frozen. Fresh ginger can be a little fibrous, overpowering and stringy. Frozen ginger is not.

1/4 cup (35g) pumpkin seeds
1/2 teaspoon chilli flakes
1 cup (100g) whole buckwheat
  grain, rinsed
2 red apples, grated
up to 1 cup (135g) gooey,
  dark, dried apricots,
  chopped
splash of extra virgin
  sesame oil
good lump of fresh ginger,
  peeled and frozen (see
  note above)
lime juice, to serve
tamari, to serve
dried nori flakes, to serve

Serves 4 as a side

Toast the pumpkin seeds with the chilli flakes by heating a dry frying pan or wok over a flame and listening for the pumpkin seeds to start popping. Stir briskly and remove when they look pregnant and crispy. Try not to let the pan smoke on a high heat.

Bring 1 1/2 cups seasoned water to the boil. Reduce the heat to a rolling simmer, add the freshly rinsed buckwheat and cook with a lid on for 8-10 minutes, until all the water has been absorbed. Turn off the heat and let the grain steam with the lid on for another few minutes. It should have a bite to it, but not a crunch. Drain any excess liquid and rinse with cold water.

Toss the buckwheat with the toasted pumpkin seeds, grated apple, chopped apricots, a splash of sesame oil and plenty of grated ginger. Serve with a squeeze of lime if you have one or a trickle of tamari and dried nori flakes.

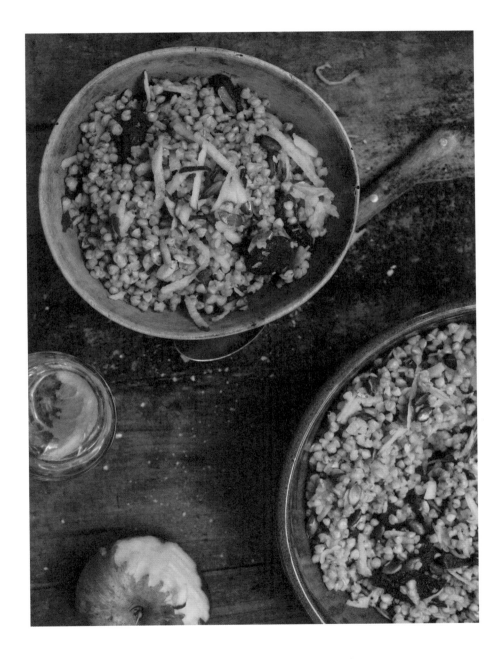

Suppers

One month of eating like this will have you feeling
like you're plugged into an electrical socket.

1 British cup = 250ml

Cooking has never been just about the recipes. It's about navigating your creativity and flirting with flavours. It's about sensuality as much as science. To me, it's the ultimate form of self-expression, where you set out to nourish your body and those you love.

Self-love is distilled in healthy eating. Feeding your body with nutrient-rich food is like plugging into an electrical socket. It has the ability to transform energy levels and resurrect brain cells. Athletes see food as their body's artillery. It's probably about time we did too. Processed food has little nutritional purchase, leaving the body bereft of the vital nutrients necessary for us to function well. Think three-toed sloth or puma: which would you prefer?

So how can you clean up your diet without losing your personality or taste buds? It's easier than you think. Here are a couple of tips.

Get your hands on a copy of Wham's greatest hits. I'm not sure if their groove transfers to my fingers, but something cosmic happens to my serotonin and my pies. Turn up the volume and get jiggy with it.

Next step is to share the results of your kitchen adventures with friends. Everyone loves to be fed. There's no easier way of getting hooked on a new habit than receiving rampant adulation.

The more you surround yourself with healthy people, the more you start to think like them. I subscribe to great blogs to get ideas for healthy eating in my inbox every week. Think of it as a form of helpful 'advertising'. Cleaning up your diet may seem slow in the beginning, but persistence will make way for a new and better you. Just think: if you make one of my recipes every week, you'll have mastered 52 seriously healthy dishes by this time next year. Your body is sure to levitate. Ready?

BROWN RICE AND HIS COUSINS

xxxxxxxxxxxxxxxxxxxxxxxxxxxxxxxxxxxxxxxxxxxx

At one stage, American actress Mariel Hemingway made brown rice so fashionable that Californian grocers struggled to keep it in stock. Mariel is a bit of a beaut, so it's hardly surprising to find brown rice, lentils and chickpeas at the heart of her diet.

You see, whole grains like brown rice contain those mighty B vitamins responsible for fuelling our batteries and busy bods. Vitamin B3 in particular can help lift your mood, like daydreaming about James McEvoy or making small changes to politicians' Wikipedia pages. There's far less B3, fibre and manganese in the white starchy stuff. We need fibre to service our pipes and regulate our poops. Nothing nice about constipation. Manganese seems crucial to an antioxidant enzyme called SOD, the maestro of all antioxidants. One cup of brown rice delivers almost 100% of our daily manga-needs! Manganese comes from the Greek word for magic. Nuff said.

There are legions of whole grain rice to choose from; here are the best ones. Soaking rice apparently improves digestibility and shortens cooking time. There's no downside to soaking rice, so it's probably a sensible thing to do.

I use my rice cooker all the time. Exact cooking times and instructions are on my blog: www.susanjanewhite.com.

Wild rice

Very expensive, so it's advisable to add 1 tablespoon into other varieties of rice instead of serving it straight. Cooks in 45 minutes.

Brown jasmine

Rinse. Simmer 2 parts water to just over 1 part rice and a pinch of salt. Follow the directions on the packet, but 30-40 minutes should be just about right. Brown jasmine rice usually takes less time to cook than long grain rice. During the final few minutes of cooking, remove the lid and boil off any remaining water.

Brown basmati

This is the fastest brown rice to cook. Rinse and simmer 1 cup brown basmati with 1 3/4 cups seasoned water. Ready in 22 minutes (check the cooking time suggested by the manufacturer on the packet). Add 1 teaspoon of caraway seeds for a smack of Bombay.

Brown long grain

Most popular but least impressive. Simmer 2 parts water to 1 part rice. You can add 1 tablespoon of millet, quinoa, wild rice or amaranth to 1 cup of long grain brown rice and cook for 45 minutes. It will be stickier than regular long grain rice, but very nourishing alongside a curry or stew.

Short grain

Rinse. Simmer 2 parts seasoned water to 1 part rice. Ready in 45 minutes. Soaking rice apparently improves digestibility and shortens cooking time. We often do 1 1/2 cups short grain rice with 1/2 cup whole barley in the rice cooker. Works beautifully.

Sticky brown sushi rice

Wash sushi rice very well in cold water. Transfer to a saucepan with 1 3/4 cups cold water to 1 cup sushi rice. Soak for 30 minutes, then boil for 35 minutes. Remove from the heat and leave to dry-steam until all the water is absorbed. It's best to use a plastic spatula to avoid splitting the grain and mushing it.

Red (camargue) rice

Good for beginners. Rinse and simmer in 2 parts seasoned water to just under 1 part rice for 40-50 minutes. Be watchful of the final few minutes to avoid burning.

Sweet brown rice

Our absolute favourite. It's a cross between sticky white rice and short grain brown rice. Rinse. Simmer 1 part rice to 2 parts water. Cook for 35 minutes or until all the water is absorbed. Remove from the heat and allow to dry-steam with the lid on for a further 10 minutes.

EGGY FRIED RICE

xxxxxxxxxxxxxxxxxxxxxxx

Every time you make rice, try to remember to make enough for this meal the following day. Then you can high five your genius when you come home from work and spend 90 seconds whizzing up your supper.

Black garlic keeps for a year in the fridge and is useful for days when you can't dart to the grocers for fresh stuff. In fact, most of these ingredients will already be lurking in your kitchen. And therein lies its USP.

There's a knack to good fried rice. The first is to cook the eggs completely before adding the rice. The second is never to add soya sauce - it should be served alongside the dish instead. Ready? Let's see if we can get this from fridge to plate in 90 seconds.

1 tablespoon extra virgin
  coconut oil
1/2 cup (70g) frozen petits
  pois
3 eggs
2 cups leftover rice
3 black or fresh garlic
  cloves, chopped
pinch of arame ocean veg
  (optional)
tamari soya sauce, to serve

Serves 2

Melt the coconut oil on a medium heat in your best frying pan. Make sure the heat isn't too high. While the oil is melting, place the peas in a separate bowl and pour boiling water over them.

Crack the eggs into the pan and poke the yolks so they break. Coat the pan with the eggs. Don't scramble or mix them, but allow them to slowly cook through (around 20 seconds). Now add the rice and stir to coat. Drain the peas and pop them in with the garlic. The arame is optional if you have it in your cupboard (this is an ocean veggie that lasts for up to 3 years in the packet, so it's very handy for suppers like this). Arame demands 10 minutes of soaking too, which would hamper our 90-second challenge right now. But it's something to consider for next time.

Plate up once hot and serve with a bottle of tamari.

BUCKWHEAT CRÊPES WITH PINE NUT RICOTTA AND SPINACH

xxxxxxxxxxxxxxxxxxxxxxxxxxxxxxxxxxxxxxxxxxxxxxxxxxxxxxxxxxxxxxxxxxxxxxx

I never get my fill on Pancake Tuesday, partly because I always forget it's coming - bit like Mother's Day and Visa deadlines. Pancakes are so darn delicious, it's rather puzzling why we don't tuck into them every Tuesday. Why reserve them for one special day a year?

To make the pine nut ricotta, drain the soaked cashews. Whizz everything together in a mini blender or food processor. A hand-held soup gun won't work - something more powerful is needed. Scoop into a glass jar and top with crushed black peppercorns.

Boil the frozen spinach in 2cm of water for 5 minutes. Drain thoroughly. Salt and pepper it up. Keep warm in the oven or on top of the cooker until the pancakes are ready to rock.

As you cook each crêpe, keep them warm on a wire rack and cover with a tea towel. Tinfoil will make the crêpes sweat and turn them soggy. At home, I just serve as I go. There's usually a queue of children at my ankles.

When everyone is seated, dish up the pancakes and dot with pine nut ricotta and a generous dollop of spinach.

1 x crêpe recipe on page 78
600g frozen spinach

For the pine nut ricotta:
1 cup (150g) raw cashew
  nuts, soaked overnight
1/2 cup (140g) pine nuts
1-2 garlic cloves
3 tablespoons water
2 tablespoons extra virgin
  olive oil
2 tablespoons lemon juice
3/4 teaspoon good-quality
  sea salt
a few turns of the black
  pepper mill

Makes 8 crêpes

CHILDREN'S STICKY RICE WITH CAULIFLOWER CONFETTI

xxxxxxxxxxxxxxxxxxxxxxxxxxxxxxxxxxxxxxxxxxxxxxxxxxxxxxxxxxxxxxxxxxxx

1 cup cooked short grain,
  sweet or brown sushi rice
3 tablespoons cultured
  coconut yoghurt
floret of purple cauliflower

Serves 2

Rice and quinoa can be tricky for children to master. You can make a 'glue' by using mashed sweet potato or coconut yoghurt to bind it all together. Using a zester or microplane, grate the purple cauliflower over each bowl of sticky rice to make purple confetti. Cauliflower has never been so cool!

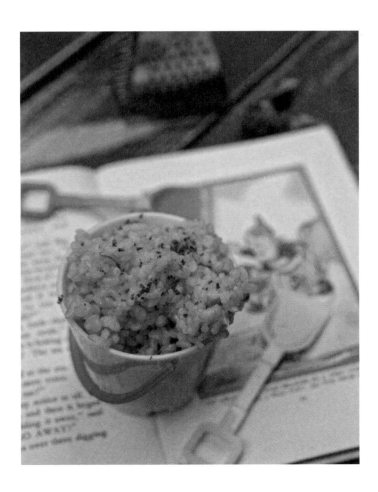

SNAZZY BROCCOLI AND SOBA NOODLES

xxxxxxxxxxxxxxxxxxxxxxxxxxxxxxxxxxxxxxxxxxxxxxxxxxxx

Broccoli is a crusader, backing up your front line defences with vitamin C, chlorophyll, antioxidants and other handsome phytonutrients. I tell my boys broccoli are edible Lego trees and then they plunder the entire plate.

Famed for its cancer-fighting properties, broccoli is an affordable superfood. When choosing a head, just make sure the florets have not turned yellowish or look limp and tired. With age, broccoli loses those supersonic nutrients.

Cook the soba noodles according to the instructions on the packet. They usually take 8 minutes.

Meanwhile, break the broccoli into bite-sized pieces. Steam for 3-4 minutes.

Whisk the garlic with the sesame oil, tamari, Brazil nuts, miso and cayenne. Reverently drizzle over the warm broccoli, toss with the cooked noodles and watch your friends and family go bonkers.

1 portion 100% buckwheat
  soba noodles
1/2 head of broccoli
2 garlic cloves, crushed
1 tablespoon sesame oil
1 tablespoon tamari
1 tablespoon roughly chopped
  Brazil nuts (optional)
1 teaspoon miso paste
pinch of cayenne pepper

Serves 2-3

BEGINNER'S QUINOA

xxxxxxxxxxxxxxxxxxxxxx

The rapid increase in wheat and gluten sensitivities is good news for quinoa. This grain practically swaggers with its impressive stash of B vitamins (energy), protein (repair), iron (strength), magnesium (circulation) and zinc (sexy skin). Quinoa is really quite the starlet and should be given centre stage on your shopping list. The United Nation's Food and Agriculture Organisation considers it to be as nutritionally complete as whole milk.

Quinoa is ideal for picnics, packed lunches, alongside curries, tossed in salads, scattered into soups or to accompany a tray of roasted veg on indolent evenings.

1 cup (200g) quinoa
1 1/2 cups (375ml) stock or
  seasoned water
8-12 juicy baby tomatoes,
  halved
flesh of 1 avocado, roughly
  chopped
1 mild chilli, deseeded and
  sliced (optional)
handful of rocket, chives,
  cress or coriander,
  roughly torn
3-4 tablespoons extra virgin
  olive oil
1 tablespoon finely chopped
  red onion
sea salt flakes and a few
  twists of the black
  pepper mill

Serves 2

Wash the quinoa very well in a sieve under running water. Transfer to a heavy-based saucepan. Bring to the boil with the stock or seasoned water and cook for 12-15 minutes with a lid on. The longer you cook it, the softer and stickier it becomes. Take the pan off the heat as soon as the quinoa has drunk up all the water. Let it sit on the countertop and fluff up in the residual heat of the lidded saucepan. Some rice cookers have a special 'grain' setting that works perfectly for quinoa.

Leave the quinoa to cool a little before stirring through the remaining ingredients. Give the black pepper mill a few twists and add a smattering of sea salt flakes. You could pack the quinoa into an empty container for lunch at the office. I use the cardboard ones from my local deli's salad counter. They seem far snazzier than my manky old Tupperware.

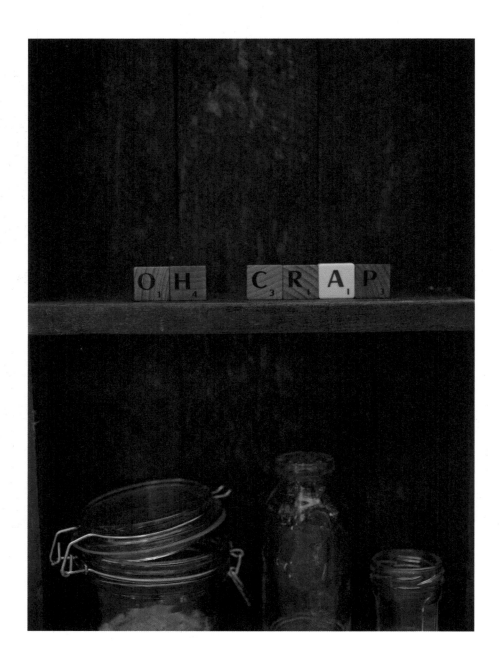

NOTHING-IN-MY-CUPBOARD QUINOA

xxxxxxxxxxxxxxxxxxxxxxxxxxxxxxxxxxxxxxxxxxxxxxxxx

When the fridge looks bare and you can't find the energy to resuscitate your sleepy brain cells, reach for a packet of quinoa. Uncooked, quinoa will store for ages in your cupboard, making it a very attractive last-minute meal. Here's one to get you started. Cooked quinoa will happily samba in the fridge for a few days.

Soak the arame in water for 10 minutes if using. Drain, and set aside for the quinoa collection. The arame is optional if you have it in your cupboard. Arame is an ocean veggie and lasts for up to 3 years in the packet, so it's very handy for suppers like this.

Thoroughly rinse the quinoa in a sieve under running water. You'll be tempted to skip this step, but try not to or you'll end up with a bitter residue. Drop the rinsed quinoa into your saucepan of boiling salted water. Add the turmeric if you have it and simmer for 12–15 minutes with a lid on it. Drain any excess water from the pan by manoeuvring the lid very slightly so that you can pour off the liquid into the sink without losing the heat from the pan. Let the quinoa dry-steam in the saucepan on your countertop for a few more minutes. This step eliminates the threat of soggy quinoa.

When it's done (taste and see), let the quinoa cool a little and toss through the remaining ingredients. The coconut looks better tickled on top. Add as much curry powder as you fancy and a spot of citrus if you feel like it. Olives, capers, pomegranate seeds and herbs are cracking additions should you find any loitering in your pantry.

pinch of arame ocean veg (optional)
1 1/2 cups (300g) quinoa
2 cups (500ml) seasoned water
1 teaspoon ground turmeric (optional)
1/2 cup (75g) raisins
1/4 cup (20g) desiccated coconut
2 garlic cloves, crushed or minced
1 tall spring onion, sliced
zest of 1/2 orange
1 tablespoon Madras curry powder
good glug of extra virgin olive oil
smattering of pistachios or any other nut

Serves 3 as a main or 6 as a side

SMOKED PAPRIKA AND CUMIN QUINOA

xxxxxxxxxxxxxxxxxxxxxxxxxxxxxxxxxxxxxxxxxxxxxxxxxxx

Cooking quinoa is a lot easier than pronouncing it. Insiders call it keen-wah rather than quin-oh-ah, but nobody seems to care what I call it. This curious carb looks and feels the same as couscous, except that it tastes a whole lot nicer. Once you give quinoa a shot, you'll be outraged that couscous ever seduced you.

With its encyclopaedic mineral and vitamin profile, quinoa is by far the healthiest grain in my cupboard. It's real fast food with a nutritional halo. Each seed is host to an army of minerals to help service our adrenal glands. These are the call centres for stress and mood. Athletes love quinoa for its low glycemic value. All this means is that a bowl of quinoa can drip feed your body, brain and dimples for longer than white bread or pasta. Apparently, it also has higher levels of calcium and protein than dairy. Hail quinoa!

1 cup (200g) quinoa
1 1/2 cup (375ml) hot
  chicken stock or boiling
  water
2 teaspoons ground cumin
1 teaspoon smoked paprika
2-3 eggs
generous splash of extra
  virgin olive oil
a few turns of the black
  pepper mill
bunch of rocket, dill,
  chives, parsley or
  coriander

Serves 2-3

Rinse the quinoa in a sieve under running cold water for a good 30 seconds (some grains have a bitter coating). Knock the wet quinoa into a small saucepan. (Bits will stick to the sieve. No matter.) Add the hot chicken stock or boiling water to the quinoa, sprinkle in the spices and simmer on a medium heat for 15 minutes with a lid on. The kitchen will smell incredible. You can tell quinoa is cooked once the tail of the seed comes away from the grain. A nifty trick is to remove the pot from the heat after 12 minutes, drain all the water and cover the pot with a tightly sealed lid for another 5 minutes. This way, the quinoa won't stick to the base or burn. Any residual heat left in the pot should fluff the grains up nicely.

To poach eggs, make sure you have the freshest eggs possible, left at room temperature, otherwise the eggs may become very disobedient. Using a small heavy-based saucepan, bring 8cm of water to a simmer. Swirl the water in a circular motion like a whirlpool and slide the raw egg into the middle. Many chefs swear that adding cider vinegar to the water will make the egg white behave. Your call. Watch carefully, and remove with a slotted spoon after 60-90 seconds to drain the water off your plump little treasure. Don't worry if it looks like half the egg white is floating in the saucepan. That always happens

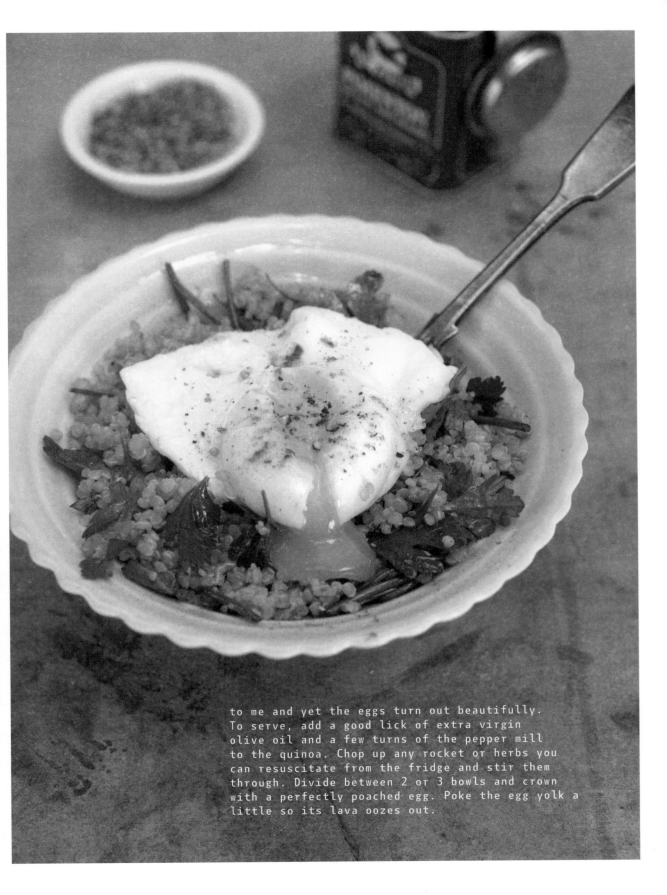

to me and yet the eggs turn out beautifully.
To serve, add a good lick of extra virgin
olive oil and a few turns of the pepper mill
to the quinoa. Chop up any rocket or herbs you
can resuscitate from the fridge and stir them
through. Divide between 2 or 3 bowls and crown
with a perfectly poached egg. Poke the egg yolk a
little so its lava oozes out.

HARISSA QUINOA WITH ROASTED LEMON FENNEL

xxxxxxxxxxxxxxxxxxxxxxxxxxxxxxxxxxxxxxxxxxxxxxxxxxxxxxxxxxxxxxx

Harissa is a spicy North African paste guaranteed to send your blood beating like a bodhrán. While it looks like a lot of ingredients, you'll find most of them in your cupboard. This should make enough harissa to last 2 weeks in the fridge or 4 months in the freezer.

For the lemon fennel:
4 fennel bulbs
splash of olive oil
zest and juice of 1/2 lemon

For the quinoa:
2 cups (400g) quinoa, well
  rinsed
2 cups (750ml) vegetable
  stock or seasoned water

For the harissa:
3-4 red peppers
6 red chillies
4 garlic cloves
1 tablespoon cumin seeds,
  ground
1 tablespoon caraway seeds,
  ground
1 tablespoon smoked paprika
1 tablespoon tomato purée
1/2 teaspoon sea salt flakes
1 tablespoon red wine or
  apple cider vinegar
3-5 tablespoons extra virgin
  hemp seed or olive oil

Serves 4-6

Preheat the oven to 180°C/160°C fan/350°F.

Cut each fennel bulb lengthways into quarters. Don't be tempted to slice the bum off, as the bulb will fall apart and you will be left with loads of bitty pieces rather than thick wedges. Throw onto a large baking tray.

Now slice the red peppers for the harissa into chunks, discarding the inner white film, stalk and seeds. Toss on the baking tray with the fennel and a splash of olive oil. Roast for 30 minutes.

While the peppers and fennel cook, bring the quinoa and stock to a rolling boil. Reduce the heat until it's puttering away politely. Put a lid on it and cook for about 12 minutes. Drain (if the stock is not thoroughly absorbed), place the lid back on and let the grains fluff up from the residual heat of the saucepan for another 5 minutes.

While the quinoa and roasted veg do their thing,
let's get going on the fresh harissa. Wearing
disposable gloves, cut the chillies down the side
and scoop out the seeds and pith with a teaspoon.
Discard. Or rub on husband's toothbrush if he
hasn't taken out the bins. Blitz the chillies
with the garlic, spices, tomato purée and salt
until it forms a smooth paste. I find a hand-held
blender much better than a food processor for
this. Now, and no sooner, add the roasted red
peppers (pick them out from the tray of roasted
fennel) and the vinegar. Pulverise to your satisfaction. Stir through the hemp oil or olive oil
and scoop into your serving dish. Avoid adding
the oil while pulverising the rest of the ingredients or the harissa will turn pink and no one
will eat it, not even your Barbie-loving toddler.

To serve the whole lot, gloss up the quinoa with
a smidge of olive oil. Divide between 4-6 plates,
top with a couple of fennel wedges, the zest and
juice of a little lemon and a royal dollop of
harissa.

QUINOA WITH STRAWBERRY AND MINT GREMOLATA

xxxxxxxxxxxxxxxxxxxxxxxxxxxxxxxxxxxxxxxxxxxxxxxxxxxxxxxxxxxxx

This is the kind of dish that will make you purer simply by looking at it. If you haven't cooked quinoa before, it's the perfect food for taking into work and dining al desko. Bring an extra fork to ward off envious colleagues forced to queue for manky canteen food.

If you're worried about evacuating the office at lunchtime with your honking breath, fear not: parsley can help neutralise garlic breath. Crushed walnuts are another stealthy trick to remember. Failing that, peppermint oil capsules from health food stores are a winner and will make you giggle when you have gloriously refreshing burps.

2 cups (400g) quinoa
3 cups (750ml) stock or seasoned water
1 teaspoon ground turmeric (optional for colour and nutrition)

For the strawberry mint gremolata:
2 garlic cloves
1 lemon
1/2 cup (125ml) extra virgin olive oil
generous helping of salt flakes and crushed black pepper
25g curly parsley
25g mint leaves
1/4 cup (25g) dried strawberries (fresh won't work)

Serves 2 as a main or 4 as a side

Rinse the quinoa under running water for 30 seconds, rubbing the grains together with your fingers. A sieve is helpful. Knock the rinsed quinoa into a saucepan (don't worry about the bits that stick to the sieve, these are designed to test your patience and are destined for the kitchen sink). Add the stock and turmeric. Bring to a rolling boil, lower the heat and fit a lid on top. Cook for 10-15 minutes, until all the liquid is absorbed. You'll know it's cooked as soon as you see a little tail on each grain. If you like it soft, keep the lid on and let it dry-steam on the counter for a further 5-10 minutes. This will make the grain nice and fluffy without the risk of burning.

To make the strawberry mint gremolata while the quinoa cooks, finely grate the garlic and lemon rind. Squeeze a tiny bit of juice from the lemon into a jam jar and add the olive oil, salt and pepper. Chop the parsley and mint into it. Give everything a jolly good mix in the jar by shaking it all wildly.

Let the quinoa cool a little before dressing it up. I find hot quinoa always absorbs more than I'd like it to, resulting in disappointing, squidgy quinoa. When it feels cooler, tumble in the dressing and dried strawberries.

KATE MOSS QUINOA

xxxxxxxxxxxxxxxxxxxxxxxx

Every time I eat quinoa, I feel like a supermodel. This elegant grain contains around 17% complete protein, making it white-hot for vegans, athletes and professional nuts (nutritionists). Celebs love the stuff. Bloggers are possessed by it. And over-priced restaurants have hijacked its pulling power with an excitement usually reserved for a Disney premiere. This grain is going places.

Quinoa is perfect to bring in for lunch at the office. Black+Blum sell dinky bento boxes and lunch sets online (see page 253). Purchase one, and you'll save a fortune on junk food and dodgy sangers.

Rinse the quinoa under cold running water for at least 30 seconds, using your fingers to rub the grains together. Plonk the now-wet grain into a small saucepan and add the stock and turmeric. Bring to boiling point, cover with a lid, turn down the heat slightly and cook for 12 minutes, until all the liquid has been soaked up. Remove from the heat and allow the saucepan to stand on the kitchen counter for a further 5 minutes with the lid on. This step is important if you like fluffy quinoa. Taste and decide for yourself. As soon as you're happy with it, let the grain cool down (I spread it out on a large flat plate).

While your quinoa is puttering away, prep the remaining ingredients. Slice the red onion in half and thinly shave into semi-circles using a sharp knife. Soak in the red wine vinegar for 15 minutes. Cut the pomegranate into quarters and peel back the white pith to reveal lots of ruby-red seeds. You're aiming for about 1/4 cup of pomegranate seeds.

In a large bowl, add the pom seeds, blueberries, dill, garlic and olive oil. I recommend using 8 cloves of creamy roasted garlic and mashing them into a paste with the oil. Drain the red onion before adding it to the remaining ingredients (you'll need to discard the vinegar).

Once you're satisfied with the texture of your quinoa, add to your prepped ingredients and give it a nice tumble and tickle. Crown with extra blueberries, or lamb cutlets for carnivores.

1 cup (200g) quinoa
1 1/2 cups (375ml) vegetable
  stock or seasoned water
1/4 teaspoon ground turmeric
1 small red onion
3 tablespoons red wine
  vinegar
1 small pomegranate
handful blueberries
1 bunch (30g) dill, stems
  removed
1 clove freshly minced
  garlic or 8 cloves roasted
  garlic (see page 94)
4 tablespoons extra virgin
  olive oil

Serves 2 as a main or 5
  as a side

CHILDREN'S QUINOA

xxxxxxxxxxxxxxxxxxxxxxxxxxx

Quinoa is a carb indigenous to Peru. As a grain, it's sort of like couscous only nuttier in taste and significantly healthier. Quinoa provides essential amino acids that the body requires for optimum functioning, making it a first-class plant protein. No wonder those wily Peruvians can skip up the Incan altitudes with the ease of greyhounds at a marathon. My children love the stuff.

Quinoa is even powdered down and sold in capsule form, such is its nutritional bounty. This children's recipe has a stash of other immune-enhancing superfoods, such as sweet potato, mango, goji berries, virgin coconut oil and turmeric. No nursery bug will stand a chance!

1 cup (200g) quinoa
1 1/2 cups (375ml) filtered
  water
2 tablespoons goji berries
  (optional nutrition)
1 teaspoon ground turmeric
2 tablespoons extra virgin
  coconut oil
1 sweet potato, baked whole
1/2 mango (optional
  nutrition)

Serves 2-4

Rinse the quinoa very well under running water. A sieve is useful. Knock the wet quinoa grains into a saucepan (don't worry about the bits that stick to the sieve, these are designed to test your patience and are destined for the kitchen sink). Add the water, goji berries (if using) and turmeric. Bring to a rolling boil, lower the heat and fit a lid on top. Cook for 12-15 minutes, until all the liquid is absorbed. You'll know it's cooked as soon as you see a little tail on each grain. Children like it soft, so keep the lid on and let it dry-steam on the counter for a further 10 minutes. This will make the grain nice and fluffy without the risk of burning. Add the coconut oil and replace the lid.

Peel and roughly mash the baked sweet potato (it won't matter what size it is). Finely chop the mango. Mix into the fluffy quinoa. The mash acts like a glue to bind the quinoa together, making it easier for children to eat.

BASIC LENTILS

xxxxxxxxxxxxxxxxxxxxx

Heart disease is Ireland's biggest killer, chased closely by bowel cancer. If you're worried about either condition, make friends with your health insurer. Or lentils. You don't have to be a member of the Green Party to enjoy them or start campaigning against animal cruelty. Just a little mustard and garlic, and in no time you'll be the best of friends.

Lentils are the heavyweight champion of fibre. Why is this important to you? Fibre helps maintain a healthy cholesterol range by deporting excess bile from the body. The lower your cholesterol range, the lower your risk of heart disease (CVD, in doctor speak). At the same time, fibre gives your pipes a first-rate servicing. A cup of lentils holds a stonking 17 grams of fibre. That's more than half our recommended daily intake. These tiny legumes have other salubrious gifts for your ticker, such as potassium and magnesium. See ya later, paltry pasta!

The Blue Zones Diet, also dubbed the Centenarian's Diet, is a compilation of foods we should be paying close attention to if we are planning to cavort well into our nineties. The diet reveals how centenarians across the world manage to live longer and better and still look buff at 99 without pills or Crème de la Mer. And you know what? Beans and lentils are among their top foods. Here are a few good recipes to bring into the office with you. Lentils love dining al desko.

Simmer the lentils gently with a lid on for 15-20 minutes (if you're using Canadian or brown lentils, they'll need more water and an extra 10-15 minutes). Lentils are cooked when they look like they're yawning. A bit like mussels, only 20 times smaller. Puy lentils cook rapidly and hold their shape very well compared to other varieties.

Try not to add salt until afterwards, or the lentils' skin can toughen. Once cooked, or when the cooking liquid has evaporated, lick with extra virgin olive oil, raw cider vinegar and a smattering of celery salt. They're not very demanding.

1 cup (210g) Puy lentils
1 1/2 cups (375ml) stock or
  water
extra virgin olive oil
raw cider vinegar
celery salt

Serves 2

MAPLE MUSTARD LENTILS

xxxxxxxxxxxxxxxxxxxxxxxxxxxxxxxxxx

1 x Basic Lentils recipe
  (page 157)

For the dressing:
1 small garlic clove,
  crushed
3 tablespoons extra virgin
  olive oil
2 tablespoons balsamic or
  raw cider vinegar
1-2 teaspoons maple syrup
1 tablespoon smooth Dijon
  mustard
1 teaspoon black or mixed
  peppercorns, crushed
handful of salad leaves or
  fresh herbs

Serves 2 as a side

Cook the lentils as outlined on page 157. Combine all the dressing ingredients (except the herbs) together before pouring over the warm lentils and then stirring through some herbs. A great side plate to fish and meat. We tend to add finely chopped anchovies to ours, but I realise not everyone shares our anchovy fetish.

Leftover dressing can be refrigerated in a clean jam jar for 2 weeks.

PUMPKIN AND BLACK GARLIC LENTILS

xxxxxxxxxxxxxxxxxxxxxxxxxxxxxxxxxxxxxxxxxxxxxxxxxx

1 small organic pumpkin
extra virgin coconut or
  olive oil
1 x Basic Lentils recipe
  (page 157)
6 cloves of black aged
  garlic, finely sliced
a couple of anchovies, finely
  sliced (optional)
coconut yoghurt, to serve

Serves 6 as a side

Preheat the oven to 220°C/200°C fan/425°F.

Quarter the pumpkin using a sharp knife (and even sharper concentration - no one wants roasted fingers). Deseed the flesh and roughly chop into 5cm pieces - no need to peel the skin. Splash with coconut or olive oil and make sure everything is well coated. Roast on a baking tray for 45 minutes, shaking the tray halfway through the cooking time. Remove the pumpkin once the sides start to caramelise. Tumble into the cooked lentils and sprinkle with the black garlic and anchovies (if using). Tuck your creation into a lunch carton, ready to pack into your briefcase the next day. Try not to scoff it all at the bus stop in the morning or you'll weep at lunchtime.

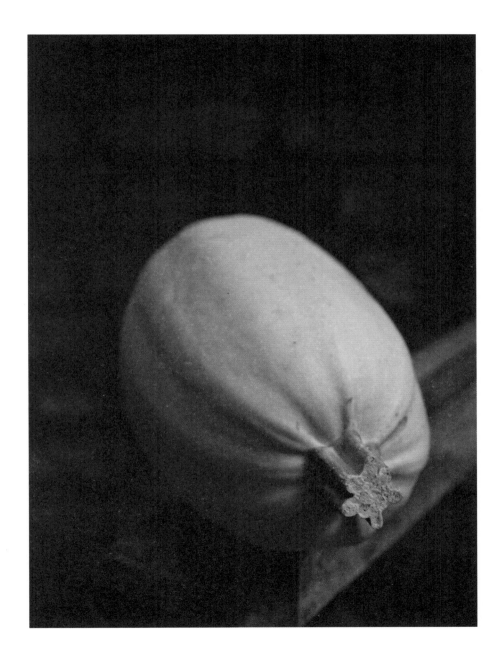

TINNED SARDINES FIVE WAYS

xxxxxxxxxxxxxxxxxxxxxxxxxxxxxxxxxxxxxxx

Tinned sardines are an excellent source of omega-3, calcium, protein and vitamin D. Let's not go into bone density here, but suffice it to say that if you want to groove on the dance floor well into your sixties, get 'em into ya! There ain't nothing sexy about brittle bones. Here are a couple of ideas to get you foxtrotting with sardines again.

Chermoula-kissed Sardines
This North African chermoula has been Irishified with a touch of seaweed. Arame only requires a little soaking before it's ready to dance. Don't be afraid of using seaweed in your cuisine - it's easier than opening a can of beans!

good pinch of arame seaweed
4 garlic cloves
1 teaspoon whole black peppercorns
1 cup flat-leaf parsley, chopped
1 cup coriander, chopped
1/2 cup (125ml) extra virgin olive oil
2 tablespoons ground cumin
2 tablespoons lemon juice
1/2 teaspoon cayenne

Soak the arame seaweed in water for 10 minutes while you prep the other ingredients.

Crush the garlic and peppercorns in a pestle and mortar. Briskly stir in the remaining ingredients with a fork. This is traditional chermoula.

Drain the arame and discard the soaking liquid. Finely chop and stir through the chermoula. Moroccans love it on hardboiled eggs, white fish or tumbled into chickpeas. I think it's cosmic with sarnies.

Smoky Sarnies
Drain the tinned sardines. Mash with crushed garlic and a good pinch of smoked paprika. Serve on top of half an avocado.

Mediterranean Sardines
Drain the tinned sardines and mash with chopped sun-dried tomatoes, olives, parsley and lemon zest. Tastes great on dehydrated linseed crackers if you can find them. My boys eat these every week.

Balsamic Sardines
Drain the sardines of their oil or brine and combine with a splash of balsamic vinegar and chopped chives (or any herb from your window farm). Use celery sticks and red pepper strips as edible spoons.

Curried Mayo and Sarnies
You can make your own curried mayo using health-enhancing oils (see page 48 and add 3 tablespoons of curry powder at the beginning). The mayo will last for 3 weeks in the fridge. Just reach for a tin of sarnies and crown on top of a simple salad of Cos lettuce leaves and chopped apple. Go for papaya or mango if you're dead fancy.

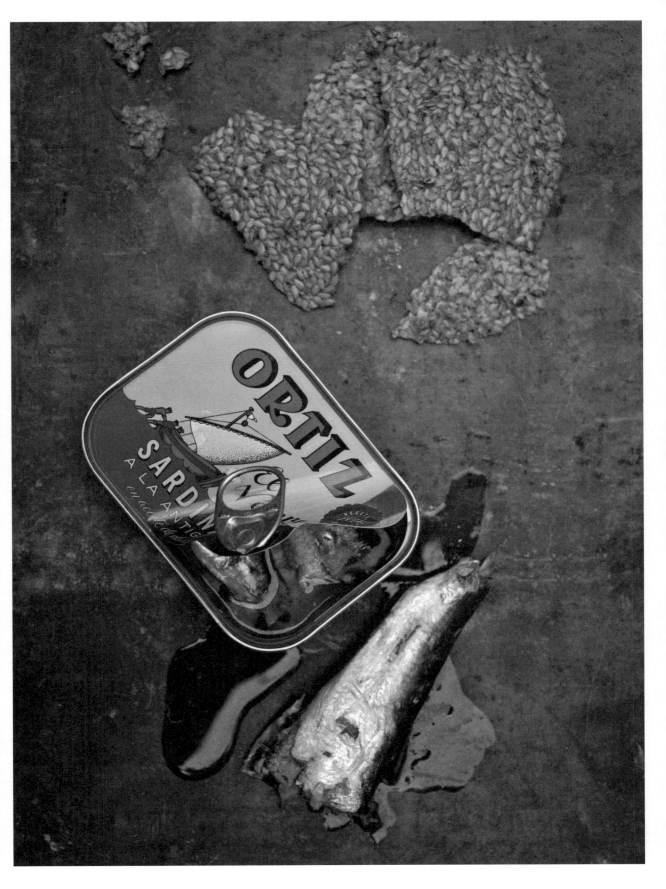

MACKEREL PÂTÉ WITH ANCHOVY AIOLI

xxxxxxxxxxxxxxxxxxxxxxxxxxxxxxxxxxxxxxxxxxxxxxxxxxxx

This is the short-top-and-sides of evening meals.

It's clear we need to look for sustainable fish if we want our grandchildren's kids to know what tuna and salmon taste like. Overfishing is leading to extinction. Our choices affect real-time demand in the marketplace, and fishing is a demand-driven industry. If you're unsure, look for the Marine Stewardship Council (MSC) label of approval or the Responsible Irish Fish logo.

Mackerel is on tap in Ireland. It has to be the tastiest, cheapest and most plentiful fish I can get my greedy mitts on. If gutting or filleting fresh fish is too much for your blood pressure, ask Mr Terribly Kind Fishmonger to do it for you.

2 hardboiled eggs
1 large fillet cooked/smoked
  mackerel or 1 x 125g tin
  of mackerel
3 tablespoons anchovy aioli
  (page 48) or coconut
  yoghurt
1-2 tablespoons chopped
  spring onion or fresh dill

Serves 2

Pulse the eggs, fish and aioli or yoghurt in a food processor before adding the chopped herbs. Make it as chunky or smooth as you wish, but don't whizz the herbs or you'll end up with what looks like remnants of Kermit the Frog.

Tinned mackerel works best with aioli and smoked mackerel with yoghurt. It's great on half an avocado or the Your New Wheat-free Bread (page 51). Bring leftovers into work the next day in a jar for a sneaky mid-morning dining al desko experience. Fishavores might like to alternate mackerel with kippers or tinned wild salmon and capers.

BAKED HAKE WITH LEMONGRASS SALSA

xxxxxxxxxxxxxxxxxxxxxxxxxxxxxxxxxxxxxxxxxxxxxxxxxxx

Farmers know all about the importance of nutrient-rich soil to grow top-quality produce. It's no different for us - nourish your body and your body will nourish you.

With that in mind, get your entire five a day with this mango and lemongrass salsa. It's also ace to bring to a BBQ. Word of caution - this salsa is the prima donna of accompaniments, made to outshine all others. Your host will hate you.

Preheat the oven to 200°C/180°C fan/400°F.

Season the hake with salt and pepper and place onto a piece of tinfoil. Secure into a tent-like parcel, transfer the tent onto a baking tray and cook for approximately 15 minutes. I always dot the fish with extra virgin coconut oil and a splash of mirin or ume, but you decide. The basic message I want to convey is that cooking fish is easy peasy. The razzmatazz is up to you.

You'll know it's cooked when it falls apart with pressure from your thumb. Raw fish won't. While the hake bakes, get going on your salsa.

There's no need to peel your mango straight away. Using a sharp knife, slice down either side of its flat, oblong stone. Cut each slice into 5 or 6 strips. Similar to a slice of melon, run your knife along the skin of each strip of mango to free its flesh. Lick your fingers and chop into small chunks. The mango, not your fingers. Peel the ginger, discarding its gnarly skin, and freeze its core for 15 minutes. Freezing fresh ginger makes it easier to grate straight into salads.

Gently toss all the salsa ingredients together. Remove the ginger from the freezer and grate it over the salsa.

When your hake is happy, serve on a big plate with the salsa running over the fish. It will end up like a large cross on the plate - the idea is not to hide the fish under the salsa. If you have any black olives lurking in your cupboards, scatter a couple over the fish for a touch of *Blue Peter*.

1 large piece of hake
a few turns of the salt and
  peppercorn mill

For the salsa:
1 mango
thumb-sized piece of fresh
  ginger
1 cup cherry tomatoes,
  quartered
3 spring onions, chopped
1 red chilli, deseeded and
  sliced into circles
1 lemongrass stalk, white
  part finely minced
1/3 cucumber, cut into small
  chunks
handful of chopped coriander
juice and zest of 1 lime
decent glug of extra virgin
  olive oil

Serves 2

SIMPLE SALMON WITH ASPARAGUS SOLDIERS AND WHIPPED GREEN TEA

xxxxxxxxxxxxxxxxxxxxxxxxxxxxxxxxxxxxxxxxxxxxxxxxxxxxxxxxxxxxxxxxxxxxxxxxxxxxx

The latest research on folic acid is rather titillating. Sufficient quantities of this B vitamin can help prolong sexual orgasms. I wonder who signed up for those trials. And whether the placebo group were just plain boring? Suddenly, folic acid seems as important to my hedonistic rights as my favourite chocolate pie.

Where can we stock up on this much-coveted substance? Your local grocery store. Asparagus is full of folate (folic acid). That's why they call it vegans' Viagra.

2 salmon or trout fillets
  (certifiably sustainable if
  possible)
dot of extra virgin coconut
  or sesame oil
large bunch of asparagus
2 tablespoons toasted sesame
  oil

For the whipped green tea:
flesh of 1 large, ripe
  avocado
juice of 1 orange
1 teaspoon wasabi powder or
  paste (Dijon mustard will
  do)
1 teaspoon matcha green tea
salt and pepper

Serves 2

Preheat the oven to 200°C/180°C fan/400°F.

Prepare the salmon by wrapping the fillets in a parcel of tinfoil and dotting with the oil. I use extra virgin raw coconut oil, but use whatever you're happiest with. Make sure there's lots of space above the fillets – it's more like a tent than a parcel. This way the fish steams in its own juices.

Transfer the tent of salmon onto a baking tray and roast for 10-15 minutes, depending on how big the fillets are. Check by pulling the flesh apart. If they're not done, just reseal your tent and pop them in the oven again. When you've become familiar with this method of cooking, crank it up another level by adding smashed lemongrass, maple syrup, chilli, cumin, kaffir lime leaves or whatever tickles your appetite on any given evening.

To roast the asparagus, start by removing the tougher ends of each asparagus spear. Gently bend each spear until it snaps. Trust the veg – it's sort of like natural selection. Discard the stalky parts and tumble the tender heads in a baking tray with the sesame oil. Roast for 10-15 minutes (same as the salmon tents), which should make them tender but not squishy.

To make the green tea whip, give the avocado, orange juice, wasabi, matcha and a touch of seasoning a jolly fine whizz with a hand-held blender. That's all there is to it. Taste, and add more wasabi if you need to ignite a dull evening or a vexatious guest.

Smear your dinner plates with a generous serving of the whip and place a fillet on top. You can arrange the asparagus on top of the salmon Jenga-style if you're brave enough.

SALMON FISHCAKES WITH CURRIED COCONUT YOGHURT

xxxxxxxxxxxxxxxxxxxxxxxxxxxxxxxxxxxxxxxxxxxxxxxxxxxxxxxxxxxxxxxxxxxxxxxx

Wild salmon is the Rob Kearney of the ocean: indecently tasty and hard to catch. Not bad for the heart and circulation either.

This supersonic fish is hailed for its cargo of omega-3, vitamin D and niacin. But before I get too misty eyed about the benefits of eating salmon, I should stress that not all salmon 'products' are created equally. Smoked, tinned, farmed or wild - each has a different nutritional purchase. While smoked might be the tastiest and the most popular, its tinned counterpart offers a lot more calcium without the smoky nitrates. Nitrates are under the watchful eye of food scientists, given their possible correlation to an increased risk of certain cancers. But then, we also have to temper our love of tinned food with questions hanging over the chemicals used in the cans. Put down the iPhone. Nothing to tweet about. Just something to be aware of should you be gobbling industrial quantities of the stuff.

Then there's the ubiquitous farmed or caged salmon, most of which are fed with dodgy colourings and antibiotics. Farmers in the US choose how pink or red they want their salmon from a colour wheel called the Salmofan. Nostril-flaring stuff. However, unlike its wilder cousin, farmed salmon is a fraction of the price and available fresh all year round. Two important factors for prudent parents.

So what does the savvy shopper do? Look out for organically farmed Irish salmon or Marine Stewardship Council endorsements, eat moderate amounts of the smoked stuff and drop into your nearest four-letter German supermarket to stock up on frozen wild salmon cutlets.

These are definitely better and cheaper than any fancy fishcake we've sunk our teeth into at restaurants. You can easily personalise this basic recipe by introducing your favourite spice: try some crushed cumin seeds, nutritional yeast flakes, caraway and fenugreek, coriander or pummelled black onion seed.

With a fork, stir the potato, spring onions, salmon, chilli, garlic, egg, lemon zest, ginger and salt and pepper together.

Heat your frying pan with a blob of extra virgin coconut oil. When your pan is sufficiently hot, drop a dessertspoonful of the fishcake mixture onto the pan, pat with a fish slice and turn down the heat a little to prevent it from burning. Cook both sides until lightly coloured.

Meanwhile, mix together the yoghurt and the curry powder. Serve the fishcakes cold or at room temperature (not hot) with a dollop of spicy yoghurt. The Vietnamese mint dipping sauce on page 170 is pretty special too. Chill them overnight if packing for a sneaky breakfast on the bus to work.

1 1/2 cups (300g) lightly mashed potato
2 spring onions, chopped
1 fillet cooked salmon, flaked (see page 164)
1 chilli, sliced (not chilli powder)
1 fat garlic clove, minced
1 small egg, beaten
zest of 1/2 unwaxed lemon
good hunk of fresh ginger, peeled and minced
generous seasoning
extra virgin coconut oil, for frying

For the curried coconut yoghurt:
1 small tub of natural or coconut yoghurt, like CoYo
1 tablespoon sweet curry powder

Makes 8 fishcakes

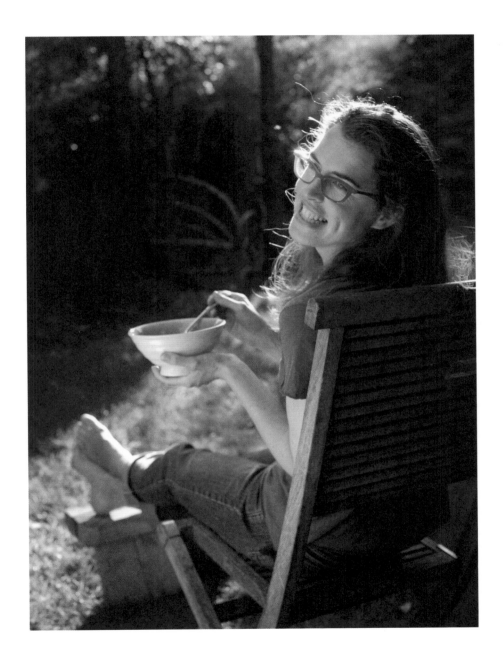

CHIA CRAB CAKES WITH VIETNAMESE MINT DIPPING SAUCE

xxxxxxxxxxxxxxxxxxxxxxxxxxxxxxxxxxxxxxxxxxxxxxxxxxxxxxxxxxxxxxxxxxxxxxxxxxx

Chia is an optional lah-di-dah. These tinchy seeds deliver a whackload of omega-3 brainpower. But if you can still remember how to solve a polynomial root with the factor theorem, you can probably leave them out.

The Vietnamese dipping sauce will leave a really refreshing taste in your mouth. If you can't be bothered making it, just add some miso paste to the mashed potatoes and wrestle some dill in there too.

For the Vietnamese mint dipping sauce:
1 red chilli, seeds removed and finely sliced
juice of 1 lime
4-6 tablespoons very finely chopped mint
1 tablespoon fish sauce (nam pla)
1 tablespoon sesame oil
1 tablespoon tamari
1 tablespoon raw honey, raw agave or yacón syrup

For the crab cakes:
2 tablespoons chopped dried mango, soaked overnight
1 1/2 cups (300g) lightly mashed potatoes
1/2-1 cup (200g) crabmeat
1 fat garlic clove, crushed
1 tablespoon chia seeds soaked in 2 tablespoons water
1 teaspoon Szechuan or black peppercorns, crushed
squeeze of lime juice
generous seasoning
2 tablespoons brown rice flour, to dust (optional)
extra virgin coconut oil, to fry
bean sprouts, to serve
Little Gem lettuces, to serve

Makes 10 small crab cakes

To make the dipping sauce, whisk everything together. Honey can be sticky, but don't worry, it eventually submits.

To make the crab cakes, start by draining the soaked mango pieces. Fresh mango won't work quite as well as its dried equivalent. Using a fork, crush with the remaining crab cake ingredients except the brown rice flour and coconut oil. If you're not making the dipping sauce, be sure to add some miso or nutritional yeast flakes to the mix for oomph. Mould into 10 small crab cakes and dust with brown rice flour (if using).

Heat a large frying pan with a little coconut oil and briefly brown each crab cake. Allow to cool completely before serving, otherwise they'll fall apart in your hands and you'll curse me. Really tasty served alongside bean sprouts and Little Gem lettuce - use the lettuce leaves to scoop up the minty mess.

FISH FINGERS WITH BEETROOT KETCHUP

xxxxxxxxxxxxxxxxxxxxxxxxxxxxxxxxxxxxxxxxxxxxxxxxxxxxxxx

Beetroot is still ranked as one of the most underused and misunderstood veggies. It's easy to find in supermarkets, yet it doesn't always mosey its way into our baskets. Dr Jonny Bowden, nutritional adviser to Hollywood's elite, rates it amongst his top superfoods. Good news for recessionistas and eco warriors because it's cheap, plentiful and comes with a low carbon footprint. We make ketchup from it. It goes devastatingly well with a salad of grated carrots, celeriac, pear and hazelnuts, for example, and keeps very well in the fridge.

You don't have to use nutritional yeast flakes in the crumb coating, but they're seriously handy to have in your cupboard. Dubbed the vegan's Parmesan, yeast flakes give your dish a nutritional upgrade and some real spine. There's also seaweed, which may sound gross but is in fact outrageously healthy. It helps bring the classic fish finger to another cosmos. Without it, we'd only hit the clouds.

These freeze exceptionally well (provided you're not using frozen fillets), so try to double the batch. They're the quickest healthy supper you can have for growing children without breaking into a sweat.

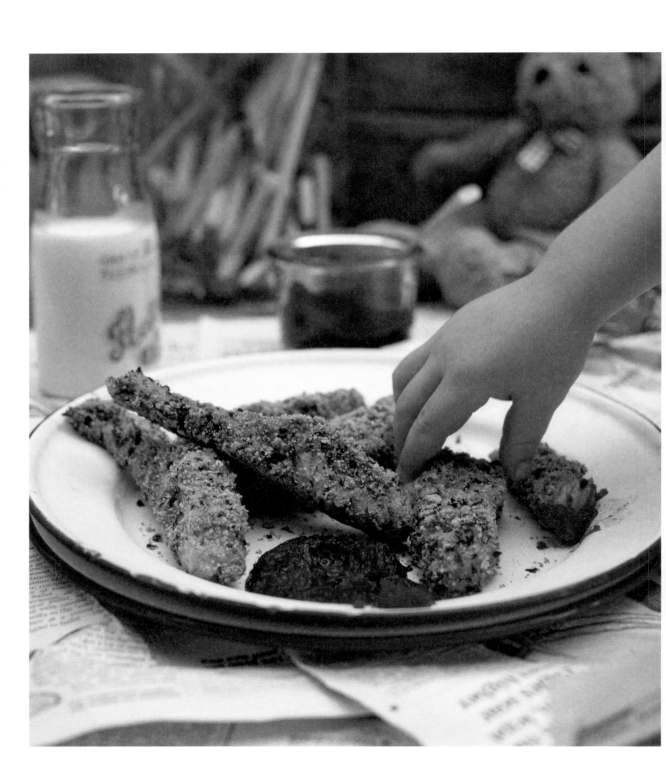

Preheat the oven to 200°C/180°C fan/400°F. Line a baking tray with parchment paper.

To make the beetroot ketchup, dice the beetroot. If using vacuum-packed beetroot, ensure there is no vinegar added as a preservative. Purée the ketchup ingredients with a hand-held blender until sumptuously smooth. Adjust the sweetness or sharpness to your preference. The honey or agave will sweeten the ketchup, while cider vinegar gives it attitude. A tiny amount of each makes a noticeable difference. Season.

To make the fish fingers, whizz the seaweed, yeast flakes and lemon zest in a food processor until they are uniform. Now stir through your almonds and transfer the mixture onto a large plate.

On another plate, lay out your chosen flour – rye, quinoa, oat, whatever you have. Pour the beaten egg onto a third plate and the pieces of fish on a fourth plate. You're ready to rock.

Using a fork – your hands need to be dry – scoop up a piece of fish, dust with flour, dip into the egg and dunk into the crumb coating. That's one fish finger. Settle on the lined baking tray and repeat until all the pieces of fish are coated.

Cook in the oven for 8–16 minutes, depending on the thickness of your fish. Lemon sole will only take 8 minutes, while thicker wedges of fish can take up to 16 minutes. Serve with the beetroot ketchup, a mini bowl of peas or diced avocado. Seriously snazzy.

For the fish fingers:
1/2 cup (20g) mixed dried seaweed, finely chopped (we use Clearspring)
1/2 cup (20g) nutritional yeast flakes (optional)
zest of 1 lemon (optional)
2 1/2 cups (250g) ground almonds or wheat-free breadcrumbs
1/2 cup (60g) flour of choice (chickpea flour doesn't work)
1 large egg, beaten
4 fillets wild salmon, pollock or lemon sole, cut into strips

For the beetroot ketchup:
4 medium-sized cooked or vacuum-packed beetroots
1 garlic clove, crushed
1 tablespoon cider vinegar
1 tablespoon raw honey or brown rice syrup
2 teaspoons organic soya or coconut yoghurt
salt and pepper

Makes 16–20 fish fingers

CHOPPED HERRING AND THE LAUREATES

xxxxxxxxxxxxxxxxxxxxxxxxxxxxxxxxxxxxxxxxxxxxxxxxxxxxxxx

This is a classic Jewish recipe. Considering 58% of Nobel Prize winners in economics are of Jewish descent, it would be fair to conclude that Jewish mamas know how to nourish their brood.

Mood and activity in the brain are dependent on a series of chemical signals that cross each membrane with the help of neurotransmitters. This intricate process is referred to as transduction — sort of like a messaging service or a call centre. Now that we know omega-3 fats are a core component in every cell membrane, they are deemed crucial for signal transduction. In other words, happy call centre staff.

If, like me, you'd rather supplement your diet naturally with food and not pharma, then fill your shopping basket with foods rich in omega-3: herring, mackerel, wild salmon, sardines, anchovies, flaxseeds, chia seeds or hemp seeds. All provide better flavour and fun than those fish-oil bullets. This book sets out to help you include them in your diet. After all, where's the decadence in a tablet?

Not just an antidote to depression, the omega-3 fats in herring guard against cognitive decline (what we Irish refer to as our senior moments). No need to agonise over a pesky Rubik's cube every day. Go boost your brainpower with this laureate-loving recipe instead.

4 pickled herrings (rollmops
  will do)
2 hardboiled eggs
1 small red onion
1/2 apple
mega bunch of flat-leaf
  parsley
toast, to serve (try Your
  New Wheat-free Bread on
  page 51)

Serves 2-3

With your sharpest knife, finely dice the herring. Repeat with the eggs, onion and apple. Roughly chop the parsley and tumble everything together. You may want a little yoghurt to bring it all together, but this is not considered authentic.

SOLE AND SATAY

xxxxxxxxxxxxxxxxxxxxxx

Getting teens to eat oily fish can be as easy as stuffing toothpaste back into its tube. That's why we've come up with a satay sauce using nutritious Udo's Oil. They'll get a sneaky dose of omega-3 while tucking into this stonkingly good dish. Shhh.

Chop the baby potatoes in half and steam for 20 minutes.

Meanwhile, finely chop your ginger and crush to a paste in a pestle and mortar. The base of a heavy object can sometimes work too, but can worry the neighbours and end up unreasonably messy. Mix with the remaining satay ingredients.

As soon as the potatoes are done, spoon the satay sauce over them and give it all a clumsy stir. The mess is half the charm.

Now is the time to flash-fry each sole fillet. Heat a pan on high. Dot with coconut oil and place each fillet on top. Let the teens do this part – with a bit of luck they'll surprise you one evening in the near future! Lemon sole is delicate, so gently turn after 30 seconds and flash fry the other side without letting it turn brown. If the pan is not sufficiently hot, the fish may need longer and will brown in the interim. It's a matter of taste I suppose, but I prefer mine snow white.

Plate up, sprinkle with anything green you may have lurking in the fridge (coriander? chives? rocket?) and serve with the potato satay. This is *real* fast food, to nourish your body and your creativity.

1 fillet lemon sole per
  person
extra virgin coconut oil, to
  flash fry

For the potato satay:
enough baby potatoes for 4
1 x 2.5cm piece of fresh
  ginger, peeled
6-8 tablespoons crunchy
  peanut butter
4 tablespoons Udo's Oil
3 tablespoons tamari
2 tablespoons mirin
1-2 tablespoons raw honey or
  barley malt extract
1 garlic clove, crushed
juice of 1/2 lime

Serves 4

CORIANDER AND POMEGRANATE CEVICHE WITH BOWLS OF FLOPPY FENNEL

xxxxxxxxxxxxxxxxxxxxxxxxxxxxxxxxxxxxxxxxxxxxxxxxxxxxxxxxxxxxxxxxxxxxxxxxxxxxxxxxxxxxxxxxxx

Freshly torn from its plant, coriander transforms a sad excuse of a salad into a party on a plate. And you're invited.

Unless you have a hotline to Diarmuid Gavin's brain, growing coriander can be a trifle tricky. Best tip? Don't bother with the supermarket plants. They are merely dejected relatives of the real thing and never live longer than their first haircut. Instead, follow these cinchy steps: (1) Sow salad seeds in a 25cm deep, well-drained pot. (2) Feed with at least 8 hours' sunlight on a windowsill. (3) Keep well watered. (4) Brag to everyone in the office that you GYO and let them rub your halo.

This will feed 4, but we double the quantities for supper parties. Very little work involved.

For the floppy fennel:
juice of 2 limes
1 tablespoon fish sauce (nam pla)
1 tablespoon toasted sesame oil
2 teaspoons maple syrup
1-2 red onions, finely sliced into semi-circles
1 fennel, topped and tailed and finely sliced

For the ceviche:
400g super-fresh fish like wild sea bass, cod, mackerel or salmon
juice of 1 blood orange
juice of 1 lime
2 tablespoons extra virgin olive oil
1 tablespoon Maldon sea salt flakes
bunch of fresh coriander, leaves only
a few tablespoons pomegranate seeds

Serves 4

To make the floppy fennel, whisk together the lime juice, fish sauce, sesame oil and maple syrup with a fork. Depending on the size of your limes, you may need to adjust the tartness by adding a smidgeon more sesame oil. Taste. Hover. Leap. Prostrate.

Pour over the thinly sliced red onions and fennel. In a few minutes, the vegetables will turn floppy and sweet, as if inebriated by the dressing. Leave them be and get going on the ceviche.

Ask your fishmonger to skin and bone the fish. If he's really nice, he'll cut them into bite-sized pieces for you too. Otherwise, you'll have to see to all three steps yourself before making the ceviche. Tumble the fish with the citrus juice, olive oil and flakes of salt. Allow to infuse for 1 hour or more in the fridge, but anything past 4 hours will turn the fish rubbery.

Tumble through the torn coriander and pomegranate seeds. Serve in a large glass bowl and have everyone help themselves alongside the bowls of floppy fennel. Plain quinoa is a great side too with a couple tablespoons of desiccated coconut.

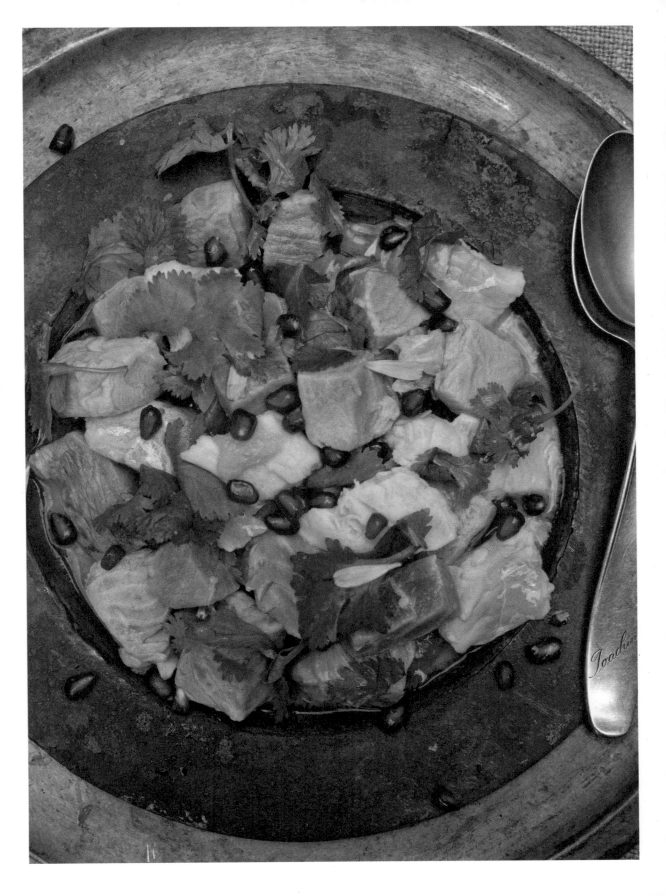

TOMATO AND BANANA BEAN CURRY

xxxxxxxxxxxxxxxxxxxxxxxxxxxxxxxxxxxxxxxxxxxxxxx

A recent study of half a million people confirmed that eating more than 20g of processed meat a day was linked to early death. Twenty grams! That's a lick of chorizo. The research covered 10 European countries over 13 years. In other words, it's fairly bulletproof.

This news was announced in the wake of the horsemeat scandal. The clamour of worried shoppers scrambling towards the vegetarian aisles in super-markets is, frankly, unprecedented. Sales of tofu rocketed by 500%.

It's clear that our love affair with sausie sangers and shish kebabs has long needed a re-evaluation. And possibly even a P45. It takes up to seven fields of grain to feed one field of cows. No wonder there isn't enough food to feed the world - Daisy's scoffing most of it. With the intensification of global warming and the planet's population ever escalating, never has the case for cutting down on meat been more compelling. But quitting altogether? No thank you.

This is our RDA curry, squeezing loads of nutrient-dense fruit and veg into one small pot. It's enough for 5 tummies, freezes well and also keeps in the fridge for a few days. It's pretty dishy served on a bed of wilted spinach and doesn't require Birkenstocks to enjoy it. Beans are one of the most common foods found in a centenarian's diet, so if you want to live longer and look like vegan superstar Alicia Silverstone, start by Sello-taping this recipe to your cupboard door.

1 large onion, diced
2-3 tablespoons extra virgin
 olive oil
2 x 400g tins chopped
 tomatoes
1 x 400g tin mixed beans
5 dried apricots, chopped
2 bananas, sliced into rounds
2 tablespoons raisins
2 tablespoons curry powder
squeeze of lemon juice
2-3 garlic cloves, crushed
great handful of fresh
 parsley, to garnish
dollop of natural coconut
 yoghurt, to serve
a few turns of the black
 pepper mill
sweet brown rice (see page
 141), to serve

Serves 5

Normally the best way to begin a curry is by sweating the onion in olive oil on a low heat in a heavy-based saucepan until translucent, but on those seriously swift evenings, just bung it all in together. Add the tomatoes to the onion and bring to a low simmer, at which point you can add the beans, apricots, bananas, raisins, curry powder and lemon juice. Cook for 15 minutes.

The key to this recipe is to stir through the crushed garlic as soon as the curry is ready, and not before. Divide between 5 plates and drizzle reverently with extra virgin olive oil and torn parsley. Crown with a dollop of live coconut yoghurt and maybe a few turns of the black pepper mill and serve with short grain or sweet brown rice. You will feel your toes sing.

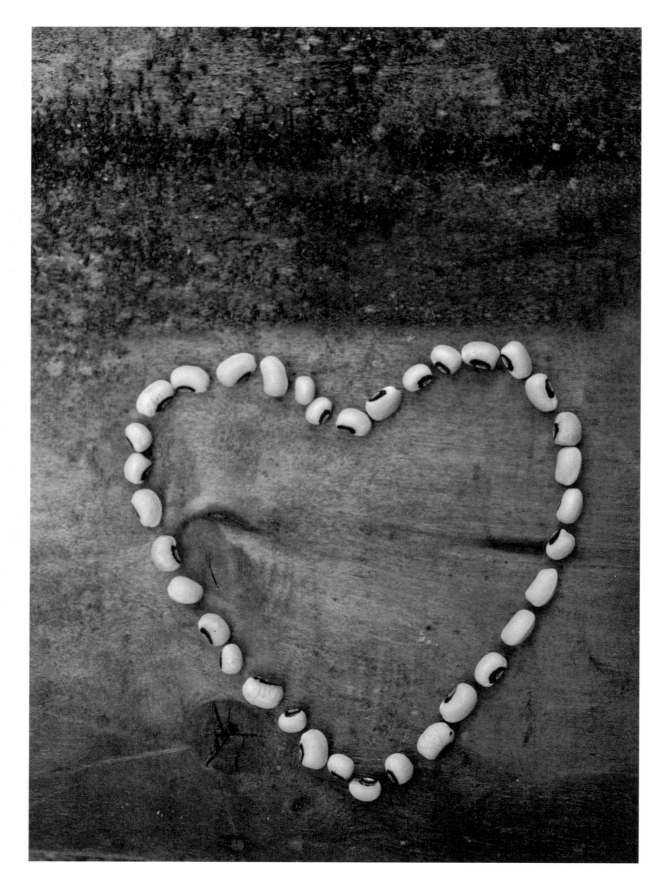

CENTENARIAN'S PINEAPPLE AND GOJI BERRY CURRY WITH RAITA AND SPINACH

xxxxxxxxxxxxxxxxxxxxxxxxxxxxxxxxxxxxxxxxxxxxxxxxxxxxxxxxxxxxxxxxxxxxxxxxxxxxxxxxxxxxxxxxxxxx

Gastroenterologists (the specialists who look after your pipes) recommend eating 30-35g of dietary fibre every day. That's because they know that high-fibre diets can lower the risk of developing colon and gastric cancers by 40%. One cup of cooked red kidney beans provides 11g, while adzuki beans ring in at 17g per serving. Want to know the average daily intake in Ireland? A measly 10g. So forget that hideous childhood rhyme and start loving beans. They love you.

There's a secret bonus in this recipe. Pineapple, goji berries, red onions, ginger, garlic, chilli and turmeric are all members of an anti-inflammatory squad. Many are flush with flavonoids too, otherwise known as heavyweight antioxidants that fight ageing and disease.

You can play around with the flavours here - try vindaloo, Bengali or Chinese five spice blend. The Green Saffron spice specialists do over 30 different Indian spice mixes. Let your taste buds vote. No need to stick to canned beans either. We often cook adzuki beans for 20 minutes or butter-beans for 90 minutes before adding them to the tomato base.

For the bean curry:
3 cups (450g) chopped butternut squash or
  sweet potato
splash of extra virgin coconut oil
3 red onions
2 red peppers, deseeded and chopped
2 x 400g tins whole tomatoes
1 cup (250ml) chicken or vegetable stock
1 x 400g tin mixed beans, drained
4 slices of pineapple, skin removed and
  chopped
1/2 cup (50g) dried goji berries
2 tablespoons hot curry powder
1 teaspoon fresh or ground turmeric
2 garlic cloves
1 red chilli, deseeded if necessary
1 x 8cm piece of fresh ginger, peeled
sea salt flakes

For the spinach:
1 x 450g packet of frozen spinach for every
  2 people
salt and pepper
extra virgin olive oil
1 garlic clove, crushed

For the raita:
cucumber
mint leaves
squeeze of lemon juice
1 teaspoon honey
natural or coconut yoghurt

Serves 8

Preheat the oven to 180°C/160°C fan/350°F.

The method employed here is more practical than traditional. Tumble the chopped butternut or sweet potato with a little oil and roast for 40 minutes, until caramelised and soft. You can leave the skin on the butternut if it's organic. Quarter the red onions and toss with the chunks of pepper and a splash of oil. Roast on a separate tray from the butternut or sweet potato for 20 minutes, until semi-soft. I keep a little raw red onion to mix through the curry before serving. It's up to you.

While the veg softens in the oven, find your largest casserole dish or stockpot and heat up the tinned tomatoes and stock. Add the drained beans, chopped pineapple, goji berries, curry powder and turmeric. Let this gurgle away for 10-15 minutes, by which time the roasted onions and peppers will be ready.

Remove the tray from the oven and shake the veg into your pot of spicy tomatoes. Your nostrils should be levitating by now. Turn down the heat very low and prep the last few ingredients while the butternut is finishing off in the oven.

Crush the garlic, chilli and ginger together with a sprinkle of sea salt flakes in a pestle and mortar to make a seriously fragrant paste. These are heroic immune-boosting anti-inflammatory foods. Stir the paste through the curry. The idea is not to cook these ingredients, but rather warm them so their medicinal qualities are not significantly diminished.

Pour 3cm of boiling water over the spinach and boil for 2 minutes in a small saucepan with a fitted lid. When it's defrosted (no need to murder it), drain very well in a sieve, give it a few turns of the salt and pepper mill, tickle with olive oil and maybe another lick of garlic.

The raita is a cinch - chop a bit of cucumber and mint. Add a spot of lemon juice and/or honey to natural yoghurt, taste, and adjust to your preferences. Spinach and raita are pretty special additions to this meal. Without them, think gin with no tonic.

As soon as the butternut or potato is soft, add it to the tomato curry, ramp up the heat and roar at everyone to take their places at the dinner table. Time to plate up.

PUMPKIN FALAFEL

xxxxxxxxxxxxxxxxxxxxxxxx

It's a shame Halloween has monopolised the pumpkin. They're far too fabulous to be dismissed for 11 months of the year.

This vegetable's buttery flesh is stuffed with goodness. There's potassium for hangovers, vitamins A and C to slay superbugs (think Uma Thurman in Kill Bill) and extra carotenoids for those who can't afford to keep up their Botox instalments. That's a lot of ammunition for a supposedly ghoulish vegetable.

On the antioxidant radar, pumpkins are almost up there with blueberries and spinach. We like antioxidants because they help prevent the bad LDL cholesterol in our bloodstream from oxidising. Once oxidation occurs, the likelihood of cholesterol depositing onto blood vessel walls significantly increases. Not sure I like the sound of that.

Heart surgeon Dr Oz Mehmet has even devised a recipe for pumpkin brownies to entice his clients into eating more of this useful vegetable. According to Dr Oz, pumpkins are probably one of the best foods we ain't eatin'.

Here's our recipe, based on Allegra McEvedy's (one of my favourite chefs). Deep-frying falafel may taste delish, but isn't recommended for our waist-lines or arteries. Shame. More alarmingly, deep-frying food can make your mouth feel like a camel's armpit. Luckily, Allegra designed hers to be baked.

around 500g roasted pumpkin pieces
125g chickpea flour (aka gram flour) or chestnut flour
2 garlic cloves, crushed
zest and juice of 1/2 lemon
2-3 tablespoons extra virgin coconut or olive oil
2 tablespoons chopped spring onions
2 teaspoons ground cumin
black sesame seeds, to garnish

Makes 8-12 falafel

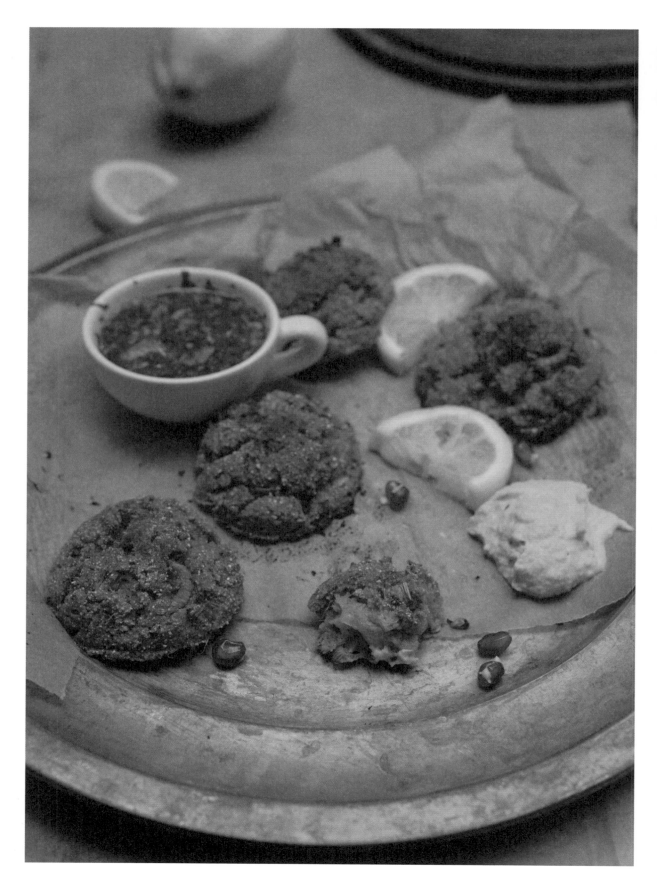

Preheat the oven to 170°C/150°C fan/340°F.

This recipe isn't a science. You're aiming
for the falafel to be one-quarter chickpea or
chestnut flour. It's really that simple, so use
whatever amount of pumpkin you have and adjust
the recipe as appropriate.

Roasting pumpkin is a cinch too - no peeling
necessary. Just make sure to avoid the monstrous
Cinderella ones. Start by cautiously hacking
the side of the pumpkin. Chop this flesh into
matchbox-sized pieces and continue to work your
way around the pumpkin. The hardest part is that
first slice. Tumble the pieces into a roasting
tray with a good splash of coconut or olive oil.
Cover with foil. Roast for 45-60 minutes, until
sweet and tender. Pumpkin is better overcooked
rather than undercooked.

Remove the tray of pumpkin and let the pieces
cool completely before handling. If you've
roasted more than you need, count yourself
lucky. Whizz any leftover pieces with coconut
milk, sautéed onions and a pinch of curry powder
to make soup. Or freeze a batch for your next
falafel craving.

Raise the oven temperature to 200°C/180°C
fan/400°F. Line a baking tray with parchment
paper or grease with a lick of olive oil.

Using clean hands, mash all the falafel ingredients except the black sesame seeds together.
Put the falafel mix in the freezer for 15-30
minutes to firm up. Mould the chilled mixture into
falafels and place on the lined baking tray. I
find an ice cream scoop is the best way to shape
falafel. If you use teaspoons and patience,
you'll double the portions and halve the baking
time. Sprinkle with black sesame seeds and cook
in the oven for 20-45 minutes, depending on their
size.

Try serving alongside thick natural or coconut
yoghurt, smooth hummus, Maple Mustard Lentils
(page 158) or a big bowl of peas. The messier,
the better.

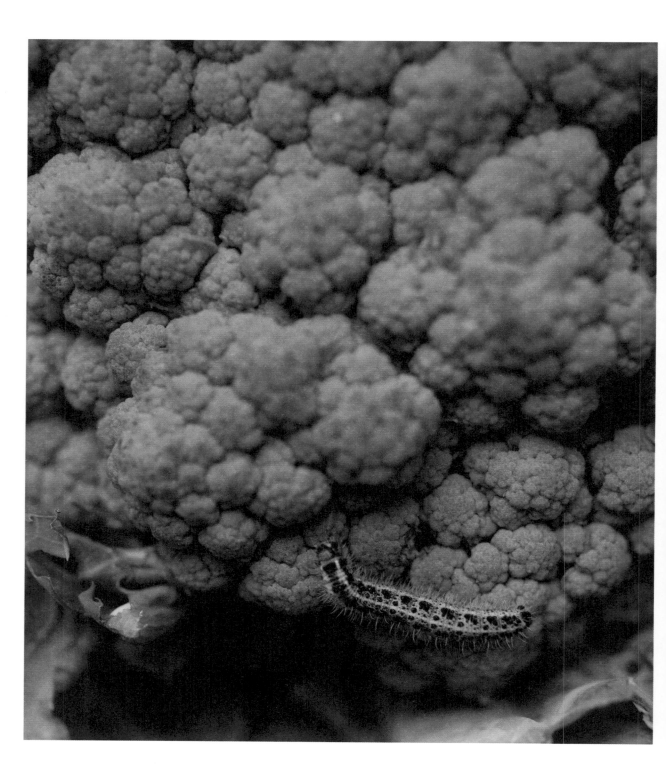

ANTI-INFLAMMATORY ALOO

xxxxxxxxxxxxxxxxxxxxxxx

This famous dish gets its psychedelic glow from poor man's saffron (turmeric). Its high veggie content also helps it feel like a big bowl of sunshine. Anti-inflammatory Aloo isn't the sexiest of names for a Saturday night curry, but did you know that inflammation relates to heaps of common conditions, such as psoriasis, bruising, swelling, hay fever, joint pain, chest infections, IBS and asthma?

You'll find a hub of ingredients in this aloo to help reduce menacing prostaglandins in the body. There are good prostaglandins and bad prostaglandins. Both manage the inflammatory process. The bad ones morph into inflammatory markers in your bloodstream and can make your body feel like a rusty BMX with a 20-ton rhino on the Tour de France. Anti-inflammatory foods like turmeric, ginger, goji berries, onions and chilli can help interrupt the life cycle of bad prostaglandins so that less of them end up circulating in your body. Pretty nifty, huh?

Start by peeling and finely chopping the onion and ginger. Heat a heavy-based casserole pot on your lowest setting with a few tablespoons of oil and add your chopped onion, ginger, chilli, cumin, mustard seeds and turmeric. Sweat for 10 minutes. Your nostrils will applaud.

Cut the baby potatoes into generous mouthfuls. Prepare your cauliflower by discarding the outer leaves, breaking into Lego-sized florets and cutting the centre stalk into rough cubes. Be sure not to throw this part out - it adds wonderful texture to your aloo. Toss the potatoes, cauliflower and butterbeans with the sautéed onion, coating everything with the spice's golden glow. Pour over the stock and add the goji berries (if using). Bring to the boil, cover with a lid and let it gurgle for 20-25 minutes, until the veggies are soft but not soggy. They will joyously soak up most of the stock while simmering away. Taste, and season with sea salt and a few turns of the black pepper mill. Serve with fresh coriander stirred through the gobi.

Other aloo gobi variations include a tablespoon of garam masala, shrimp, peanuts, desiccated coconut or raw minced garlic stirred through at the end, or a squeeze of lemon just before serving. Let your taste buds vote.

1 large red onion
thumb-sized piece of fresh
  ginger
splash of extra virgin
  coconut or peanut oil
1 green chilli, deseeded and
  finely chopped
1 tablespoon ground cumin
1 tablespoon black mustard
  seeds (optional)
2 teaspoons ground turmeric
6 baby potatoes
1/2 head of cauliflower
1 cup cooked (see page 118)
  or tinned butterbeans,
  drained
2 cups (500ml) chicken, fish
  or veggie stock
1/4 cup (25g) goji berries
  (optional)
salt and pepper
fresh coriander, to serve

Serves 4

RED DAAL WITH WILTED SPINACH AND A PLUMP POACHED EGG

xxxxxxxxxxxxxxxxxxxxxxxxxxxxxxxxxxxxxxxxxxxxxxxxxxxxxxxxxxxxxxxxxxxxxxxxxxxxx

This dish requires little or no kitchen experience. Unlike beans, red lentils do not need pre-soaking or hours of patience. You'll find most of the ingredients already lurking in your cupboard, making it particularly attractive for unexpected callers.

Research from the British Journal of Pharmacology shows that garlic and ginger contain anti-bacterial and anti-inflammatory compounds to help soothe anything from swollen tonsils to achy limbs. Did you know most common skin complaints involve inflammation? Dandruff, psoriasis, acne and eczema - all would benefit from a good frolic with garlic and ginger. Besides, they're outrageously tasty, dead cheap and will vastly improve a dull date.

1 onion, diced
2 tablespoons extra virgin
  coconut or olive oil
1 cup (190g) dried red
  lentils, washed
6-8 cloves
2 garlic cloves, finely
  chopped
1 tablespoon mustard seeds
  (wholegrain mustard would
  do)
1 tablespoon minced ginger
1 teaspoon whole black or
  white peppercorns, smashed
chicken stock or water
3 handfuls of baby spinach
  leaves
3 poached eggs (see page
  150)
nice squeeze of lemon juice
  (optional)

Serves 3

Start by sweating the onion in the oil on a low setting for 10 minutes, until they appear slightly glassy. A heavy-based saucepan is perfect to avoid the onions 'catching' on the bottom of the pan and burning. If you fry the onions at a higher temperature, the oil will chemically change and play with your arteries. It doesn't matter if you use the best cold-pressed extra virgin oil money can buy. High heat, as opposed to gentle warmth, chemically disfigures oil and spoils most of the health benefits it carries. If you suffer from cholesterol or weight problems, it might be worth writing this on the inside of your kitchen cupboard to remind you!

As the onions sweat, in another medium-sized saucepan combine the lentils, cloves, garlic, mustard seeds, ginger and peppercorns. Add enough chicken stock or water to cover the lentils by about 2cm and bring to a boil. Sometimes we do a blend of carrot juice and water to give the lentils a fabulously rich colour and sweetness. Adjust the heat so that the lentils putter away rather than violently bubble. Cover and cook for about 12 minutes, then remove from the heat, keep the lid on and allow to stand on the countertop until tender. Ideally, daal should be saucy, not soupy, so keeping the lid on the pan will naturally steam the lentils for another couple of minutes.

Remove the cloves from the cooked lentils (it
helps if you remember exactly how many you popped
in) and add the baby spinach and the sautéed
onion. Divide between 3 bowls and slip your
poached egg on top. Finish off with a generous
squeeze of lemon and love.

FLASH-FRIED PLAICE WITH PINK PEPPERCORN SALT AND LEMON DUST

xxxxxxxxxxxxxxxxxxxxxxxxxxxxxxxxxxxxxxxxxxxxxxxxxxxxxxxxxxxxxxxxxxxxxxxxxxxxxxxxxxx

That gorgeous Italian Laura Santtini has bewitched me with her Flash Cooking. It's not a diet or a fad. It's a masterclass in creativity and time poverty. Santtini's mission is to arm your kitchen with an arsenal of explosively tasty spices, finishing salts and scented yoghurts. They are guaranteed to transform your meals, and possibly even your life.

Plaice is a super-slim fish that cooks in less than 90 seconds. Not so good from the freezer, so make sure your plaice is hyper-fresh. I buy the white-bellied fillets as opposed to the black side because the soft white skin is the best part. Plaice camouflage themselves in the ocean – one side is dark and mottled so that predators above the plaice can't differentiate them from the ocean floor. Their underbelly is white so that predators below them think they are shards of light glistening in the water. Poor things never accounted for crafty fishermen.

a dot of extra virgin
  coconut oil
2 x plaice fillets
zest of 1 small lemon
1 teaspoon pink peppercorns
pinch of sea salt flakes,
  like Maldon
black olives, to serve
roasted fennel (page 152),
  to serve

Serves 2

Heat a large frying pan on high. When the pan is piping hot, dot with coconut oil and immediately drop the fillets over the oil. Each side should only take 20–40 seconds to cook, during which time you can zest the lemon and crush the pink peppercorns in a pestle and mortar. Mix the zest and peppercorns with the flakes of salt and dust each fillet with this finishing touch as soon as you plate up. You'll need to work at an inflammable speed.

Plaice is too delicate for lemon juice, so the zest is perfect. A simple bowl of black olives and lightly roasted fennel serves us well.

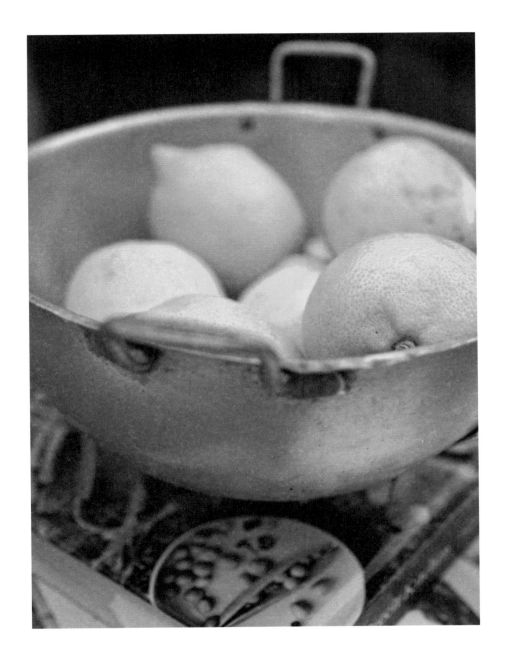

UMAMI BEEF STEW

xxxxxxxxxxxxxxxxxxxxxxxx

Domini Kemp is a badass Irish chef who women want to be and men want to meet. This is her flavour bomb. One of Domini's restaurants, Hatch & Sons Irish Kitchen, pencils it on the menu from time to time. I've seen fans bless themselves in its presence.

Umami is our fifth taste sensation, often underserviced. Scientists refer to this neglected fifth taste bud as the lip-smacking point. Think anchovies, Parmesan cheese, miso, tamari soya sauce and prosciutto. Domini uses streaky rashers in the original recipe, but given the fatwa on piggies in our house, we subbed it with umami-rich seaweed and mushrooms.

This freezes really well, so tuck some away for those evenings when you couldn't be bothered to knock up a meal from scratch.

a good few splashes of extra
  virgin olive oil
800g stewing beef or lamb,
  cut into 2-3cm chunks
500g wild mixed mushrooms
  (dried won't work)
2 large onions, chopped
1/2 head of garlic, peeled
  and sliced
large glass of red wine
strip of dried wakame or
  kombu (optional)
1.5 litres stock
1 x 50g tin anchovy fillets
2 heaped tablespoons tomato
  purée
3 bay leaves

For the sweet potato purée:
6 large sweet potatoes
seasoning

Or a carrot and mango purée:
8 medium carrots, unpeeled
handful of dried mango
  pieces
extra virgin coconut oil

Serves 8

Preheat the oven to 160°C/140°C fan/325°F.

It's quicker to have 2 pans frying simultaneously. Using a heavy-based pan, brown the meat all over in batches. This should take 10-15 minutes. Make sure the meat almost looks caramelised.

Take your biggest ovenproof pot (ideally a cast iron, heavy-bottomed casserole dish like Le Creuset) and sauté the mushrooms, onions and garlic in small batches in some oil. As they soften and colour, transfer to a large plate with the browned meat. Work like this for 15 minutes, until all the beef, mushrooms and onions are coloured and ready to rock. The reason we don't bung them all into one pan is because they will sweat rather than caramelise.

Once the beef has finished browning, deglaze the pan with a large glass of red wine and transfer to the ovenproof pot. Let the mushrooms, onions, garlic and kombu or wakame (if using) join the party. Add the stock, anchovies, tomato purée and bay leaves and bring to a simmer.

Pop it into the oven and cook for about 2 hours with a lid on. Turn the heat way down to 120°C/100°C fan/250°F. Cook for another 60 minutes.

To make the sweet potato purée, pop the spuds whole into a hot oven for 1 hour. They will naturally steam in their skins, provided they are not cut or slit. If the potatoes are massive, you'll need an extra 30 minutes' cooking time. Adjust as you feel fit. Sweet potatoes are best when they are really soft, and not al dente. Once they are properly cooked, their skins will peel off easily. Mash with tasty seasoning like Herbamare or celery salt. You can purée them in a food processor to achieve a silky-smooth finish. Sweet potatoes behave differently to regular white spuds and can be put through a blender without turning into glue.

For the carrot and mango purée, chop up the carrots and steam with the dried mango for 10-15 minutes. Make sure they are very soft before whizzing in a food processor or a hand-held blender. Add a drop of coconut oil for cream-iness.

All 3 dishes can be made 1 or 2 days in advance of a dinner party and reheated when required. In fact, the stew tastes even better when the beef gets a chance to absorb all those umami semi-quavers. Amen.

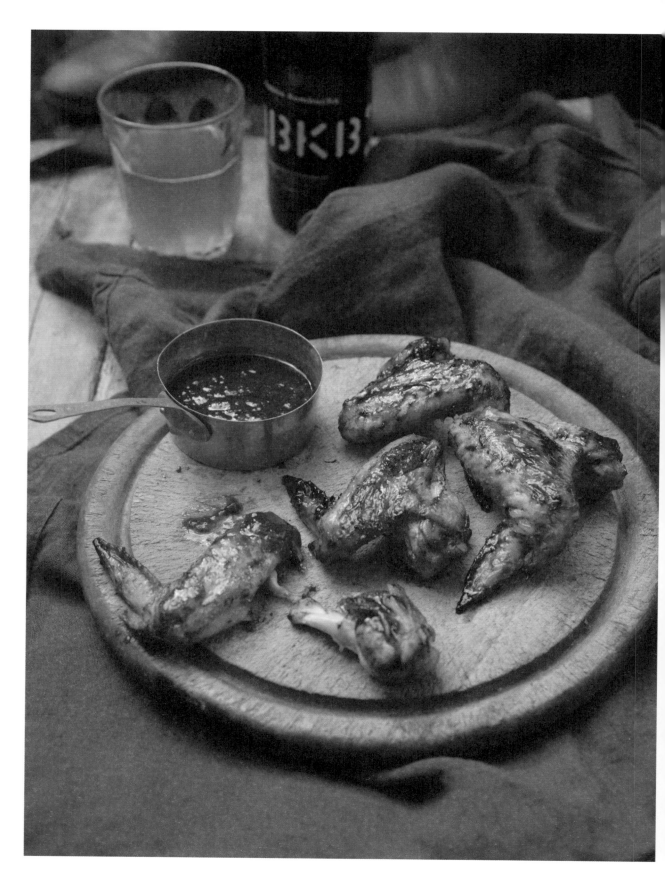

LICKY-STICKY WINGS WITH CHILLI SAUCE

xxxxxxxxxxxxxxxxxxxxxxxxxxxxxxxxxxxxxxxxxxxxxxxxxxxxxxxxxxx

I think cutlery is really odd. Touch is a sense that can heighten taste. Try this recipe and see for yourself. Serve with your favourite bean sprouts, dressed with freshly juiced ginger if possible or a tray of roasted parsnip and carrot.

Preheat the oven to 200°C/180°C fan/400°F.

Carefully remove any stray feathers from the wings and discard. Throw the wings onto a roasting tray and drizzle with the lemon juice, honey, oil and peppercorns. Give everything a jolly good tumble to coat well. Roast for 40 minutes, shaking the tray whenever you remember to.

If you are cooking enough wings for 4 people, you will need 2 trays. The magic in browning wings is to give them plenty of space and independence on the roasting tray. The same principle applies to roasting veg – an overcrowded tray generates too much steam between the ingredients, resulting in a soggy, insipid meal.

To make the chilli sauce, knock it up with a hand-held blender or stir together with a fork and strength. The wings are sufficiently tasty on their own, but the sauce amps up the reverie. There's something so primal about chicken wings and great big bowls of licky-sticky yummy.

around 12 chicken wings
juice of 1 large lemon
2 tablespoons honey (not agave)
2 tablespoons extra virgin coconut oil
1 tablespoon black or Szechuan peppercorns, smashed

For the chilli sauce:
2-3 tablespoons barley malt extract, raw agave or yacón syrup
2 tablespoons fresh miso paste
2 tablespoons cold-pressed toasted sesame oil
1/2 teaspoon cayenne

Serves 2-3

ROAST CHICKEN WITH IRISH GREMOLATA AND CHARRED PUMPKIN

xxxxxxxxxxxxxxxxxxxxxxxxxxxxxxxxxxxxxxxxxxxxxxxxxxxxxxxxxxxxxxxxxxxxxxxxxxxxx

Chicken is a special treat in our home, when an occasion demands. We don't think meat is evil. I like Mark Bittman's idea of using meat as a garnish instead of giving meat the lead role. Hugh Fearnley-Whittingstall built on Bittman's idea by publishing a book with vegetables as its entire cast. This may not seem unusual, except that Hugh is Britain's High Priest of Carnivore-ville.

Scientists warn that the amount of meat we eat is unhealthy and unsustainable. Therein lies the problem. If Bittman's resolution seems too darn difficult, another smart option is to only buy meat when it is free range and unprocessed. Meat piracy is a curse.

1 large organic, free-range
  or higher-welfare chicken
1 large fennel bulb
  (optional)
1 large, juicy lemon
2 tablespoons extra virgin
  coconut oil
sea salt flakes

For the Irish gremolata:
pinch of sea veg (arame is
  excellent)
4 garlic cloves
zest and juice of 2 lemons
1 cup extra virgin olive oil
50g parsley, finely chopped

For the charred pumpkin:
1 small organic pumpkin
extra virgin coconut or
  olive oil

Serves 6

Take your chicken out of the fridge 40 minutes before cooking. It's also a good idea to clear the kitchen sink so that when you wash your hands after touching the bird, you don't transfer bacteria to your dishes.

Preheat the oven to 230°C/210°C fan/450°F. Quarter the fennel (if using) and place in the centre of a roasting tray. Carefully remove the chicken's packaging and gently place the bird on top of the fennel. Wash your hands thoroughly after handling the bird, especially if you have children dancing at your heels.

Roll the lemon under the palm of your hand (an Aga or microwave will briefly warm it up to get the juices spilling). Halve the lemon and rub the bird all over with it. Squeeze the juice into the tray and pop the empty lemon halves in the bird's cavity. Dot with the coconut oil and season with a flurry of salt flakes.

Place the tray into the oven and turn it down to 200°C/180°C fan/400°F. Cook a 1.6kg bird for approximately 1 hour 20 minutes. The top of the chicken leg bones will look dry and prominent once the bird is cooked and the meat should easily come away from the bone. If not, leave in the oven for longer.

Meanwhile, to make the Irish gremolata, soak the arame in water for 10 minutes to rehydrate.

If you've chosen a different sea veg, follow the
instructions on the packet. Discard the soaking
water once it's ready and roughly chop. Use a
kitchen grater to mince each clove of garlic.
Follow with the lemon zest. Squeeze the juice from
both lemons and add the oil. Add the parsley and
give it all a good shake in a jam jar. Set aside.

Slice the pumpkin into wedges using vigour and
vigilance. Scoop out its stringy nest and dice
the flesh into matchbox-sized pieces. If it's
organic, keep the skin on - saves on time and
gives extra nutrition. We've also noticed that
organic pumpkins are 10 times tastier than
conventional ones. Tumble the pumpkin pieces onto
a large baking tray and give it a good lick of
coconut or olive oil. Roast on high for 45-65
minutes, or until it starts browning and caramelising around the edges. The same temperature as
the chicken is fine. Shake the tray once or twice
during roasting to share the juices around the
pan and let your nostrils party.

The pumpkin can start cooking 1 hour before the
chicken finishes cooking so that it all comes out
of the oven at the same time. While the chicken
rests, you can switch off the oven, leave the door
ajar and keep the pumpkin and guests warm.

If you have time, roast a tray of carrots too or
prepare the carrot and mango purée on page 192.
This will help stretch the meal to 8 and bump up
your veggie intake.

10-HOUR SHOULDER OF LAMB WITH CRUSHED CHICKPEAS AND THE BEST SAUCE YOU'RE EVER LIKELY TO TASTE

xxxxxxxxxxxxxxxxxxxxxxxxxxxxxxxxxxxxxxxxxxxxxxxxxxxxxxxxxxxxxxxxxxxxxxx

Here's some slow-cooked lamb that effortlessly falls off the bone. Let it cosy up to some messy chickpea smash and a scorching hot Middle Eastern mojo. This recipe was designed to help mend marriages.

For the slow-cooked lamb:
1 shoulder of mutton (an older lamb)
2 tablespoons balsamic vinegar
a few tablespoons sumac (optional)

For the crushed chickpeas:
500g dried chickpeas
1 teaspoon bicarbonate of soda
1 strip of kombu seaweed (optional)
1/2 cup (140g) cashew nut butter
3 garlic cloves, crushed
3 tablespoons tamari (or generous seasoning)
squeeze of lemon juice

For the hot anchovy mojo:
1 x 50g tin anchovies (8-10 anchovies)
3-5 mixed medium chillies, deseeded
3 garlic cloves, crushed
1 red pepper, finely chopped
1 yellow pepper, finely chopped
2 large bunches of fresh coriander
1 tablespoon ground cumin
1 tablespoon dried oregano
juice of 1 lemon
dash of sherry vinegar (to taste)
great big glug (120ml) of extra virgin olive oil

Serves 5

Start tonight by soaking the chickpeas in cold water. Tomorrow, drain and discard the soaking water. Tip the chickpeas into your largest heavy-based pan with the bicarb and ramp up the heat. Stir for 30 seconds without burning the bum off the pan. Pour in 2-3 litres of water and the strip of kombu seaweed (if using). Bring to a rolling boil and cook for 1 hour. While you want the chickpeas to be soft and cooked, try not to let them go mushy. Taste a chickpea every so often and decide how soft you like them to be. A good test is to press one between your middle finger and thumb - the chickpea should just about submit to pressure.

Remove from the heat, drain and set three-quarters of the chickpeas aside. Blitz the other one-quarter in a food processor with the cashew nut butter and garlic. Add a good few splashes of ice-cold water from the fridge, just to loosen it up. Finish whizzing to a smooth cream.

Roll the cream into the drained chickpeas and gently crush some of the chickpeas to let in the flavours of the smooth sauce. Douse with enough tamari and lemon juice to suit your fancy. You can leave this big pot of crushed chickpeas covered in a warm oven until required.

To make the hot anchovy mojo, give all the ingredients a jolly good whizz in your food processor, but not with a hand-held blender. Food processors give chunkier textures, whereas hand blenders are basically creamers. As spicy, captivating and sparkling as that first kiss, this sauce is high octane.

To cook the lamb, preheat the oven to 220°C/200°C fan/425°F.

Rub the lamb with the balsamic vinegar and sumac (if using) and place on a roasting tin with high edges. Bring to room temperature before blasting at high heat in the oven for 20 minutes. Turn down the heat to 140°C/120°C fan/275°F and cook for 8 hours.

Pull some meat away from the bone after 6-8 hours to check how it's doing. If you are doubling up to feed 10, then make sure to give the lamb a few extra hours. Increasing the quantity of food in the oven often dilutes the heat and can result in undercooking, especially at this temperature. Similarly, if the lamb is a small spring shoulder, it probably only needs 6 hours and will feed fewer people. The meat is done as soon as it falls from the bone and practically dissolves in your mouth.

We find the best way to serve this is by piling everything on the table. A simple crisp salad dressed in lemon juice and black pepper can help stretch out the number of mouths to feed.

CHOCOLATE CHILLI CON CARNE WITH COCONUT YOGHURT AND JAZZY ONIONS

xxxxxxxxxxxxxxxxxxxxxxxxxxxxxxxxxxxxxxxxxxxxxxxxxxxxxxxxxxxxxxxxxxxxxxxxxxxxxxxxxxxxxxxxxxxxxxx

*If you are a feral carnivore, like my husband, here's a good way of intro-
ducing more beans and veg to your diet without feeling oppressed. The
overtones are there (what man won't wolf down a Chilli Con Beast?), but so
is the nutritional purchase. It doesn't actually taste of chocolate, but
rather, utilises cacao powder as another spice in the mix.*

*By downloading some good podcasts at RadioLab.org, you'll prep this before
you even realise it. Put your feet up, and enjoy the dance your nostrils
will do over the next 2 hours. Serve with great big dollops of cultured
coconut yoghurt, macerated red onions and exceptional company.*

1 1/2 cups (270g) dried kidney beans, soaked overnight
2 onions
2 red peppers
1 large carrot
4 garlic cloves
extra virgin olive or coconut oil, for sautéing
2 tablespoons tomato purée (optional)
1 tablespoon dried oregano
1 tablespoon raw cacao powder
1 tablespoon sweet or hot paprika (optional)
1 cinnamon stick
good pinch of dried chilli flakes
large pinch of coconut sugar
500g minced beef
2 x 400g tins chopped tomatoes
just over 300ml vegetable or beef stock
salt and pepper
1 tablespoon ground cumin
2-4 squares dark or raw chocolate (optional)

To serve:
1 small red onion
1 really juicy lime
1 tablespoon nam pla (optional)
fistful of fresh coriander (optional)
natural coconut yoghurt, like CoYo

Serves 10-12

First off, soak the dried kidney beans overnight.
The next day, prep the veggies. I find the easiest
way to dice the onions is to cut each onion
in half, from root to toe. Peel and place the

flat part on the chopping board. With a slicing action, make little matchsticks from the onion lengthways, but not quite cutting all the way to the root end so that they are still held together. Now slice across the matchsticks.

Roughly chop the peppers and carrot into bite-sized chunks, discarding the pepper seeds and stalks. Slice your garlic and line up all your dried spices and herbs. Now you're ready to cook.

Heat a little oil in your largest sauté pan or frying pan (I have 2 going at the same time to speed things up). Sweat the onions first, stirring regularly for 10 minutes, until they become glassy. Put them aside, then sauté the peppers and carrot until soft but not browned. Add the garlic towards the end, along with the tomato purée, spices and coconut sugar (if using). Cook for a good 5 minutes and let your nostrils samba. Remove from the heat and pile on top of the resting onions.

Now whack up the heat and brown the mince all over. Mince needs to be browned or the end result will be disappointingly insipid. You may need to do this in 2 batches.

Tip in the soaked kidney beans (tinned is okay in an emergency), tinned tomatoes and stock. Don't worry if it looks a little icky. The pot will transform in a few hours. Stir in the veg, pop a lid on and let it paddle on a low heat for 2-3 hours. It's done as soon as the beans are soft, but not mushy.

Taste, tickle with salt and pepper and add the cumin and dark chocolate to liven it up. If you feel it needs more pungency, add some yeast extract, blackstrap molasses or chopped anchovies. Sometimes we do, sometimes we don't.

To serve, cut the red onion in half and finely slice into semi-circles. Squeeze the lime over the onions, and allow them to party with the nam pla. Top each bowl of chilli con carne with a little macerated red onion, fresh coriander (if using) and a great big dollop of cultured coconut yoghurt in place of sour cream. It's the holy trinity to a good con carne.

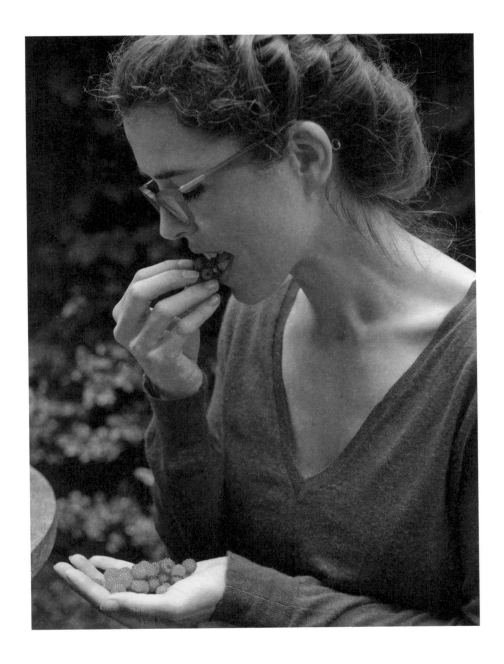

Extra Virgin Treats

I'm through with guilt.

1 British cup = 250ml

Looking back, I could never get enough sugar hits. I was an addict. Everything I did related to or led to my next sugar fix. I even convinced myself that college projects required kilos of coffee and Curly Wurlies to charge my brain cells. I couldn't possibly perform without them.

Sound familiar?

Having to give up junk food was like a bad break-up with the love of my life. Sudden. Undesired. Unexpected. Grief smothered my senses like a diaphanous veil over my entire body. I struggled deeply to wave goodbye to the things I loved in life: my chocolate bars, ice cream, cupcakes, panna cotta. Clearly, they did not love me back. Like all cases of unrequited love, I had to get over myself, move on, or drown in a pool of self-pity.

Here were my choices - ignore the medical advice I was given and dig my way to the grave with my teeth?
Or nosedive into an apron and role-play with
Heston Blumenthal?

I chose the latter.

Today, my body is in balance. There are no sugar binges or episodes of overeating. That's because my cravings are satisfied with real food that nourishes my neurotransmitters in a way that white sugar and flour never could.

It's *sooo* good to leave the wheat-sugar-dairy circus, to let your body samba to something less generic and more wholesome. Do it! If you feed your body, your body will feed you. So here are loads of treats to help turn your naughty cravings into a nutritional hit. A word of caution - your wings will go wild and your toes may take off.
Sláinte!

Visit page 12 to learn more about my alternatives to refined cane sugar.

Raw Cacao Nib Toffee -------------

----------- Goji Berry Smudge

GOJI BERRY SMUDGE

>>>>>>>>>>>>>>>>>>>>>>>>

This is like a smoochy fudge. It's quite possibly my favourite recipe.

We know that good bone health is intimately linked to what we eat. Dr Marilyn Glenville, specialist in women's health, is dubious about dairy's monopoly on calcium in our diet. Why, Glenville asks, is our rate of osteoporosis much higher than Japan's, where they don't even eat dairy? A good question. Glenville is not alone. New York Times best-selling author Dr Joel Fuhrman doesn't rate dairy at all. Fuhrman's medical research and experience as a GP have entirely reversed his thinking about dairy. Worthy of further head-scratching.

So let's explore alternative sources to dairy without having to mourn our cheese board. These include tinned salmon and sarnies, barley grass, chickpeas, broccoli, figs, sesame seeds, tahini, almonds, hazelnuts and green leafy veg. This Goji Berry Smudge is a great place to start.

Melt the coconut oil on a very gentle heat. Stir in the maple syrup, vanilla and salt. The grooviest salt to use in desserts is a vanilla-infused organic salt from Halen Môn in Wales. Find it online or in Fallon & Byrne, Dublin 2.

With a fork, beat through the tahini, goji berries and hemp seeds (if you don't have hemp seeds, no worries). Keep some gojies to tickle the top. Scrape half the mixture into a small rectangular container lined with cling film. Dribble runny honey over it and scrape the remaining mixture on top of the honey. Prod it with a fork and give it a swirl to move the honey about without incorporating it into the tahini. Think caramel swirls.

Freeze for 4 hours. Just like ice cream, it must be stored in the freezer or else it will melt into a holy mess. Slice big wedges from it and marvel at its virtuous decadence.

3 tablespoons extra virgin coconut oil

up to 1/2 cup (125ml) maple or brown rice syrup

1 teaspoon vanilla extract or powder

1 teaspoon Maldon sea salt flakes

1 x 340g jar light tahini

4 tablespoons goji berries

2 tablespoons hemp seeds (optional nutritional boost)

2-3 tablespoons runny raw honey

Makes 30 servings

RAW CACAO NIB TOFFEE

>>>>>>>>>>>>>>>>>>>>>>>>>>>>>>

Apparently, women think about chocolate more then men. Some scientists think this is because eating cacao helps release a cavalry of dopamine in the female brain, the same substance released during orgasm. It's even been suggested that when women eat raw chocolate, it affects activity in the cerebral hemisphere responsible for regulating sexual desire. Only one way to find out…

1/2 cup (125ml) date syrup
3 tablespoons extra virgin
 coconut oil
1 x 340g jar light tahini
3 tablespoons raw cacao nibs
2 tablespoons carob powder
2 teaspoons vanilla extract
pinch of sea salt flakes

Makes 25-30 servings

Melt the date syrup and coconut oil together over a low heat. Add the remaining ingredients, mushing with a fork. Ensure the oil is well mixed. Taste, and adjust with vanilla or sweetener. Work quickly, as the oil will begin to separate from the other ingredients as soon as it starts cooling. It needs a warm environment.

Line a small rectangular container (a little lunchbox perhaps?) with cling film so that it comes out over the sides. Transfer your gorgeous gooey gloss into the lined container and tickle with more cacao nibs (if you have any left).

Transfer to the freezer for 4 hours before indulging. Store it there too, as it melts quite quickly at room temperature.

FANCY PANTS LÚCUMA FUDGE

>>>>>>>>>>>>>>>>>>>>>>>>>>>>>>>>>>

I'm a firm believer in the idea that healthy eating should never tax your taste buds. This recipe has an authentic fudgy feel, but with none of the wicked additives or cosmetic gunk. It practically levitates with goodness.

Ever look 20 years older on a Sunday morning? Or sport a dirty big hangover? This recipe will help. Lúcuma is a fancy pants fruit from South America, good enough for the gods and maybe even for Satan. Its creamy flesh falls between an avocado and an egg yolk - a killer combo. Its perfume will even drive your senses wild. Sadly, lúcuma is just too perishable to find fresh in Ireland. Instead, its flesh is freeze-dried before exporting. For helpful online sources of where to find it, see page 253.

Line a very small container with cling film. Gently melt the coconut oil over a low heat and stir in the remaining ingredients with a fork. If you intend using the vanilla pod, split it along the side lengthways, carefully peel the pod open and using the blade of a knife, scoop out its fabulous black seeds. Add to the fudge mix, which should look like wet sand by now. Taste, and adjust the sweetness or saltiness to your preferences.

Spoon into your lined container and let it set in the fridge before cutting into chunks of fudge. It should be ready to devour in 1 hour.

4 tablespoons extra virgin coconut oil
8 tablespoons ground almonds
3 tablespoons lúcuma powder
2 tablespoons maple syrup or raw honey
1 vanilla pod (optional) or 1 teaspoon vanilla powder
sprinkle of decent unrefined salt, like Himalayan pink rock salt

Makes 12 servings

LEMON WHOOPIE PIES

>>>>>>>>>>>>>>>>>>>>>>>>

Whoopie pies are teeny custard cream cakes with a personality all of their own. Every time my son confides that these whoopie pies are his 'favourite burgers in the world', my chest swells. I think he's an aspiring vegetarian. Or con artist. It's so hard to tell at three, but the pride is definitely undisputed and comical in equal measures.

When I'm baking for kiddies' birthday parties, I use organic cream cheese instead for the vanilla custard cream. If any of their buddies are lactose intolerant, the filling below does the trick.

For the whoopie pies:
1/2 cup (65g) coconut flour
1/2 cup (50g) ground almonds
zest of 1 small lemon
2 tablespoons desiccated
  coconut
2 teaspoons baking powder
1/2 teaspoon ground turmeric
1/2 teaspoon unrefined
  organic salt
4 medium eggs
1/2 cup (125ml) extra virgin
  coconut oil
1/2 cup (125ml) runny honey
  or brown rice syrup (not
  maple)
good squeeze of lemon juice

**For the vanilla custard
  cream:**
1 cup (150g) cashews, soaked
  in water overnight
1/2 cup (125ml) water
1/4 cup (60ml) raw agave,
  barley malt extract or
  brown rice syrup (not
  maple syrup)
2 teaspoons vanilla extract
  (powder is visually
  better)
squeeze of lemon juice
  (optional kick)
1/2 cup (125ml) extra virgin
  coconut oil, melted

Makes 10 large or 20 small
  pies

Preheat the oven to 170°C/150°C fan/340°F. Line 2 trays with parchment paper.

To make the biscuit base, you'll be using 2 separate bowls. In the first bowl, stir together the dry ingredients. The second bowl wants the wet ingredients (eggs, oil, natural syrup and lemon juice).

Add the dry ingredients to the wet and mix well. Spoon little puddles onto the lined baking trays. You may need to cook the whoopies in batches, especially if they're teeny tiny ones. Bake large whoopies for 15-18 minutes. If you made smaller whoopies, they'll only require 12-15 minutes.

Remove from the oven and allow to set for 15 minutes before transferring them from their tray and sandwiching with the vanilla custard cream.

To make the vanilla custard cream, discard the soaking water from the cashews. Blitz the nuts in a high-speed food processor with the fresh water, natural syrup, vanilla and optional lemon for a good 2 minutes.

Meanwhile, gently melt the solid coconut oil until liquid. While the motor is still running, slowly add the coconut oil to the whizzed cashew (like you would if making mayonnaise). Blitz until smooth rather than grainy. The custard cream tends to thicken once chilled for a few hours, so don't panic if it looks like milk.

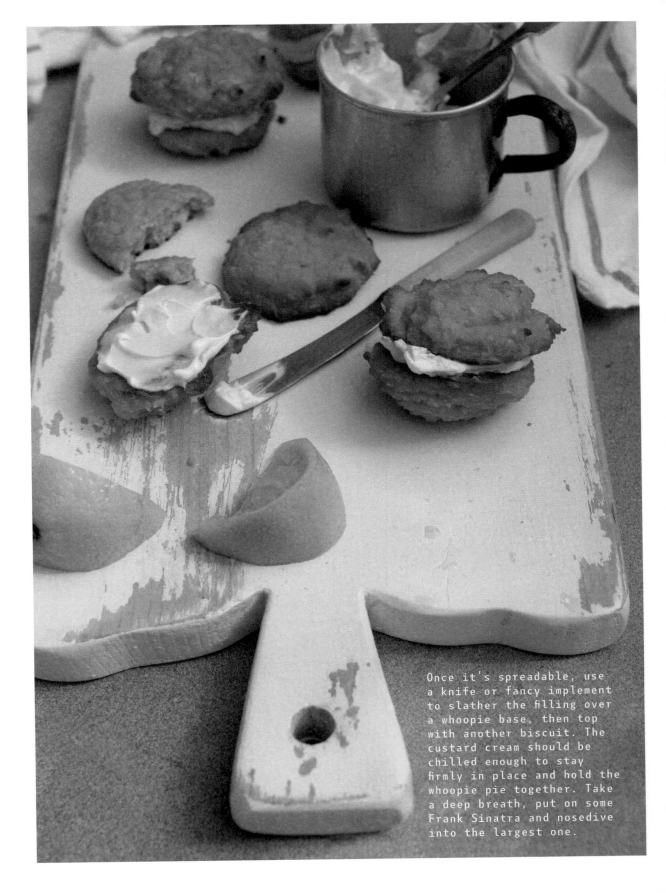

Once it's spreadable, use a knife or fancy implement to slather the filling over a whoopie base, then top with another biscuit. The custard cream should be chilled enough to stay firmly in place and hold the whoopie pie together. Take a deep breath, put on some Frank Sinatra and nosedive into the largest one.

DELINQUENT BROWNIES

>>>>>>>>>>>>>>>>>>>>>>>>>

These brownies will fool the most ardent of brownie bingers. Not as saccharine as regular cane sugar, coconut blossom sugar offers a burnt toffee kick to everything it caresses. It's not heavily processed either. The sap of the coconut flower is dehydrated to form honeyed crystals. While coconut sugar can be classified as a palm sugar, it is not to be confused with regular palm sugar, which is no friend to the diabetic. Coconut sugar is thought to have a low glycemic value - good news for hyperactive children, diabetics and bored sedentary workers.

I've used goat's butter in response to many requests over the years to include it in my online recipe portal. This won't suit everyone, but it can be a great alternative for those who react to cow's milk, like my mother. Goat's milk and goat's butter appear to be more alkaline than cow's milk, appealing to those on a calcium-retention diet or alkalising menus.

The ingredients for these brownies need to be measured in grams. For more on this, see page 8. Don't panic - it's just a fling.

250g 85% dark chocolate
200g goat's butter
100g ground almonds
2 teaspoons gluten-free
  baking powder
4 medium eggs
250g coconut blossom sugar

Makes 16-20

Preheat the oven to 180°C/160°C fan/350°F. Line a 30cm x 25cm baking tray with parchment paper and set aside.

Slowly melt most of the chocolate (keep back 30-40g) with the goat's butter over a bain marie. All this means is a saucepan of 2cm of water simmering away and a shallow bowl fit snugly on top in place of a lid. This is where you'll melt the butter and choccie. If the bowl gets too hot the chocolate will go lumpy, so take it off the heat as soon as you see the ingredients melding. Sometimes the water can turn from a mannerly simmer to a violent boil when you're not watching.

Chop the remaining chocolate into mini buttons, throw into a separate bowl and stir through the ground almonds and baking powder.

In a very large bowl, beat together the eggs and sugar with an electric whisk until creamy. The mixture will aerate and change colour slightly, so don't be overly alarmed. Fold in the ground almond mix and the melted chocolate. Swiftly transfer to your prepared tin with a spatula, before all the lovely air bubbles pop.

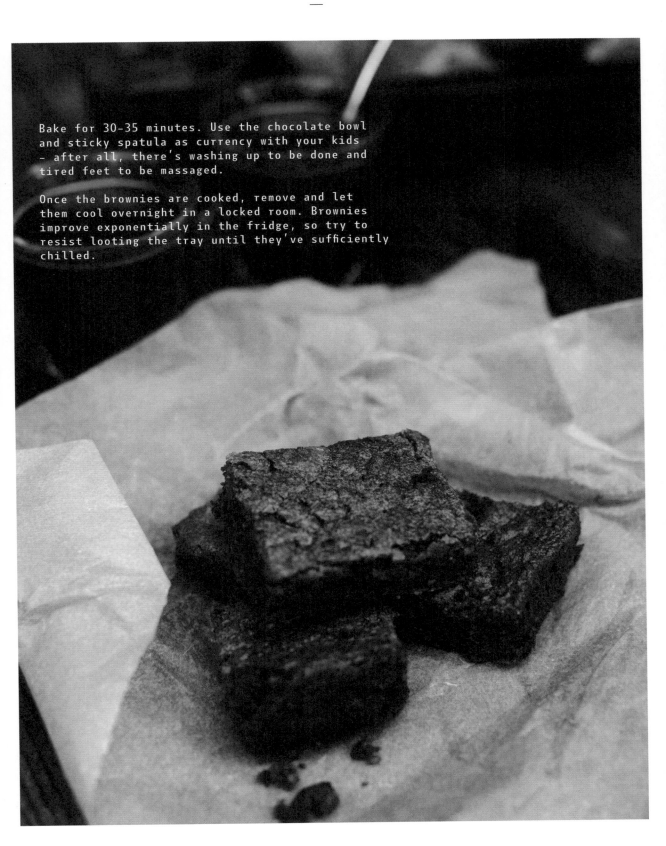

Bake for 30-35 minutes. Use the chocolate bowl
and sticky spatula as currency with your kids
- after all, there's washing up to be done and
tired feet to be massaged.

Once the brownies are cooked, remove and let
them cool overnight in a locked room. Brownies
improve exponentially in the fridge, so try to
resist looting the tray until they've sufficiently
chilled.

DARK PEANUT BUTTER BROWNIES

>>

Chocolate is a vaccine against bad moods. Something explosive happens in my veins as well as my mouth. According to scientists, this is because of a neurochemical called dopamine. Once stirred, dopamine can initiate an electrical cavalry through the veins and hit every imaginable spot. And I mean every spot. High levels of dopamine are associated with increased motivation, neuro-aerobics and general rí rá agus ruaile buaile - all diplomatic speak for better nookie.

Luckily for us, Mother Nature gave the cacao bean lots of heart-healthy flavanols and magnesium. Both nutrients are loyal friends of the cardio-vascular system, helping blood flow and circulation. In fact, I believe the smell of chocolate can send a feline's pulse into a frenzy. Quite the defibrillator.

This endorsement of chocolate comes with a rather large qualification: it must be raw or dark. Untreated, raw cacao is the nutritional heavy-weight champion of chocolate. Next best is 85% dark chocolate - indecently rich and muscular. Anything else is disqualified, especially the white or milk varieties. Now for some irritating information: caffeine (in coffee or chocolate) prompts the body to release stored sugars in our system. This is bad news for diabetics or candida warriors. Caffeine's physiological effect can be just as pernicious as sugar. Too much, and we're in trouble.

The ingredients for these brownies are best measured in grams. For more on this, see page 8.

4 tablespoons crunchy peanut butter
1-2 tablespoons maple syrup
125g 85% dark chocolate
100g goat's butter (see note on p.212)
2 medium eggs
125g rapadura sugar or coconut blossom sugar
75g ground almonds or hemp protein powder
1 teaspoon gluten-free baking powder

Makes 10-12

Preheat the oven to 180°C/160°C fan/350°F. Line
a small square baking tray (20cm x 20cm) with
greaseproof paper.

Beat the peanut butter and maple syrup together
in a cup using a fork and litter the lined baking
tray with baby blobs. Set aside.

Slowly melt the chocolate with the goat's butter
over a bain marie. All this means is a saucepan
of 2cm of water simmering away and a shallow bowl
fit snugly on top in place of a lid. This is where
you'll melt the butter and choccie. If the bowl
gets too hot the chocolate will go lumpy, so take
it off the heat as soon as you see some action.

In a very large bowl, beat together the eggs
and sugar with an electric whisk until creamy.
Stir through the ground almonds or hemp and the
baking powder, then fold in the melted chocolate.
Swiftly transfer to your prepared tin with a
spatula. Bake for approximately 18 minutes.

Once the brownies are cooked, remove and let them
cool overnight in a locked room. Store in the
fridge or other chilled hiding place.

ITALIAN AND RICH

>>>>>>>>>>>>>>>>>>>>>>>

Make Paul Daniels proud - turn your cravings into a nutritional hit by using avocado in place of cream, and prunes in place of sugar. If you're leery about using them, don't be. Their flavour is muted by the cacao content. This Gianduja-style torte is so darn scrumptious, it feels illicit.

For the base:
6-8 soft prunes or soaked
  dates
1 cup (135g) roasted
  hazelnuts
1/4 cup (25g) cocoa or cacao
  powder
1/4 cup (60ml) maple or date
  syrup
handful of walnuts or pecans
2 tablespoons ground
  linseeds

For the ganache topping:
2 Medjool dates, pre-soaked
1 large avocado, stone and
  skin removed
1/2 cup (50g) cacao or cocoa
  powder
1/4 cup (60ml) maple or date
  syrup (not honey)
2 tablespoons hazelnut
  butter
1 tablespoon tamari
1 teaspoon vanilla extract

Serves 14

To make the base, add the listed ingredients to your food processor and pulse until it starts to stick together. You're looking for a clumpy nut texture, not a purée. Make sure your prunes or dates are plump and juicy, otherwise the mixture won't behave. Soak them in a spot of water for 10 minutes before using if you think this will help.

Once pulsed, scrape the base mixture into a pre-lined tin, one that's about half the size of a magazine page. Refrigerate straight away - I find the base easier to manipulate into place later, when it's chilled.

Now get going on your filling. Whizz all the filling ingredients together with a hand-held blender or food processor. Process until lusciously smooth. Taste to see if it reaches your serotonin and dimples. If not, adjust accordingly: more maple to sweeten, more tamari for depth, more cacao for richness. Set aside.

As soon as the base is cold, press firmly down with the back of a spoon or your fingertips. Fold the filling on top and set for 4 hours in the fridge. Provided it remains in the fridge, it should last for up to 6 days. Pending diligence and discipline, of course.

SEA SALT PROBIOTIC CHOCOLATES

>>

Probiotic means pro-life. Naturally fermented food like yoghurt is brimming with live probiotic bacteria to keep your internal ecosystem in balance. I understand how foul this may sound, but trust me, these guys are on our side. Without healthy strains of live bacteria, our food would not be sufficiently broken down in our guts or absorbed by our bodies. Thrush, bloating and dodgy bowel movements tend to be the most common symptoms of intestinal imbalance.

If you can't have natural yoghurt, look for alternative sources of probiotics in fermented foods such as sauerkraut, kimchi, unpasteurised miso and coconut yoghurt. Or these chocolates. We use them as currency in our house when necessary. Our toddlers will sing Humpty Dumpty in Mandarin for them. So will my husband.

Melt the cacao butter in a bain marie. All this means is placing the broken shards of butter in a shallow bowl set over a pan of barely simmering water. Make sure the bowl is at least 10cm above the simmering water. Remove from the heat and let the cacao butter naturally melt over the hot water for 5 minutes.

Blitz the remaining ingredients (except the raw cacao powder for dusting) in a food processor. Keep the motor running and slowly add the melted cacao butter in a steady stream. The addition of 1/4 teaspoon cayenne pepper is rumoured to make your tongue dance and your pulse quicken. Just saying.

Refrigerate in the same bowl, with the blade intact, for about 3 hours. If the mixture seems too hard or you've forgotten about it in the fridge, blitz it again to loosen it up. (That's why it's useful to leave the blade in.)

Put the raw cacao powder in a bowl or shallow plate. Roll the mixture into little bonbons between your palms, then drop into the raw cacao powder. They can be frozen for up to 3 months. Glory be to the icebox!

65ml melted cacao butter

1/2 cup (125ml) raw agave, barley malt extract or brown rice syrup

1/3 cup (35g) cacao or cocoa powder

1/4 cup (70g) cashew nut butter

2 tablespoons water

2 tablespoons hazelnut butter (or more cashew butter)

1 tablespoon probiotic powder (we use Udo's)

1 teaspoon vanilla extract or powder

1/2 teaspoon good sea salt, like Maldon flakes

3 tablespoons raw cacao powder, to dust

Makes 40-50

BEETROOT CANDY

>>>>>>>>>>>>>>>>>>>>

Tiny titans of flavour, no one would guess these candies are scrupulously healthy. Underneath their neon pink dusting lies some of Mother N's finest superfoods: beetroot, seaweed and raw almonds.

That bold pigment that gives beetroot its Harry Potter glimmer is where the magic lies. Deep red-coloured foods like beetroot and onions store powerful chemicals called betacyanins. These compounds love your liver and are believed to support the body's detoxification process. This might be why beets have charmed every detox clinic from North America to the West of Ireland.

You don't need to stick to beetroot powder for the recipe to work - try a Peruvian powdered fruit called lúcuma. Apparently lúcuma is the maple syrup of South America. A mere whiff of this ambrosial substance has the ability to drive the feline persuasion wild. Move over, Justin Bieber, there's a new fixation on the block.

15 plump Medjool dates
2 tablespoons almond or
  cashew nut butter
2 tablespoons extra virgin
  coconut oil
1 tablespoon spirulina
1-2 teaspoons tamari
2 tablespoons beetroot
  powder, to dust

Makes 30-35 candies

Destone the dates before dropping them into a food processor. Add the remaining ingredients except the beetroot powder for dusting later. Whizz on a low speed for 1-2 minutes.

Using a teaspoon amount, mould the candy mix into teeny bonbons. Your hands will become slippery, aiding the process. Expect to get around 30-35 candies from the batch, depending on how many times the teaspoon fell into your mouth.

Chill for 24 hours before rolling in the beetroot powder. Any sooner, and the candy will drink up the coating. No harm in looting one or seven in the meantime. Store in the fridge for up to 1 month.

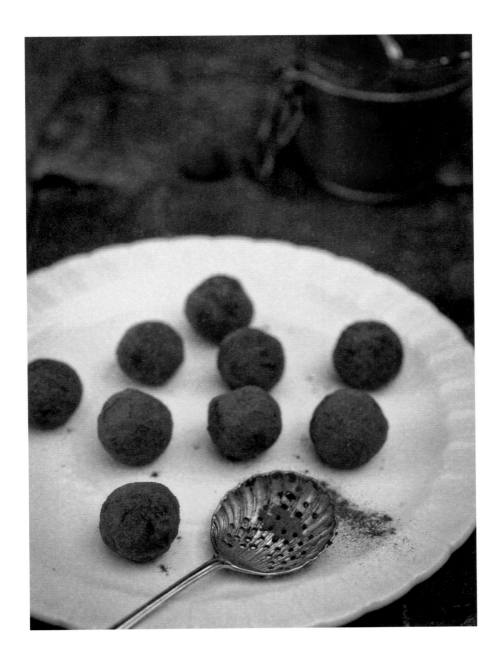

FIG AND PRUNE CRUMBLE WITH GINGER-LACED YOGHURT AND DATE SYRUP

>>>

This crumble will unleash some serious goodness into your system and prompt a fervent tail-wagging session around the kitchen table.

Whether fresh or dried, figs are a surprisingly good source of calcium. This mineral is the Holy Grail for strong bones, so throw a packet of dried figs in your office drawer to ward off sugar cravings and dodgy hips.

It's worth keeping your health antennae out for cold-pressed extra virgin coconut oil. Once refined, coconut oil's immune-boosting properties substantially diminish. I should add that there is quite a price difference. A large jar of copra, the refined coconut oil that you don't want, is available for the same price as a big bar of chocolate. The equivalent size, raw and unrefined, will be four times more costly. But as Michael Pollan so sensibly exhorts, 'It's better to pay the grocer than the doctor.'

For the filling:
6 small or medium eating
  apples
1 tablespoon ground cinnamon
splash of lemon juice
6 fresh or dried figs,
  stems removed and roughly
  chopped
roughly 1 cup (180g) prunes,
  stones removed and chopped

For the topping:
2 cups (180g) jumbo oat flakes
4-5 tablespoons maple or
  brown rice syrup, honey or
  raw agave
4 tablespoons extra virgin
  coconut oil
1 cup (120g) mixed seeds
  (sunflower, linseeds,
  pumpkin)
sprinkle of sea salt flakes

For the yoghurt:
coconut or organic soya
  yoghurt
3 tablespoons grated frozen
  ginger
date syrup, to serve

Serves 8

Preheat the oven to 170°C/150°C fan/340°F.

To make the topping, briefly blitz the oats with the syrup and coconut oil (which is solid like butter at room temperature) in a food processor until it clumps together – 5 seconds should do the trick. Stir in the seeds and salt and mix well. It's a good idea to soak the linseeds in twice as much water for 60 minutes or overnight, but it's not essential.

To prep the fruit, chop the apples into bite-sized pieces, binning the core. Don't remove the skins, as these soften once cooked and can add terrific texture and nutrition. In a small saucepan filled with 3cm of boiling water, add the apples, cinnamon and lemon juice. Cover and cook on a medium heat until semi-squishy (anything between 8 and 20 minutes, depending on the variety of apple used). Remember not to let it turn into mush, as it will have additional cooking time in the oven later (but if this happens, don't panic – it will still taste damn fine!). Once it's soft, add the figs and prunes. Pour the filling into an oven dish. Top with the oaty crumble and press down.

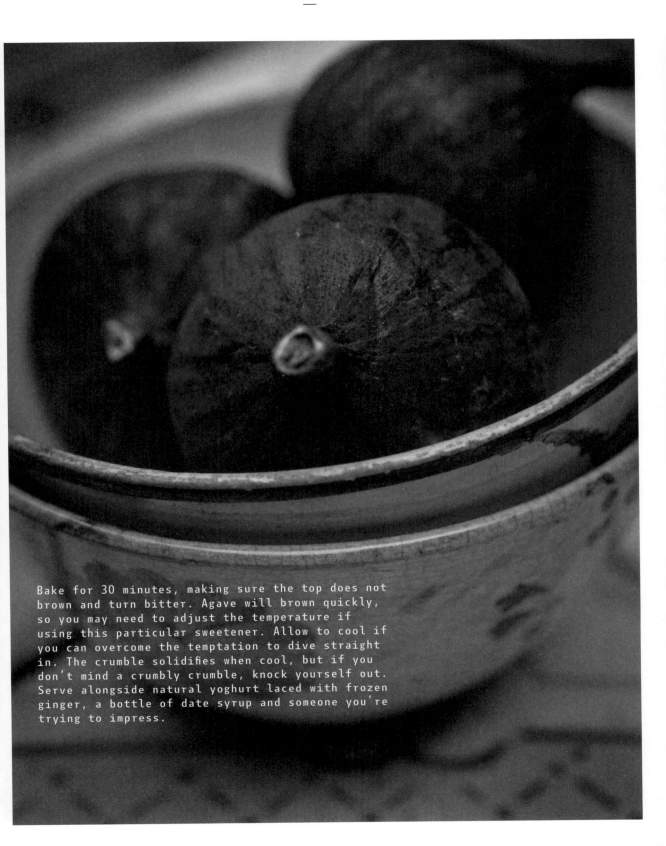

Bake for 30 minutes, making sure the top does not brown and turn bitter. Agave will brown quickly, so you may need to adjust the temperature if using this particular sweetener. Allow to cool if you can overcome the temptation to dive straight in. The crumble solidifies when cool, but if you don't mind a crumbly crumble, knock yourself out. Serve alongside natural yoghurt laced with frozen ginger, a bottle of date syrup and someone you're trying to impress.

MACADAMIA AND PASSIONFRUIT CUSTARD PIE

>>

This recipe will help exorcise those overactive sugar cravings. The base is both crunchy and creamy, in a way that only a team of macadamia can achieve. You'll be getting a fair whack of heart-healthy magnesium and cholesterol-lowering oleic too, something junk food could never brag.

The passionfruit filling is sweet and buttery, with a halo hovering over it. Don't be afraid of egg yolks, as they contain a brain-boosting compound called choline to help find those bloody car keys. And while coconut oil is a source of saturated fat, its unique chemical structure allows us to utilise it as energy straight away.

The snazziest pie dish to use is a 20cm loose-bottomed one, but play with whatever you have. This pie will taste sensational regardless of where you put it. Grease the base and sides with coconut oil.

Using a food processor, briefly pulse all the crust ingredients until they start to clump together in a doughy ball. Scrape into your pie dish and press along the sides and bottom with clean fingers to cover the entire dish and form a crust. If you have any mixture left over, roll into bonbons and use as bribes for stubborn toddlers and teenagers. Chill the pie crust in the freezer until later.

To make the custardy filling, first download a podcast or stick on some great tunes since you will be locked to the cooker for 8 minutes. Gently heat all the ingredients on an extra-low setting in a small saucepan. If it's too hot, the yolks will cook in seconds. Continuous whisking is crucial. When all the coconut oil has melted, keep a watch for little bubbles forming on the surface, telling you the mixture is getting hotter and hotter. By then, you should notice the mixture getting thicker, like a custard. Test it by dipping the back of a spoon into it. If the custard coats the spoon, remove it from the heat. If it runs off, keep the custard over the heat until it thickens a little more. Failure to keep whisking will result in lemony scrambled eggs.

Pour over your chilled base and set in the fridge for 2 hours before serving. Deliciously potent stuff, with a nod to the nutritional gods.

For the crust:
1 cup (140g) raw macadamia
  nuts (and/or almonds)
1 cup (150g) raisins (not
  currants)
1/2 cup (40g) desiccated
  coconut
1 tablespoon runny honey or
  maple syrup

For the filling:
4 egg yolks
2 passionfruit
juice and rind of 1 large
  lemon
5 tablespoons runny honey or
  raw agave
4 tablespoons extra virgin
  coconut oil

Makes 12-16 portions

LEMON AND PISTACHIO PIE WITH ORANGE BLOSSOM YOGHURT

>>

This recipe is designed to drive your neurotransmitters wild without driving up your blood sugar levels or gunging your arteries.

But aren't nuts fattening? Not so. Nuts contain monounsaturated fat. That's the healthy one associated with lower rates of heart disease and cholesterol. Commercial candy, on the other hand, is a source of nasty fat, responsible for bumping up your bad LDL cholesterol and haunting your arteries. Please don't confuse the two fats - they behave very differently in the body. In fact, the British Medical Journal published research on Polymeal foods that, if consumed daily, would reduce the risk of cardiovascular disease by 75%. Dark chocolate and nuts were two of the seven foods. Glee.

For the biscuit base:
3/4 cup (105g) unsalted
  cashews
1/2 cup (70g) shelled
  pistachios
1/3 cup (50g) sultanas
juice and zest of 1 small
  lemon
2 tablespoons raw agave,
  maple or brown rice syrup
1/4 teaspoon unrefined salt

For the filling:
1 1/2 cups (200g) raw
  unsalted cashew nuts,
  soaked overnight
1/2 cup (125ml) raw agave or
  brown rice syrup (maple is
  not good)
up to 1/2 cup (125ml) melted
  extra virgin coconut oil
juice of 1 1/2 lemons (or 2
  small lemons)
1/2 teaspoon ground turmeric

handful of shelled
  pistachios, to decorate
coconut or soya yoghurt, to
  serve
orange blossom water, to
  serve

Makes 12 slices

Briefly pulse the base ingredients together using a food processor. Stop the motor when the dough starts to clump together. Spread the nutty dough over the bottom of a lightly oiled 18cm springform tin. These are a special type of baking tin usually used to make cheesecakes. Place in the freezer to chill while you get going on the filling.

Drain the cashew nuts and discard the soaking liquid. Cream the softened cashews with the remaining filling ingredients (except the pistachios) until smooth and glossy. This should take 2 minutes in a blender or food processor. Add more turmeric if you want to achieve an even brighter glow. Too much, though, and planes will start landing on your house. Pour over your base and return to the freezer until beckoned.

Allow to thaw for 5 minutes before cutting the pie from frozen. Crush a handful of shelled pistachios with the bottom of a saucepan and tickle the top of the pie with them. Serve with thick cultured coconut or soya yoghurt splashed with orange blossom water or culinary-grade orange oil. And maybe a pitcher of iced green tea on a sweltering summer's day.

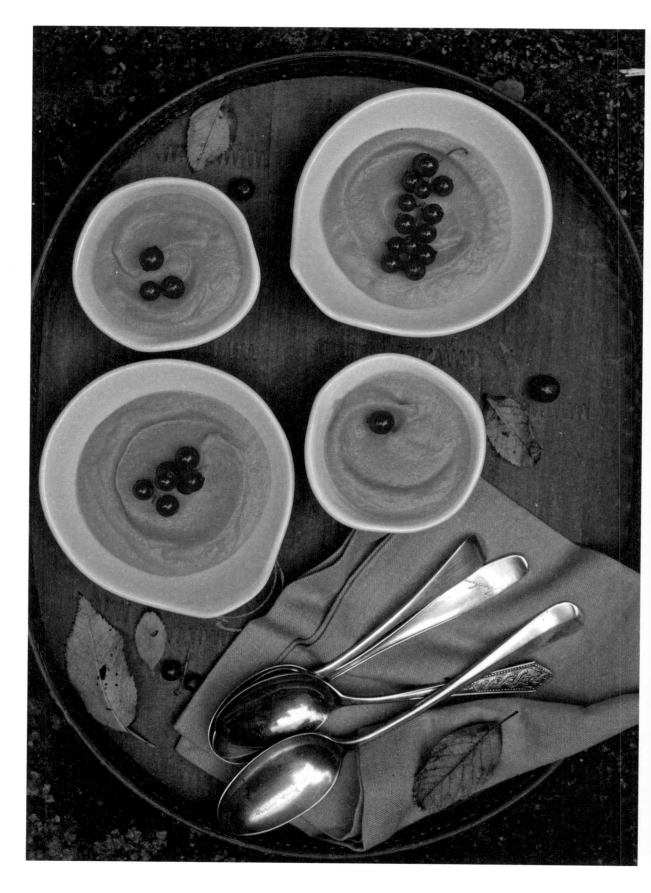

MAPLE AND PUMPKIN PANNA COTTA

>>>

The Japanese use agar as a weight-loss aid because of its stellar fibre content. This natural setting agent is made from sea algae, which is frozen and shaved. So make friends with agar, because it's good for your body. After all, you're the one who has to live in it!

Start by peeling the ginger and placing it in the freezer to firm up. Fresh ginger would be too fibrous, overpowering and stringy.

While the ginger is freezing, peel and chop your pumpkin into matchbox-sized pieces, toss in a little olive oil, season and roast on a baking tray at 200°C/180°C fan/400°F for 30 minutes, until soft and tasty. Covering the tray with tinfoil prevents any browning from occurring. Broadly speaking, it's worth cooking about 3 mugs of chopped pumpkin and gleefully gobbling any you don't use in the recipe. As soon as the pumpkin is done, mash it while it's hot and measure out 1 1/2 cups (375ml) of the purée. Grate the frozen ginger over it using the finest part of a grater. Set aside.

Sprinkle the agar flakes into the cold water and bring to a gentle simmer for 4-5 minutes without stirring.

In the meantime, throw the remaining ingredients (except the blueberries or redcurrants) into your food processor along with the pumpkin mash. Blend everything together on high speed, slowly adding the hot agar mix. Purée until sumptuous and smooth.

Pour into handy jam jars ready to bring into school or work tomorrow. If serving tonight, refrigerate in a suitable large bowl or individual ramekin dishes until set. Excite with redcurrants and a glorious drizzle of maple syrup.

1 x 4cm piece of fresh root ginger, grated
1 small organic pumpkin
a little olive oil
1 tablespoon agar flakes
1 cup (250ml) filtered water
4-5 tablespoons maple syrup, plus extra to serve
1-2 tablespoons extra virgin coconut oil
1/4 teaspoon sea salt flakes
pinch of ground cinnamon
splash of vanilla extract
tiny squeeze of lime juice
redcurrants, to decorate

Serves 5-8

HAZELNUT AND RAISIN FREEZER COOKIES

>>

It takes 4 pounds of grapes to produce a single pound of raisins. This markedly concentrates raisins' nutritional kick. Counted as one of your five a day, a handful of these chewy little candies will give you astral amounts of antioxidants and phytochemicals, equivalent to a bunch of fresh grapes. (No, not equivalent to a bottle of Merlot, but nice try. Nor does wine count as part of your five-a-day programme, except in December, obviously.)

That same handful contains blushing amounts of resveratrol too, the phyto-nutrient that furnishes our body with anti-cancer infantry. Antioxidants and phytochemicals such as resveratrol are needed to deactivate menacing molecules in our bodies, more commonly referred to as free radicals. Imagine an internal Pac-Man and you've got the idea.

Now for the down sides. Research has shown that grapes carry more pesticides and agrichemicals than most other fruit. Agrichemicals don't exactly sound synonymous with good health, but the jury is still debating this one. If you're worried, the European Working Group has a handy guide to pesticide residues, downloadable online or as an app. It's a simple list of the 'cleanest' fruit and veg and the worst-offending ones for you to consult when shopping at your grocer. The president of the EWG is eager to make the case to eat more fruit and veg, whether conventional or organic. He comes across as a smart and practical shopper rather than a loony food fascist.

With their high glycemic load, raisins are not so good for diabetics. In fact, all dried fruit carries greater glycemic indices (GI) than their fresh equivalent. This is something diabetics have to watch. Low-glycemic fruits to splurge on instead include fresh blueberries, raspberries, black-berries, redcurrants, blackcurrants and strawberries.

2 cups (200g) ground almonds
1/2 cup (125ml) extra virgin
  coconut oil, melted
1/3 cup (80ml) maple syrup
1/4 cup (40g) raisins
handful of roasted
  hazelnuts, roughly chopped
zest of 1 small unwaxed
  lemon
1 tablespoon ground ginger
1/2 teaspoon sea salt flakes

Makes 22 small cookies

Using a fork, mix everything together in a cold bowl. Grab an apricot-sized piece of dough and flatten it into a cookie shape. If it's too sticky, wait until the dough has cooled and dampen your hands slightly.

Place on greaseproof baking parchment and freeze - no need to cook. Once frozen, they can be stored in a freezer bag, ready to pillage at will. Other variations to play with include orange zest and cinnamon, a tablespoon of chia seeds for added omega-3 fuel, or carob powder and cacao nibs.

WHITE CACAO TRUFFLES

>>>>>>>>>>>>>>>>>>>>>>>>>>>>>>>>>>

These are the stunning creation of rawvolutionist Katie Sanderson. Check out her Facebook page Living Dinners for inspiration and super-cool photos. If I won the lotto, I'd have a hotline to her kitchen.

Cacao butter may require a little sat navving to find. I get mine online (see page 253), where I can bulk buy an artillery of scrummy stuff without having to leave my lazy armchair.

Melt the cacao butter in a bain marie. All this means is placing the broken shards of butter in a shallow bowl set over a pan of barely simmering water. Make sure the bowl is at least 10cm above the simmering water. Remove from the heat and let the butter naturally melt over the hot water for 5 minutes.

Cream the other ingredients in a mini electric blender or food processor. Keep the motor running and slowly add the melted cacao butter in a steady stream.

Refrigerate for about 3 hours. If the mixture seems too hard or you've forgotten about it in the fridge, blitz it again to loosen it up. You might want to chill it in the food processor's bowl with the blade still in for this reason. Using a teaspoon, take a teeny amount and form a bonbon between your palms. Drop into lúcuma powder and roll again with dry fingertips. Store in the fridge until the munchies hit. Then kick your feet up and high-five Katie.

1/3 cup (80ml) melted cacao butter
3/4 cup (200g) hazelnut butter
1/2 cup (125ml) raw agave, brown rice syrup or barley malt extract
3 tablespoons lúcuma powder, plus extra to dust
2 tablespoons water
1 teaspoon vanilla extract or powder
pinch of pink Himalayan salt

Makes 40-50 truffles

PECAN PILLOWS WITH CHOCOLATE PUDDLES

>>

These are quick and easy to whip up, with remarkably few ingredients. But surely something so tasty has to be bad for you? Nope. Pecans are a rich source of zinc, the 'fertility mineral' responsible for healthy hormones, radiant skin and a Herculean immune system. These unassuming little nuts also proffer a nice dose of age-defying vitamin E, beta-sitosterol for dirty arteries and potassium for mouldy hangovers. Jaysus, pecan, you is one talented nut.

The cacao bean happens to be one of nature's top sources of magnesium, the mineral associated with blood flow and good circulation. No yawning! Circulation affects the entire body, irrespective of what age you are. Think blood flow to the brain, depression, varicose veins, constipation, hypertension, erectile dysfunction and gorgeous skin. We love you, Pecan Pillows!

1 cup (110g) pecans
5 Medjool or other very
  sticky dates
4-5 tablespoons cocoa or
  cacao powder
2 tablespoons date, maple or
  brown rice syrup
pinch of unrefined, mineral-
  rich salt
50g 85% dark chocolate
1 tablespoon probiotic
  powder (we use Udo's)

Makes 15

Pulse the pecans, dates, cocoa, syrup and a pinch of salt in a blender until it starts resembling sticky sand. Roll into 15 apricot-sized balls between the palms of your hands. Using your thumb, press a dimple into the crown of each ball. Refrigerate.

For the probiotic frosting, gently melt the chocolate over a saucepan of barely simmering water. It's easiest to use a plate that fits snugly on top of your saucepan, with only 3cm of water beneath. As soon as the chocolate has melted, work very quickly. Remove from the heat, stir through the probiotic powder (or 1 tablespoon of yoghurt will work) and immediately fill each pecan pillow with a puddle of frosting.

Try to refrigerate for 2 hours before looting. They're best hidden behind old jars of capers and gherkins at the back of the fridge. Few will find them.

STRAWBERRY SHORTBREAD

>>>>>>>>>>>>>>>>>>>>>>>>>>>>

These chaps take a mere 3 minutes to whip up, 6 minutes to cook and 2 seconds to devour. The cookie dough can even be eaten straight from the freezer. My mother calls them her La Prairie biscuits. In other words, a cracking anti-ageing brew high in vitamin E, calcium, protein and antioxidants.

For adventurous palates, try lúcuma powder. This golden South American fruit is a scrumptious way of naturally sweetening the dough while providing niacin (vitamin B3) to fight cholesterol and depression. A toughie to find in stores, order lúcuma online or from your local health food supplier. Otherwise, stick to cheap and trusty ginger.

Preheat the oven to 170°C/150°C fan/340°F. Grease a baking tray.

Gently melt the coconut oil in a saucepan, then add the honey or maple syrup. Take off the heat and using a fork, combine with the remaining ingredients. Taste the mixture, ponder a little, and add more dried ginger or salt if you like.

When you're satisfied with your tasting session, mix well and form a squidgy ball of dough. Place on a piece of greaseproof paper and press into an oblong pizza base shape about 5mm deep with the base of your palm or your fingers. Cover with another sheet of greaseproof paper, roll over it with a wine bottle to flatten it some more, then freeze for 15 minutes. This makes it easier to shape and cut into shortbread cookies, but it also ensures they don't turn into puddles in the oven.

Remove the dough from your freezer, cut out your desired shapes with a cookie cutter and place on the greased tray. The quantity you get depends on how thin you manage to press the dough. I normally get about 30 shortbread cookies and freeze 20 of them in their raw state. Bake for approximately 5 minutes before they start to brown or colour, or for 10 minutes if cooking from frozen. Allow to set on the baking tray in a cool place, out of temptation's sight. Best stored in the fridge, or in your tummy.

1/3 cup (80ml) extra virgin coconut oil
1/2 cup (125ml) honey or maple syrup
2 1/2 cups (250g) ground almonds
3 tablespoons dried strawberries
2 tablespoons dried ginger or lúcuma powder
good pinch of unrefined salt

Makes about 30 biscuits

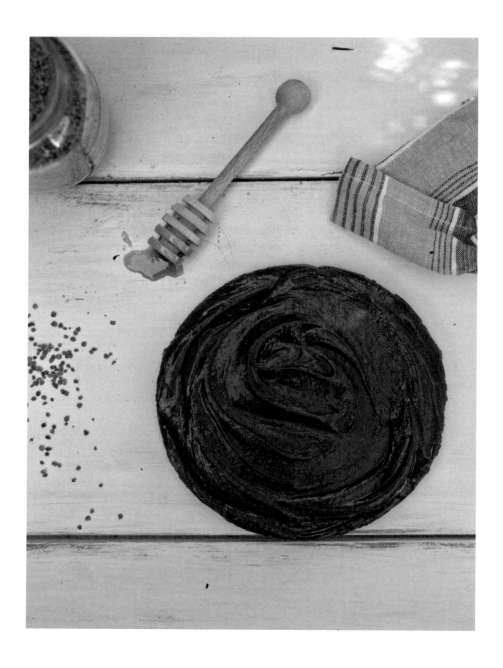

PITCH-DARK CACAO TORTE

>>>>>>>>>>>>>>>>>>>>>>>>>>>>>>

I'm through with guilt. As a woman, my brain was trained to deliver remorseful code after every bite of chocolate cake. What if you could turn your cravings into a nutritional hit? Find something sinful but saintly? Here's a recipe for you to flirt with. It's a basic dark chocolate torte, waiting for your personalisation. I decorate it with raspberry leaf tea or bee pollen, but you could try mint, ginger, sea salt, Chinese five spice, blueberry powder or adulation.

Local unpasteurised honey is thought to help introduce manageable amounts of pollen to our bodies, allowing us to prepare for the sneezy season several months in advance. Bee pollen is another unlikely remedy for hay fever. Studies have shown how this superfood can help boost immunity and acts as a natural anti-histamine. Considering the queen bee needs to lay up to 2,000 eggs per day and lives 40 times longer than a worker bee, her stamina is probably testament to this luminous superfood. I think bee pollen tastes like fermented dust balls, so I've hidden it in chocolate. But I've seen people eat it straight from a jar, sober, without flinching.

Chop the dates into small pieces. Whizz in a high-speed blender with the remaining base ingredients until thoroughly socialised. You may need the teeniest splash of water to bring it together. Press the mixture firmly into a 18cm springform circular tin. These are the funny sort of circular tins that detach from its sides. You could make a number of individual tarts too if you have a few cookie-cutter rings. Aim for a thin base. Refrigerate. Any leftover mixture? Freeze for another torte-making day or add to your morning's yoghurt with blueberries and jazz.

To make the filling, cream the cashew butter, ripe avocado (if using), water, cacao, sweetener, tamari and vanilla in a powerful blender. You should have a dense, dark, glossy ganache by now. While the motor is running, slowly add a steady stream of melted cacao butter. Taste, and decide whether you'd like more sweetness from honey or perhaps a salty kick from tamari.

Once you're happy, spread the filling over your base, decorate with bee pollen or raspberry leaf and chill in the fridge. This torte is indecently good straight from the freezer, which is where we store ours.

For the base:
1/2 cup sticky dates, like Medjool
up to 1 cup (120g) walnuts
zest of 1/2 orange
2 tablespoons carob, cacao or cocoa powder
pinch of good, organic, unrefined salt

For the filling:
1 x 200g jar cashew nut butter
1/2 ripe avocado (optional)
1/4 cup (60ml) water
5 tablespoons raw cacao or cocoa powder
4-5 tablespoons local raw honey, maple syrup or date syrup
1 tablespoon tamari
1 teaspoon vanilla extract
2-3 tablespoons (45ml) cacao butter, melted
bee pollen granules, to decorate (optional)
1 teabag of raspberry leaf tea, to decorate (optional)

Serves 16

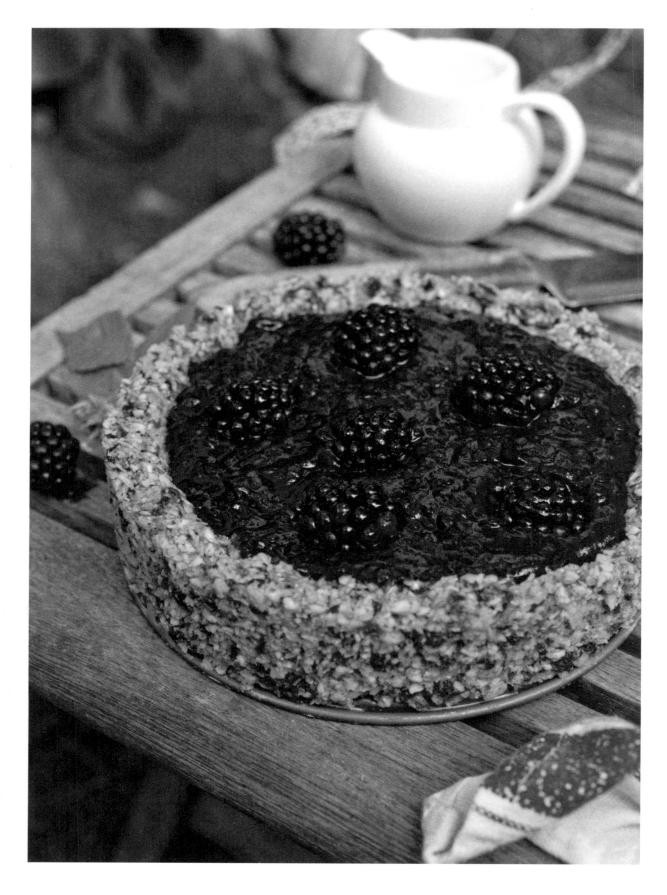

BLACKBERRY TART WITH ALMOND PASTRY

>>

Mother Nature is preparing us for the onslaught of winter bugs by supplying us with free stashes of blackberry bushes every autumn. Blackberries are honking with vitamin C and immune-boosting carotenoids. Look up your local PYO (pick your own) farm instead of shooting back Lemsip this autumn.

But that ain't all, my friends. This tart will arm your body with alarming amounts of anti-ageing artillery. This is because almonds are rich in vitamin E, the undisputed beauty vitamin, and raisins are pumped with resveratrol, a free radical assassin. Free radicals cause damage to our skin and to our bodies. Nasty things. Let's remedy that with some pie!

Using your food processor, briefly blend the pastry ingredients together until it starts to clump into a doughy ball. You might need 1 teaspoon of cold water to help it along. Scrape into a pie dish and press along the sides and bottom to cover the entire dish and form a crust. Place in the freezer.

To make the jammy filling, blitz half the blackberries with all of the remaining ingredients (except the coconut yoghurt) until smooth. Gently stir through the rest of the blackberries with a fork and spread over the chilled pastry. Let it set for 4 hours in the fridge and serve beside a good dollop of natural coconut yoghurt, like CoYo (see page 253).

For the raw pastry:
1 1/2 cups (210g) almonds
1 cup (80g) desiccated
  coconut
3/4 cup (115g) sultanas or
  raisins
zest of 1 unwaxed lemon
3 tablespoons raw honey or
  maple syrup
1 teaspoon ground allspice
  or ground cinnamon
good pinch of sea salt flakes

For the filling:
3-4 cups blackberries
8 Medjool dates
2 tablespoons raw honey or
  maple syrup (optional)
squeeze of lemon juice
coconut yoghurt, to serve

Serves 12

POTLETS OF GRAPEFRUIT, LIME AND GINGER CUSTARD

>>

This is a hummer of a recipe when your body feels like a petri dish. Each serving gives you more than 100% of your daily recommended dose of vitamin C. This is the vitamin hailed as the slayer of free radicals, active campaigner against ageing and loyal deterrent of disease. Pretty impressive for a pot of pleasure.

You'll find that freshly juiced ginger adds an extra karate kick to sore throats. Ginger is one of my top three megafoods. If you don't have a juicer at home, use your best Marilyn Monroe voice and ask your local juicing outlet to press the ginger for you. Failing this, freeze a massive 12cm peeled stick of ginger. Grate the flesh into the mixture, straight from frozen.

6 egg yolks
juice of 1 lime
juice of 1 pink grapefruit
5 tablespoons extra virgin
  coconut oil
5 tablespoons raw honey
3 tablespoons juiced ginger
  (see note above)

Serves 6

Start by downloading a good podcast. You'll be locked to the cooker for 8 whole minutes watching the custard thicken.

Using a small saucepan on a low setting, gently heat all the ingredients. Make sure you are continuously whisking with a metal balloon beater. Keep a watch for little bubbles forming on the surface, telling you the mixture is getting hotter and hotter. By then you should notice it getting thicker. Test by dipping the back of a spoon into it. If the mixture coats the spoon, remove from the heat. If it runs off, keep the mixture over the heat until it thickens a little more.

Pour into little pots and refrigerate until it's no longer possible to ignore. Particularly tasty with crushed pistachio nuts or torn mint leaves.

Don't know what to do with leftover egg whites? Whip 3 into soft white peaks and add to the granola ingredients on page 20 before baking. This gives the granola extra-large clusters. Otherwise, green tea macaroons will happily use them up. See www.susanjanewhite.com.

CHILLI CHOCOLATE MISSILE

>>>>>>>>>>>>>>>>>>>>>>>>>>>>>>>>>>>

The addition of chilli powder will give your lips a delicious sting and swell the senses. Chillies can also heighten body temperature and help release natural endorphins to keep your blood gurgling with excitement.

But wait! There's more! Folate in avocados is thought to boost histamine production, apparently necessary for optimal orgasms. Whether this is true or not, its sumptuous flesh is enough to dizzy the senses. In fact, Catholics weren't allowed to eat avocados when the Spanish conquistadors brought them back to Europe in the 16th century. They evoked pleasures of the flesh at a time when contraception was not available. And the Aztec people of South America - the same cunning chaps who invented hot chocolate - called the avocado plant the ahuacatl, which translates as testicle tree.

Cream all your ingredients together with a hand-held blender. It's best chilled for 30 minutes before wolfing, but excitement may override your sensibilities. No shame in that.

Serve in petite wine glasses and top with freshly sliced red chilli if you have it. This mousse is unreasonably tasty after a long day at work. You'll quickly feel the chilli pelt through your veins and service those stubborn limbs.

1 ripe avocado
3 tablespoons cocoa or cacao powder
2 tablespoons raw agave or maple syrup (not honey)
1 tablespoon almond, cashew or macadamia butter
2 teaspoons tamari
pinch of cayenne pepper
1 red chilli, finely sliced, to decorate (optional)

Serves 2

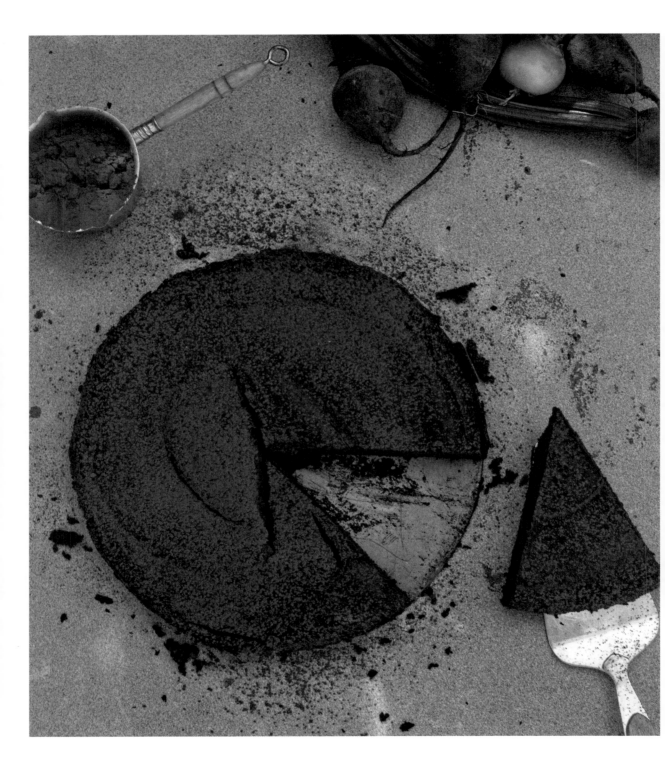

'I CAN'T BELIEVE IT'S BEETROOT' CAKE

>>>

A study in the Journal of the American Medical Association revealed that older women taking supplements might die younger than non-users. Why? Supplements may deliver too much of a good thing, since nutrients can be toxic at high doses or over long, unsupervised periods. Or perhaps pill-poppers delegate accountability for their health to multivitamins rather than addressing their diet?

We can all agree on one thing: a diet rich in fruit, veg, beans and basketball will rarely backfire. I'm not saying you'll live forever (Dragon's Den still has to crack that one), but we've nothing to lose by eating fresh, unadulterated food. A good diet is the best health insurance you can give your family, not a packet of lab-created pills.

I'm obsessed with beetroot right now. It's one of the tastiest veg on my superfood sonar. (My toddler isn't much convinced.) It may seem odd, but beetroot and chocolate are quite the couple. They get on better than Vladimir Putin and Gerard Depardieu. And the toddler is none the wiser.

Preheat the oven to 180°C/160°C fan/350°F. Grease a 20cm round cake tin or springform tin.

Boil the dates in a small saucepan with about 3cm of water for 10-15 minutes. Purée in a high-speed electric blender. This should yield about 1 1/2 cups of date paste. The recipe only needs 1 cup's worth, so freeze the rest, use it in the Apple-sauce and Cinnamon Cookies on page 71 or scoff with natural yoghurt.

Purée the cocoa powder, beetroot and tamari with the date paste until sumptuously smooth. I cheat by using vacuum-packed beetroot with no vinegar.

Blend in the eggs, oil, vanilla and baking powder until thoroughly incorporated. Immediately pour the batter into the greased cake tin.

Once the cake is in the oven, lower the heat to 170°C/150°C fan/340°F - an important step. Bake for 40-55 minutes. You're looking for a moist, rich cake, not a dry, fluffy cake. It's closer to a ganache torte. Allow to cool, making sure you give it enough time to chill before removing from its tin. Serve with plenty of coconut yoghurt and a large spoon.

2 cups (280g) pitted dates
125g cacao or cocoa powder
1 cup puréed beetroot (about 4 cooked baby beets from a vacuum packet)
2 tablespoons tamari
4 medium eggs
1/2 cup (125ml) extra virgin olive oil
2 teaspoons vanilla extract
2 teaspoons baking powder
natural coconut yoghurt, to serve (obligatory)

Serves 16-20

PRALINE CUPCAKES

>>>>>>>>>>>>>>>>>>>>>>>

I tend to yearn for childhood recipes, but I also love alchemising healthier versions - coconut flour instead of refined wheat, extra virgin oils instead of butter, maple syrup instead of white sugar. Admittedly, Abba plays a big part in it too.

You can order coconut flour from your local health food store, as it's not that common outside of the US. Coconut flour is whoppingly high in fibre and low in carbohydrates, making it an ideal ingredient for coeliacs, diabetics, paleos and anyone worried about glycemic load. However, it's imperative to follow recipe measurements and not to substitute coconut flour for any other flour. It can be quite the diva.

For the cupcakes:
1/2 cup (50g) cocoa powder
1/4 cup (35g) coconut flour
1 teaspoon baking powder
1/2 cup (125ml) raw agave or honey
3 tablespoons almond butter
3 eggs, beaten
5 tablespoons melted coconut oil
1 tablespoon tamari
2 teaspoons apple cider vinegar
1 teaspoon vanilla extract

For the praline frosting:
2/3 cup (180g) cashew nut butter
1/2 cup (125ml) maple syrup
2 teaspoons tamari

Makes 10 cupcakes

To make the cupcakes, preheat the oven to 180°C/160°C fan/350°F. Sift the cocoa powder, coconut flour and baking powder into a large mixing bowl.

In a medium bowl, beat together the agave or honey and the almond butter with a balloon whisk (those whisky-looking things you see your grandmother using to whip cream). Blend through the remaining ingredients.

Add the wet ingredients to the dry and blend thoroughly with your balloon whisk until glossy and smooth.

Prepare your muffin tray with cupcake liners and fill each one with 1/4 cup of the mixture. Expect a very runny consistency. Don't worry - you're on the right track. Bake for 20 minutes. Touch to feel if they are done. Gently remove from the muffin tray and allow to cool completely on a wire rack before icing with praline frosting.

To make the frosting, mix the nut butter, maple syrup and tamari together with a fork. Smother on top of each cupcake and gleefully tiptoe through the kitchen.

Dispatches from the kitchen: You can replace the almond butter with equal amounts of soya yoghurt. It seems rather important to stick to raw dark agave or honey. Maple syrup, barley malt and brown rice syrup misbehave with the coconut flour.

CINNAMON AND PECAN MALT ICE CREAM

>>

My husband never suspected this was dairy free, let alone sugar free and guilt free. Had I told him, perhaps his spoon would never have ventured in. It was loved, revered and annihilated in one blissful binge.

Chilled, full-fat coconut milk is the key. Go for the organic variety; inorganic can be packed with preservatives and chemical stabilisers that turn the ice cream a dodgy tinge of purple. A top idea is to chill your serving bowls in the freezer beforehand. I use tiny glass preserving jars so that everyone has a pot to themselves.

4 frozen bananas
1 x 400g can full-fat
  coconut milk, chilled
3 tablespoons barley malt
  extract or maple syrup
1/2 tablespoon ground
  cinnamon
handful of pecans, crushed,
  to decorate

Serves 3-4

Peel and chop each banana into many chunks. Try using black-skinned bananas, which are ultra ripe and much sweeter. Place the chunks on a bread-board covered with baking parchment, making sure the banana pieces are not touching each other. Freeze for 60 minutes, then transfer to a freezer bag. This is to prevent the banana sticking together and wearing down your food processor and your patience.

When an ice cream craving hits, take the chilled, unopened can of coconut milk from the fridge and blend in a food processor with your frozen bananas, sweetener and cinnamon. Process in bursts at first until the bananas soften, then continuously until they develop a creamy consistency.

Decorate with crushed pecans, and more maple syrup if you fancy.

Devour immediately, and finish every last slurp because it doesn't like the freezer. Oh well.

ICED GREEN TEA AND MANUKA HONEY CUBES

>>

When my multiple espresso regime got the heave-ho, I became possessed by the search for a worthy replacement. Decaffeinated coffee was somewhat pointless, having undergone even more chemical adulterations to remove the caffeine than Shane McGowan's liver. Floral teas were cruel. I wanted a hit, not a mug of liquid lawn.

Then I tasted chilled green tea with fresh lemon. Green tea contains one-third the amount of coffee's caffeine and up to 20 times the antioxidant activity as vitamin C. This popular Chinese tea is also bucked up with skin-enhancing polyphenols, something coffee sorely envies.

Choosing to cut down on coffee is a smart decision. Coffee's giant caffeine content releases sugar into your system in the form of glycogen and makes your blood pressure pelt. That's why you love it. But your heart doesn't. Nor does your immune system, which becomes less effective under the influence of raised cortisol levels. Besides, your skin looks parched on coffee, your mouth feels like a badger's bum and you age quicker. Onwards!

Steep the bags in a teapot filled with hot water for around 30 minutes. It doesn't matter if you have a small or large teapot because you can dilute the strength with additional water afterwards. Once cooled, pour into a tall glass jug and top up with filtered water to your preferred strength. I normally use 3 pints of water with 4 teabags as a guideline. Chill in the refrigerator.

To make the ice, *gently* warm the lemon juice and honey together. If using manuka honey, heating too quickly destroys its potency and health-giving properties. Likewise, baking or cooking with manuka honey deletes its effectiveness against bacteria - an expensive lesson to learn. This special honey's efficacy depends on whether or not it is taken on an empty stomach, so it's ideal for this iced green tea in between meals.

Add a little water to the warm lemony mix before pouring into an ice cube tray, then freeze until set. Serve the chilled tea in its jug alongside a tall glass filled with lemony manuka ice cubes for people to help themselves. And perhaps a punnet of raspberries, or a side of last night's gossip.

4 white or green teabags
juice of 2 large lemons
4 tablespoons manuka honey

Serves 8

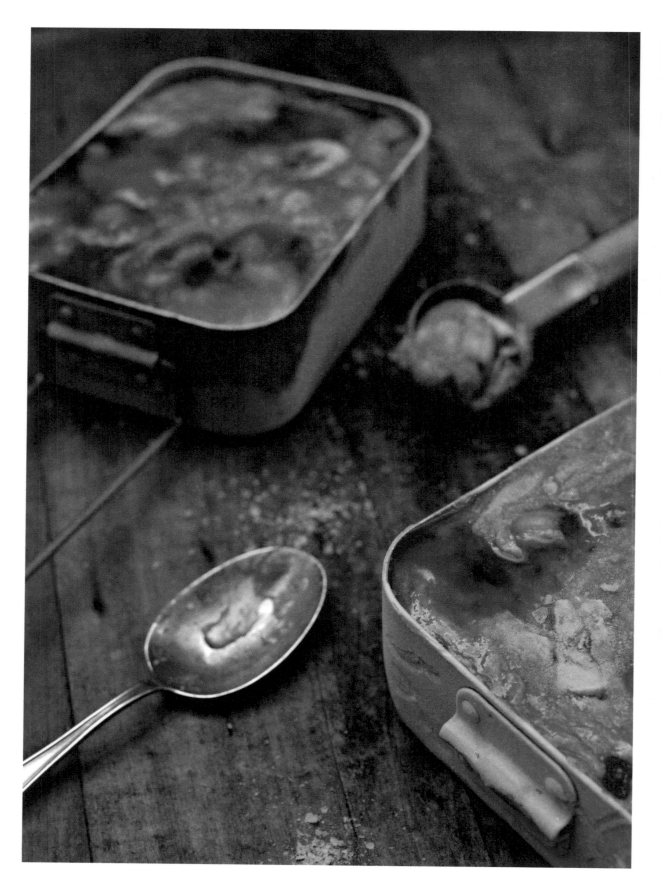

BANANA TOFFEE ICE CREAM

>>>>>>>>>>>>>>>>>>>>>>>>>>>>>>>>

Eating good food sends my hormones into party mode. It's a sensory pleasure, just like listening to great music or soaking up a swatch of unexpected sunshine. So here's my favourite ice cream recipe to feed your cells as well as your soul.

When you're looking for sweeteners, untreated honey gets my vote. Raw agave is only recommended if you suffer from wonky blood sugar levels. That's because agave has absolutely no nutritional plaudits, though it can serve as a useful alternative to sugar. For more on agave, see page 11.

Roughly mash 2 1/2 bananas with the salt flakes. Stir through the raisins or chopped dates. I use Medjool dates because they are sent from angels. Or demons. Not sure which, but I encourage you to indulge me and try a few licky-sticky yummy ones. Dried dates are fine to use too, but taste crunchy in the ice cream as opposed to squidgy. Raisins are delectably chewy and noticeably cheaper.

In a separate bowl, beat the tahini, sweetener and vanilla with a fork until sumptuously smooth. Fold in the banana mess. Now chop the remaining 1 1/2 bananas into chunks and stir through the entire ice cream mixture. You can swirl a little honey on top if you fancy - it sets like toffee. Pour into a plastic cylindrical tub, seal and freeze overnight. In the morning, you shall rejoice.

4 medium bananas
decent pinch of sea salt flakes
handful of plump raisins or chopped dates
1 x 340g jar of tahini
1/2 cup (125ml) raw honey, agave or maple syrup
1 teaspoon vanilla extract or powder
extra honey, to decorate (optional)

Makes 12 servings

COFFEE BEAN ICE CREAM

>>>>>>>>>>>>>>>>>>>>>>>>>>>>>

In Hinduism, the sesame seed stands for immortality. Eyebrows sufficiently raised? Wait until you taste this ice cream. Notions of everlasting life will become much clearer. Theoretically, it might come from the sesame's stash of lignans. These are a group of plant-based compounds associated with fighting cancer. Or perhaps such fancy can be attributed to its bank of B vitamins? This is the vitamin responsible for releasing energy, massaging frayed nerves and mending marriages. Not bad for half a cent per gram, and notably less than a psychotherapist.

Whisk the tahini, date syrup, carob, vanilla and salt crystals with a fork until sumptuously smooth. I find this a little easier if the ingredients are heated ever so gently. As you work, sprinkle in your coffee beans and good humour.

Pour the mixture into a large plastic cylindrical container, just like professional ice cream (we doubled the portions for the photo). You'll need to freeze it for 5 hours before serving.

approx. 1 x 340g jar tahini
1/2 cup (125ml) date syrup
3 tablespoons carob powder
1-2 teaspoons vanilla
 extract
1 teaspoon sea salt flakes
sprinkle of whole organic
 coffee beans

Serves 6

ICE POPS

>>>>>>>>>>>>>

Get yourself some fetching ice pop moulds on Amazon. You could also use paper espresso cups from your local café if you ask nicely! Fill three-quarters high with ice pop mixture, cover with tinfoil and gently pop a wooden stick through the centre of the foil. Freeze as usual. Ta-da! Takeaway espresso cups (as opposed to regular paper cups) are lightly lined, making it easier to remove the pop. Nifty, huh?

ISOTONIC POPS

500ml young green coconut water

Pour into moulds and freeze for 8 hours. That's it!

OCTONAUT ICE POPS

My little buddies love The Octonauts. These cartoon sea creatures eat lots of kelp seaweed. One day, Benjamin asked me for green ice cream, just like Captain Barnacles. I couldn't resist, so here it is.

4 pears, peeled and chopped
1 small avocado
1 tablespoon wheat grass or barley grass
  powder

Cook the pears in a splash of water for 6-8 minutes. Keep the lid on to retain the juices. Purée with the flesh of the avocado and the wheat grass powder. You can try adding slices of kiwi too if you think your little one will eat it.

Pour into ice pop moulds and freeze for 8 hours. Enough to fill 6 regular pops.

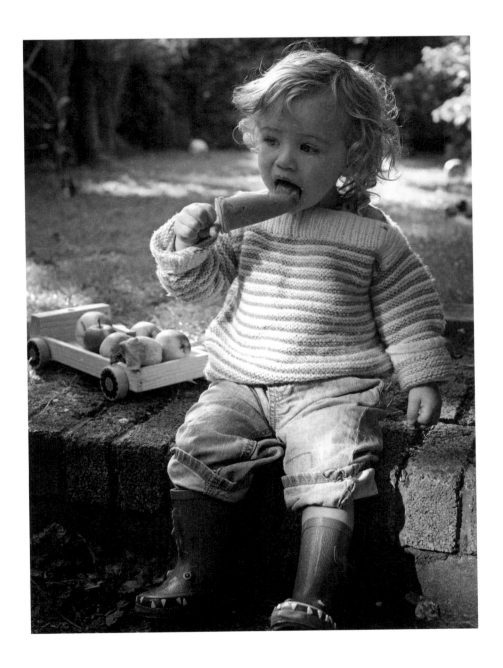

EXTRA VIRGIN TREATS

What to Read and Where to Shop

What I'm Reading

Learning about the perils of processed food is a smart move. It's the best insurance policy you can offer your body.

My heroes are authors and campaigners like Marion Nestle, Robyn O'Brien, Joanna Blythman, Bee Wilson, Felicity Lawrence and Michael Pollan. Never heard of them? Nestle, a professor in public health at New York University, has over 100,000 followers on Twitter. Pollan has 200,000. Each of them has a free blog, so it's not necessary to shell out money to access their research and opinions. Here are some great books by these authors. Many of them read like thrillers – scandalous, jaw dropping and haunting.

Not on the Label: What Really Goes into the Food on Your Plate by Felicity Lawrence

Eat Your Heart Out by Felicity Lawrence

Food Rules by Michael Pollan

The Food Our Children Eat by Joanna Blythman

What to Eat by Joanna Blythman

Bad Food Britain by Joanna Blythman

Swindled: From Poison Sweets to Counterfeit Coffee by Bee Wilson

The End of Overeating by David A. Kessler, M.D.

Salt Sugar Fat: How the Food Giants Hooked Us by Michael Moss

Basket Case: What's Happening to Ireland's Food? by Suzanne Campbell and Philip Boucher-Hayes

Gulp: Adventures on the Alimentary Canal by Mary Roach

Diet Delusion by Gary Taubes

Pure, White and Deadly: How Sugar Is Killing Us by Robert Lustig and John Yudkin

Vegan Before Six: Eat Vegan Before 6:00 to Lose Weight and Restore Your Health … for Good by Mark Bittman

Good Food: Can You Trust What You Are Eating? by John McKenna

Food, Inc. (DVD) by Eric Schlosser and Robert Kenner

Farmageddon (DVD) by Linda Faillace and Kristin Canty

Resources: Where I Like to Shop

You'll find me in quirky health stores across Dublin, organic food co-ops and specialist grocers like Fallon & Byrne. Say hi when you see me (unless my toddler is smashing his brother's head through the deli counter again).

Some of the ingredients used throughout this book require a little sat-navving. If you live outside Dublin or Ireland, I recommend exploring your nearest independent health food store, market or savvy deli. Listed below are some useful online sources. Many deliver nationwide and overseas.

www.irelandsrawkitchen.ie and www.iswari.net
Coconut sugar, raw carob, spirulina, barley grass, stevia, dried mulberries, goji berries, raw dark agave, lúcuma, acai and all manner of cacao products.

www.seaweedproducts.ie and www.clearspring.co.uk
Wild harvested Irish sea veg. My favourite is their dulse powder. Clearspring supply hijiki, arame, nori sprinkles, authentic wasabi powder, mirin and tamari.

www.wallandkeogh.ie
My local teahouse. Sells incredible loose-leaf organic tea. International delivery. Favourites include Persian Prince and Barry White. I get my beans for the Coffee Bean Ice Cream recipe on page 249 at Wall & Keogh.

www.organicsupermarket.ie and www.waitrose.com
Home delivery of organic veg, fruit, flours, grains and household sundries.

www.steenbergs.co.uk
Exceptional salts and spices. Also check out the Irish Organic Herb Co. for certified organic herbs.

www.black-blum.com
Bento boxes to transport lunches into work with you.

www.amazon.co.uk
This is where you'll find a Lurch spiraliser, nut milk bags, Tiana coconut flour, matcha green tea powder and oven thermometers.

www.avogel.ie
Three-tier large germinator or sprouter, for your bean zoo on page 126.

www.linwoodshealthfoods.com
If you don't own a coffee grinder to finely mill seeds, Linwoods does a fantastic range of freshly milled flax, sunflower and pumpkin seeds, chia seeds and even goji berries. Essential for recipes such as the Black Bread (page 54), Office Bombs (page 62), Barley Grass Balls (page 66) and Chia Bonbons (page 64).

www.highbankorchards.com
Organic apple syrup, Ireland's answer to maple syrup.

www.coyo.co.uk
Coconut yoghurt made from coconut milk.

www.udoschoice.ie
Udo's Oil is a blend of really healthy oils like linseed, wheat germ, evening primrose, sesame and extra virgin sunflower. We use it for our fresh satay sauce and lots of salads with pomegranate molasses.

www.blackgarlic.com
Fermented and aged black garlic. Keeps for weeks in the fridge.

www.pulsin.co.uk
For the Pea Protein Isolate Powder used in the Protein Grenades on page 69. See also www.sunwarrior.com for really good raw vegan protein powders.

Index